WORLD ROYAL FAMILIES

WORLD ROYAL FAMILIES

SANDRA FORTY
JUDITH MILLIDGE
ED RILEY

CHARTWELL
BOOKS, INC.

Published in 2009 by Compendium Publishing Ltd,
43 Frith Street, London W1D 4SA

CHARTWELL BOOKS, INC.
A Division of
BOOK SALES, INC.
276 Fifth Avenue Suite 206
New York, New York 10001

ISBN 13: 978-0-7858-2530-2
ISBN 10: 0-7858-2530-4

Editor: Judith Millidge
Designer: Compendium Design/Ian Hughes, Mousemat Design

Printed and bound in China

Page 1: Three generations of the British royal family – HM Queen Elizabeth II and
the Duke of Edinburgh, with their eldest son the Prince of Wales and his son,
Prince William. Taken to celebrate the 50th anniversary of the Queen's coronation.
Title pages: Schloss Vaduz, home to the royal family of Liechtenstein.

CONTENTS

INTRODUCTION

The whole world is in revolt. Soon there will be only five kings left—the King of England, the King of Spades, the King of Clubs, the King of Hearts, and the King of Diamonds.
King Farouk of Egypt, 1948

ONCE, THEY RULED THE world, but in the 21st century hereditary monarchs have become something of an endangered species. Political upheavals in the 20th century removed from power many ancient families – the Romanovs, the Habsburgs, and the Hohenzollerns – but their descendants live on, many of whom retain their courtesy titles, if not their palaces. Other noble families have survived with their crowns intact, notably the house of Windsor in Britain and the house of Orange in the Netherlands, the restored Bourbons in Spain, the Grimaldis in the principality of Monaco, and the Chakri dynasty of Thailand.

When King Farouk made his famous quip, the kings of Albania, Bulgaria, Romania, and Italy had recently been exiled in the aftermath of the Second World War, and in Spain General Franco had sidelined the Bourbons a decade earlier in the 1930s. The Greeks actually voted to restore their monarchy in 1946, but 25 years later, decided that they were surplus to the republican requirements of the new military regime. Other countries have dangled their thrones like yo-yos in front of their royal families, inviting them back for a time, before overthrowing them again as political circumstances change. The Vietnamese king was restored twice in the post-colonial years of the 1940s and

1950s, before the country was ripped apart by America's Cold War battle against Communism.

In a purely logical and rational world, where advancement should be based on a person's talent rather than their birth, the argument for hereditary monarchy is hard to sustain. For centuries, most European countries were ruled by the members of a dynastic family: in crude terms the strongest and richest noble family which succeeded in garnering enough support for their rule. William the Conqueror is the archetypal example of this. He firmly believed that Edward the Confessor had promised him the throne of England in 1064, and in 1066, nine months after Edward's death, he set off to fight the new king, Harold, by promising his followers land and money if they won. After the Battle of Hastings, William kept his promise, distributed English estates to his Norman followers, and thus guaranteed the rule of his dynasty for several generations. And the Normans – along with their peers in France, Germany, Spain and elsewhere – reinforced their material position by claiming spiritual authority from God. No man (and certainly no woman) could challenge the rule of a monarch without risking their life and their immortal soul. So hereditary monarchs were impregnable and thrones were passed, if not always from father to son, certainly among an elite group of high-born families, blessed by the Almighty with the 'divine right of kings'.

But as education became more widespread from the 17th century, the subversive whispers of democracy became louder. Writers of the Enlightenment in the 18th century reflected on the freedom of the human condition, and the French philosopher Diderot succinctly demolished royal claims to rule their subjects with God's blessing: 'Man will never be free until the last king is strangled with the entrails of the last priest', he wrote. Why should anyone have the right to rule a country just because their father or mother did? What if the heir is incapable of ruling well, or simply doesn't want the job? History is peppered with tales of unsuitable princes who have ruined their countries, such as Ivan the Terrible in Russia, Richard III and Charles I in England, Louis XVI in France. Surely, in the 21st century, the argument in favour of democratically elected rulers has been won?

Well, yes and no. There are few absolute monarchs left in the world – only Sultan Qaboos of Oman, King Mswati of Swaziland, the King of Saudi Arabia and the Sultan of Brunei rule without restrictions – and most surviving monarchies today are constitutional. In a constitutional monarchy, the hereditary ruler is head of state, and the democratically elected prime minister leads the government that is responsible for the legislature. A constitutional monarch acts upon the advice of his or her elected officials.

Elective monarchies are not new – the oldest and most venerable is the position of Pope, and this was closely followed by that of Holy Roman Emperor until 1918 – but both Malaysia and the United Arab Emirates are ruled by elected monarchs, and both were established within the last 50 years. However, an elected monarch cannot really be regarded as a democratic ruler, as in all cases, the monarch must fulfil a number of specific criteria to be eligible for the role. The pope is elected by his peers from the Catholic church's college of cardinals. The president of the United Arab Emirates is chosen from among the hereditary rulers of the emirate states, and thus far, has always been the ruler of Abu Dhabi. In Malaysia, the king is elected for a five-year term of office from among the nine rulers of the Malaysia's federated states, and is head of a constitutional parliamentary democracy.

So with most of the world opting for democratic rule, and certainly not advocating any kind of hereditary principle, it is interesting that the scions of many ancient

and noble houses retain their titles and in some cases, their fortunes, if not their powers. What is fascinating is that several countries that have recently been beset by bloody civil wars have flirted with a restoration of the monarchy once peace has been restored. For monarchies represent some sort of stability to nations which have seen their people killed and infrastructures destroyed by the machinations of politicians, elected or otherwise. A wily politician himself, King Sihanouk of Cambodia is one such survivor. King from 1941 to 1953 when he was deposed, he was a

Below: Pope Benedict XVI is the elected monarch of Vatican City.

Left: Schönbrunn Palace, Vienna was once the home of the Habsburg emperors and is now owned by the Austrian state.

fervent nationalist who led Cambodia to independence from France and trod a fine diplomatic line in the 1960s to maintain the country's neutrality while the Vietnam War raged on Cambodia's border. After the dreadful years of Pol Pot's regime, (when five of the king's 14 children were killed by the Khmer Rouge) Sihanouk returned to power in 1991 as a symbolic but immensely popular figure.

With the end of the Balkan wars of the 1990s, when Yugoslavia split into its constituent parts, both Serbia and Montenegro have invited their royal families home after nearly 50 years of exile. In both cases, the country's monarch is seen as a unifying figure, although they co-exist side-by-side with the elected politicians. Both Serbia and Montenegro are independent republics, so neither monarchical family has any real power, not even the constitutional powers accorded to monarchs who are official heads of state, such as Elizabeth II of Britain, or Juan Carlos of Spain. However, they are strong reminders of the days when their countries were independent nation states, symbols of patriotism and heritage before the imposition of Communist rule under Marshal Tito. Interestingly, neither family was regarded as responsible for the mayhem that affected the nations in the 1940s.

Perhaps the most remarkable return to power is that of Simeon Borisov Sakskoburggotski, the man formerly known as King Simeon II of Bulgaria. Simeon inherited the Bulgarian throne at the age of six in 1943, but was exiled by the Communist regime after the Second World War. He

Right: This picture gives some idea of how widely dispersed were the heirs of Queen Victoria and Prince Albert. They were the parents of nine children and 42 grandchildren, and most European royalty today are descended from them. This picture, taken in 1896 records the visit of the Russian imperial family to Balmoral Castle, Scotland. Kaiser Wilhelm II is seated next to his grandmother, Queen Victoria. Behind him is the bearded Tsar Nicholas II and his wife the tsarina, the queen's granddaughter Princes Alexandra of Hesse.

Left: Peles Castle, in the Carpathian Mountains, Romania, was the home of the Romanian royal family from 1883 until 1947.

lived happily enough in Spain until he returned to his homeland in 1996, where rapturous crowds mobbed him. Simeon founded a political party and in 2001 was elected prime minister – the world's first hereditary monarch to succeed as a democratically elected political leader.

In Germany, the ruling Hohenzollerns were sent into exile after the First World War, when Kaiser Wilhelm II shouldered the blame for Germany's defeat. The same fate awaited the Habsburgs in Austria, and neither family were regarded with much affection for many years in their native lands. The Habsburgs probably fared best after 1945, when many people acknowledged that imperial rule was infinitely preferable to Fascism. But even then, Crown Prince Otto was not permitted to return to Austria until he

had renounced his claim to the throne in 1961.

Portugal, which banished its king in 1910, regards the Duke of Braganza, the pretender to the Portuguese throne, with affection and pride. The country's Ban Law was repealed in 1950, and the current duke has spent most of his life living peacefully in Portugal, where he occasionally carries out ceremonial duties alongside the politicians.

Dispossessed royals have shown themselves to be versatile and imaginative, with a wide array of skills that have enabled them to survive away from the trappings of inherited wealth. Not least is a talent for languages. Many of them speak four or five languages fluently, driven by the need to retain the language of their native land alongside English, French or German, for example.

Some of the world's most ancient and stable monarchs reside in northern Europe – the countries of Scandinavia, Great Britain and the Netherlands have retained the hereditary principle for their head of state for over a thousand years. On the other side of the world, the Chrysanthemum throne of Japan and the kingdom of Thailand have also retained their kings, regarding them with an almost religious reverence, while gradually eroding their practical powers.

In Britain Queen Elizabeth II has reigned for over 50 years, and shows little sign of slowing down. Like other reigning monarchs, she and her family live in great comfort, in houses and palaces surrounded by wealth that the rest of us can only dream of. The price for this seems to be a rather rigid and restricted life. The royal family of Great Britain runs according to an almost unalterable timetable: Buckingham Palace is home from Monday to Thursday, with Windsor Castle for the weekend during the winter and spring months. In August the Queen decamps to Scotland and remains at Balmoral Castle until October, when she returns to London in time for the state opening of parliament. Christmas is usually spent at Sandringham House in Norfolk, and, after Ascot in June, in early July, she spends a week at the Palace of Holyroodhouse in Edinburgh, her official Scottish residence. Despite the material luxury, the life of the monarch has not been altogether easy and Elizabeth II's reign has been punctuated by a number of crises, ranging from her sister's desire to marry a divorcé in the 1950s, to the controversy surrounding the death of the Princess of Wales in 1997. The Queen has successfully steered around them, by calling on almost superhuman resources of duty, service, tradition and good sense. At the age of 21 she dedicated herself to a life of serving the nation and the Commonwealth, a vow she has adhered to ever since. 'It's all to do with the training: you can do a lot if you're properly trained,' she has apparently said, echoing the sentiments of her grandmother, Queen Mary, who once said with a flash of humour, 'You are a member of the British royal family. We

are never tired, and we all love hospitals'.

Elizabeth II is rightly regarded with great respect and can be seen as an excellent argument for the strengths of constitutional monarchy, where the ruler's role is to caution, advise, but ultimately, to sign whatever the prime minister of the day requests. Her successors, brought up in a less deferential world, are more likely to face a challenge to their position.

Over the centuries, many people have fought and died for their right to inherit a throne or a landed estate, and even when the ancestral home has become a republican people's palace, the family in-fighting continues. Several dispossessed families, such as the Romanovs, Bonapartes and the Hohenzollerns have disputed among themselves for many years over the rightful claimant to what is essentially a non-existent throne. Often, the argument centres on the fact that individuals failed to marry people of equivalent

social standing, thus removing themselves and their children from the line of succession. It seems that however impoverished a prince, they must strive to marry from the thoroughbred field of noble families to maintain their royal status.

Today, it is often more likely that princes and princesses want to disassociate themselves from their royal heritage and all the unwelcome publicity that it implies. In Holland for example, there is a differentiation between the royal family and the royal house. Since 2002, members of the royal house are those who undertake work on behalf of the state, and are usually the closest relatives of the monarch. Other relatives, who do not wish to carry out traditional royal duties, are simply members of the royal family, with no official obligations. This arrangement provides an opt-out system for those who wish to live a quiet life. In Britain, the quickest way to remove oneself from the line of succession is to marry a Catholic, as the 1775 Royal Marriages Act still upholds this rather antiquated law designed to prevent the throne falling to a Catholic monarch.

So, although the royal families of the world have been forced to adjust to changing attitudes and in many case, altered standards of living, they have certainly not been wiped out and time has proved King Farouk wrong. Royalty throughout the world remains an object of fascination, despite the fact that royal powers have been stripped back, leaving crowned heads little but their ceremonial coronets as a mark of their status.

Left: A right royal party at the wedding of Princess Alexia of Greece in 1999. Felipe, Prince of Asturias stands behind his parents the king and queen of Spain. To the left of King Juan Carlos is Queen Noor of Jordan, the widow of King Hussein. In the front row, stands Prince Nikolaos of Greece next to his uncle, Prince Henrik the prince consort of Denmark, Crown Prince Pavlos of Greece and the Crown Princess of Yugoslavia.

Far left: Queen Elizabeth II during her Golden Jubilee year, 2002.

Overleaf: The Chateau d'Amboise, France is owned and maintained by the Comte de Paris.

EUROPE

Left: The Chateau d'Amboise, France is owned and maintained by the Comte de Paris.

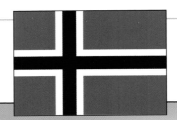

NORWAY
King Harald V

Official title	Harald V King of Norway
Country ruled	Norway
Born	21 February 1937
Accession to throne	17 January 1991
Royal house	House of Glücksburg
Official residences	The Royal Palace, Oslo
Heir	Crown Prince Haakon, (b. 1973, son)

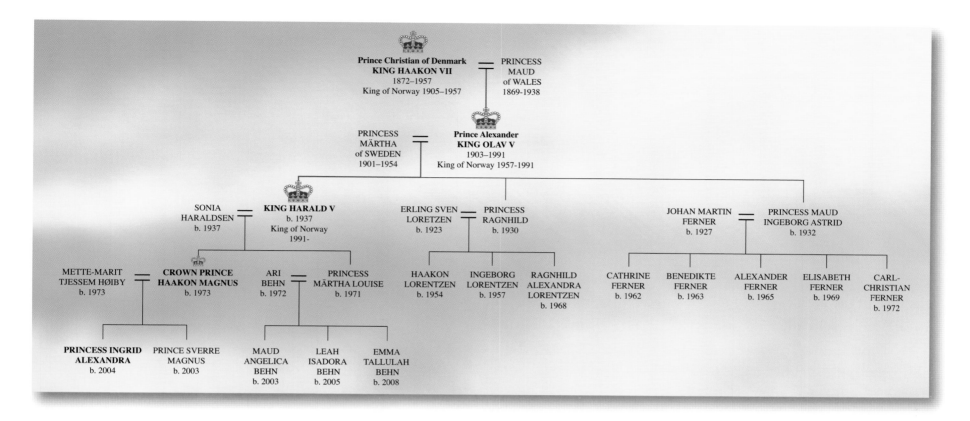

Prince Christian of Denmark
KING HAAKON VII
1872–1957
King of Norway 1905–1957

PRINCESS
MAUD
of WALES
1869-1938

PRINCESS
MÄRTHA
of SWEDEN
1901–1954

Prince Alexander
KING OLAV V
1903–1991
King of Norway 1957-1991

SONIA
HARALDSEN
b. 1937

KING HARALD V
b. 1937
King of Norway
1991-

ERLING SVEN
LORETZEN
b. 1923

PRINCESS
RAGNHILD
b. 1930

JOHAN MARTIN
FERNER
b. 1927

PRINCESS MAUD
INGEBORG ASTRID
b. 1932

METTE-MARIT
TJESSEM HØIBY
b. 1973

**CROWN PRINCE
HAAKON MAGNUS**
b. 1973

ARI
BEHN
b. 1972

PRINCESS
MÄRTHA LOUISE
b. 1971

HAAKON
LORENTZEN
b. 1954

INGEBORG
LORENTZEN
b. 1957

RAGNHILD
ALEXANDRA
LORENTZEN
b. 1968

CATHRINE
FERNER
b. 1962

BENEDIKTE
FERNER
b. 1963

ALEXANDER
FERNER
b. 1965

ELISABETH
FERNER
b. 1969

CARL-
CHRISTIAN
FERNER
b. 1972

**PRINCESS INGRID
ALEXANDRA**
b. 2004

PRINCE SVERRE
MAGNUS
b. 2003

MAUD
ANGELICA
BEHN
b. 2003

LEAH
ISADORA
BEHN
b. 2005

EMMA
TALLULAH
BEHN
b. 2008

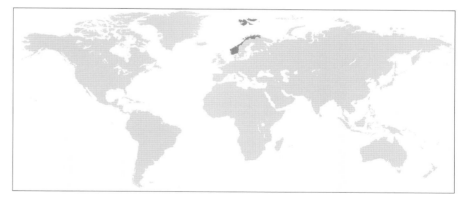

THE THIRD CHILD AND only son of Crown Prince Olav (later King Olav V) and Crown Princess Märtha, King Harald V was the first prince born in Norway for 567 years. When Germany invaded Norway in April 1940, the royal family (and most of the government) fled initially to Sweden, most then moving on to Washington DC. King Haakon VII and Crown Prince Olav moved to London, while Harald remained in Washington with his mother and sisters, princesses Ragnhild and Astrid. The royal family was reunited in Oslo on 7 June 1945 to a rapturous reception from the Norwegian people.

After attending schools in Oslo, Harald went on to the Norwegian Military Academy and then Balliol College, Oxford. He became crown prince in September 1957 on the death of his grandfather King Haakon VII, and began to work alongside his father, undertaking various state duties as preparation for his role as king. Controversially, Harald fell in love with a commoner, Sonja Haraldsen and needed special consent from his father and influential Norwegian politicians to marry her. They were married in August 1968 at Oslo Cathedra, and have two children, Princess Märtha Louise and Crown Prince Haakon.

Harald became king of Norway on the death of his father King Olav V in 1991 and was consecrated king in a thousand-year old ecclesiastical ceremony. The king's royal duties as a constitutional head of state are mainly ceremonial and representative. The king is calculated to have a personal fortune of some $27 million.

Until a change to the succession law in 1990, Norway followed Salic law, which allowed only males to inherit the Norwegian crown. From 1990, the oldest child of the monarch will inherit, but this only applies to people born after the law was enacted, so Crown Prince Haakon remains heir apparent, even though he is younger than his sister. His first born, Princess Ingrid, will succeed him.

The monarch's official residence and the royal family's main home is the Royal Palace in Oslo, which was built between 1824 and 1849. The king conducts his daily business here, as well as presiding over the Council of State, holding official dinners and granting audiences. The palace also houses most of the royal court and contains the offices of the royal family. Most official state functions take place at the Royal Palace, and foreign heads of state stay at the palace while in Oslo.

Additionally, the king has a number of other state-owned, residences in other parts of the country. In Trondheim his official residence is one of the largest wooden buildings in Scandinavia, the 18th century Stiftsgården in the centre of the city. The official residence in Bergen is Gamlehaugen, built at the turn of the 20th century in Art Nouveau influenced medieval style. The monarch has the use of Ledaal in Stavanger, an early 19th century summer residence. Norwegian monarchs traditionally spent their summer months at medieval Bygdø Royal Farm during the 20th century.

The royal family has a number of private residences. The crown prince and princess live on the Skaugum Estate in Asker. In the Jotunheimen mountains in Sikkilsdalen valley lies 'Prinsehytta', the Royal Mountain Chalet, and the Royal Lodge

Kongsseteren, located on the outskirts of Oslo, was a coronation gift from the people of Norway to King Haakon and Queen Maud in 1905. It is regularly used by the Royal Family, especially at Christmas. The king and queen have a further private modern holiday home called Mågerø at Tjøme in southern Norway.

Above: Crown Prince Haakon and Crown Princess Mette-Marit the day before their wedding in 2004.

Left: Queen Sonja and Crown Prince Harald married in 1968.

Below left: The Crown Prince and Princess with their children in 2006.

Right: Princess Martha Louise and her aunt, Princess Astrid.

Opposite, top: Harald of Norway (left) and Juan Carlos of Spain at Windsor Castle in June 2002.

Opposite, below: The coffin of King Olave was carried by members of the royal family at his funeral, 1991.

Left and below: Det Kongelige Slott — the Royal Palace — is the official residence where most royal functions are held and where the daily work of the monarchy is conducted. Located in the heart of Oslo, it sits on a slight hill at the north-west end of the main thoroughfare, Karl Johansgate. The building was designed in classical style by Hans Ditlev Franciscus Linstow and built between 1824 and 1849. It contains 173 rooms and has been modernised and changed regularly over its 150 year existence.

Right: The Breakfast Room of Royal Skaugum Manor. Skaugum Estate lies south-west of Oslo in Asker municipality and is the home of Crown Prince Haakon and his family.

Above: The Royal Yacht Norge *was presented by the Norwegian nation to King Haakon VII on his 75th birthday in 1947. Originally a British motor yacht called* Philante, *the 1,629-ton yacht served as a convoy escort vessel during World War II. She is owned by King Harald, but is manned and maintained by the Royal Norwegian Navy.*

KINGDOM OF SWEDEN
King Carl XVI Gustaf

Official title	Carl XVI Gustaf, King of Sweden
Country ruled	Sweden
Born	30 April 1946
Accession to throne	1973
Royal house	House of Bernadotte
Official residences	Drottningholm Palace, Stockholm Palace
Heir	Crown Princess Victoria (b. 1977, elder daughter)

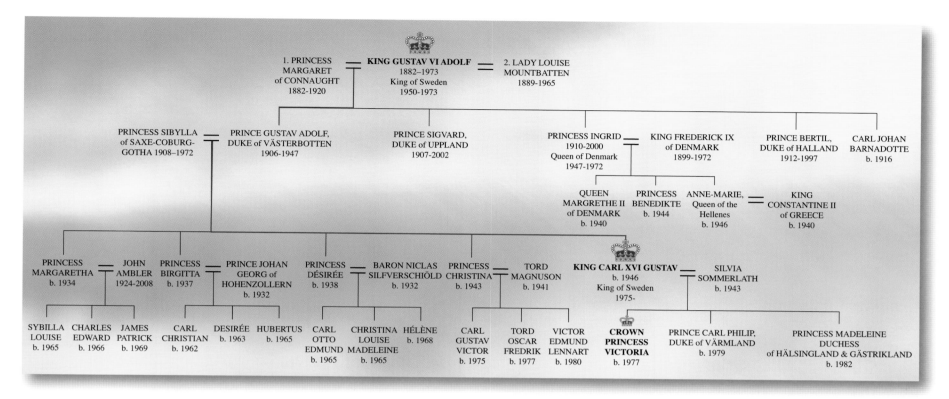

Family tree:

1. PRINCESS MARGARET of CONNAUGHT 1882–1920 — KING GUSTAV VI ADOLF 1882–1973 King of Sweden 1950-1973 — 2. LADY LOUISE MOUNTBATTEN 1889-1965

PRINCESS SIBYLLA of SAXE-COBURG-GOTHA 1908–1972 — PRINCE GUSTAV ADOLF, DUKE of VÄSTERBOTTEN 1906-1947

PRINCE SIGVARD, DUKE of UPPLAND 1907-2002

PRINCESS INGRID 1910-2000 Queen of Denmark 1947-1972 — KING FREDERICK IX of DENMARK 1899-1972

PRINCE BERTIL, DUKE of HALLAND 1912-1997

CARL JOHAN BARNADOTTE b. 1916

QUEEN MARGRETHE II of DENMARK b. 1940 — PRINCESS BENEDIKTE b. 1944 — ANNE-MARIE, Queen of the Hellenes b. 1946 — KING CONSTANTINE II of GREECE b. 1940

PRINCESS MARGARETHA b. 1934 — JOHN AMBLER 1924-2008 — PRINCESS BIRGITTA b. 1937 — PRINCE JOHAN GEORG of HOHENZOLLERN b. 1932 — PRINCESS DÉSIRÉE b. 1938 — BARON NICLAS SILFVERSCHIÖLD b. 1932 — PRINCESS CHRISTINA b. 1943 — TORD MAGNUSON b. 1941 — KING CARL XVI GUSTAV b. 1946 King of Sweden 1975- — SILVIA SOMMERLATH b. 1943

SYBILLA LOUISE b. 1965 — CHARLES EDWARD b. 1966 — JAMES PATRICK b. 1969 — CARL CHRISTIAN b. 1962 — DESIRÉE b. 1963 — HUBERTUS b. 1965 — CARL OTTO EDMUND b. 1965 — CHRISTINA LOUISE MADELEINE b. 1965 — HÉLÈNE b. 1968 — CARL GUSTAV VICTOR b. 1975 — TORD OSCAR FREDRIK b. 1977 — VICTOR EDMUND LENNART b. 1980 — CROWN PRINCESS VICTORIA b. 1977 — PRINCE CARL PHILIP, DUKE of VÄRMLAND b. 1979 — PRINCESS MADELEINE DUCHESS of HÄLSINGLAND & GÄSTRIKLAND b. 1982

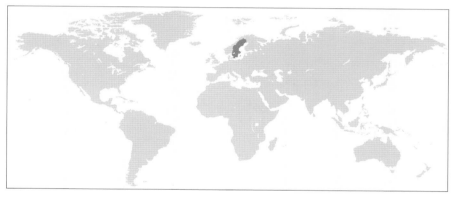

KING CARL XVI GUSTAF became the king of Sweden in September 1973. He was born at Haga Palace in Uppland only son of Prince Gustaf Adolf (1906-1947) and Princess Sibylla; he has four older sisters. His father died in a plane crash in January 1947 when he was only nine months old, leaving him second in line for the throne: he became heir-apparent aged four when his great-grandfather King Gustaf V died in 1950. Thanks to the extreme conventions of royal etiquette, Carl Gustaf was seven years old before he was told of his father's death.

Carl Gustaf served with each of the Swedish armed forces, and attended the universities of Uppsala and Stockholm and was then sent to work in a broad range of businesses to prepare him for his future role as king. On 15 September 1973 Carl became king of Sweden on the death of his grandfather, King Gustaf VI Adolf.

He met and fell in love with a German commoner, Silvia Sommerlath in 1972 at the Munich Olympics, and they married four years later, when she became Queen Silvia. They have three children, Crown Princess Victoria, Prince Carl Philip and Princess Madeleine. Sweden has had three queens regnant in the past, but otherwise has always followed Salic law and crowned the firstborn son of the monarch. However, the constitution was changed on 1 January 1980, when the 1979 Act of Succession became effective: this states that the firstborn child will inherit the throne regardless of sex, and so the law changed to allow Princess Victoria to become queen of Sweden after the death of her father. The king has publicly expressed his displeasure at the retroactive nature of the law, depriving his son Carl Philip of the throne.

The monarch has very little political power, which entirely rests with the representative democratic government. He leads the ceremonial opening of the *Riksdag* (parliament), and represents Sweden both at home and abroad. Perhaps his most important international duty is presenting the awards to the annual Nobel Prize winners. He has a personal reported wealth of some $9 million.

The Royal House of Bernadotte, the ruling house of

Sweden, is descended from Jean-Baptiste Bernadotte, a 19th century Napoleonic marshal, who had risen from his peasant roots in the Pyrénées to become Prince of Pontecorvo and one of Napoleon Bonaparte's most trusted officers. He was put on the Swedish throne when the legitimate heir Karl August died in 1810 and Napoleon intervened on behalf of his marshal. The elderly king Karl XIII and his wife Hedvig Elisabeth Charlotta officially adopted Jean-Baptiste Bernadotte as Karl Johan to give the scheme legal backing. He became Karl XIV Johan, King of Sweden and Norway in May 1818, and ruled Sweden from 1818 until his death in 1844. He established the Bernadotte dynasty, but the family's power has been gradually eroded with the rise of democracy, until in modern times the role of the Swedish monarchy is a constitutional one.

The Swedish royal family enjoys many official residences. Since 1981 they have lived at Drottningholm Palace, which sits on an island in the middle of Lake Mälaren almost five miles west of Stockholm; the royal family occupy the southern wing while the rest of the palace and grounds are open to the public. The first building was constructed here in the late 16th century for King Johan III and Queen Katarina, and it is sumptuously decorated throughout. About a century later it was destroyed by fire and was replaced by this vast palace.

The Royal Palace of Stockholm is a huge palace in the heart of Stockholm. It is the official royal residence and the location for most important state functions and ceremonies. The palace houses offices for members of the royal family and court. Containing over 600 rooms, the palace is built in baroque style and opulently decorated throughout.

The royal family like to retreat to Tullgarn Palace in the summer months. Originally built for Duke Fredrik Adolf in the 1770s, it has been a favorite of the royal family for generations.

Gripsholm Castle, Gustav Vasa's castle sits on the shores of Lake Mälaren in Södermanland. Built in 1537, it is an imposing

building which contains an 18th century theatre and features the Swedish national collection of portraits of prominent Swedes.

Gustav III's Pavilion at Haga Park was built in the late 1700s and is one of the finest examples of a royal palace anywhere. The state rooms are decorated in Pompeian style following the interest in Roman antiquity in the 1780s.

Right: King Carl XVI Gustaf and Queen Silvia. They met at the Munich Olympics in 1972 where, as Silvia Sommerlath, she was working as an educational host. They announced their engagement in March 1976 and married three months later in June.

Right: Queen Silvia of Sweden in 2002. She has three nationalities, German (from her father), Brazilian (from her mother) and Swedish (by marriage).

Below: King Gustaf and his family in the late 1970s. To his left is his oldest child Princess Victoria who, thanks to a change in constitutional law made on 1 January 1980, will succeed him on his death as Swedish monarch and become the fourth queen of Sweden in her own right. Until then Prince Carl Philip (left) was the heir apparent.

Below right: The Swedish royal family and prize winners on stage at the annual Nobel Prize award ceremony in Oslo in 1995.

Far left: King Carl Gustaf, Queen Silvia and Crown Princess Victoria in Malmoe.

Left: Carl XVI Gustaf with members of the Royal Swedish Academy of Engineering Sciences at the Progress Central Design Bureau.

Below left: Princess Madeleine, Duchess of Hälsingland and Gästrikland, Prince Carl Philip, Duke of Värmland and Crown Princess Victoria.

Right: Crown Princess Victoria. Sweden is the first country to adopt absolute primogeniture and Victoria is the only female in the world in direct line to inherit a throne.

Following page: Main picture: Drottningholm Palace is the permanent residence of the royal family.

Inset, top left: Gripsholm Castle was built by Gustav Vasa in 1537.

Inset, below left: Castle Solliden, where the royal family spend their summers.

Right: A salon in the royal private apartments of Drottningholm Palace

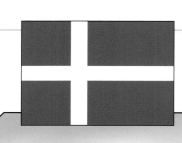

DENMARK
Queen Margrethe II

Official title	Margrethe II, Queen of Denmark
Country ruled	Denmark, Greenland, the Faroe Islands
Born	16 April 1940
Accession to throne	1972
Royal house	House of Schleswig-Holstein-Sonderburg-Glücksburg
Official residence	Winter residence, Amalienborg Palace, Copenhagen. Spring and autumn residence, Fredensborg Palace, Fredensborg. Summer residences, Marselisborg Palace, Aarhus and Grasten Palace, Grasten and the Royal Yacht *Dannebrog*.
Heir	Crown Prince Frederick of Denmark (b. 1968, elder son)

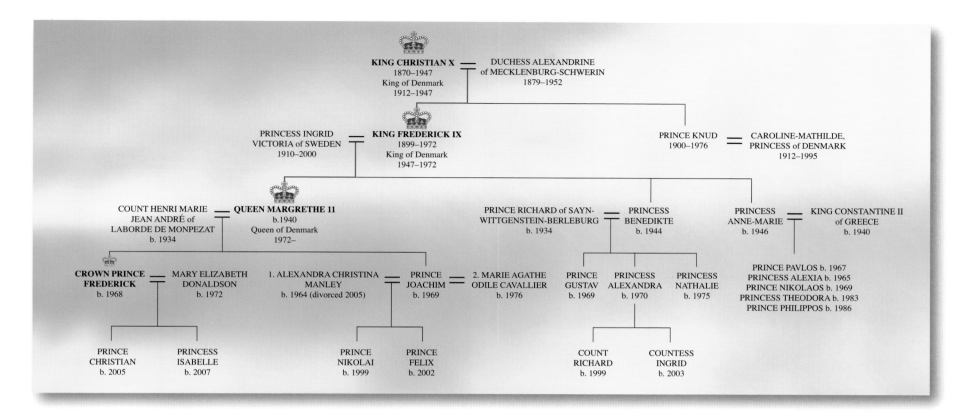

KING CHRISTIAN X
1870–1947
King of Denmark
1912–1947

DUCHESS ALEXANDRINE
of MECKLENBURG-SCHWERIN
1879–1952

PRINCESS INGRID
VICTORIA of SWEDEN
1910–2000

KING FREDERICK IX
1899–1972
King of Denmark
1947–1972

PRINCE KNUD
1900–1976

CAROLINE-MATHILDE,
PRINCESS of DENMARK
1912–1995

COUNT HENRI MARIE
JEAN ANDRÉ of
LABORDE DE MONPEZAT
b. 1934

QUEEN MARGRETHE 11
b.1940
Queen of Denmark
1972–

PRINCE RICHARD of SAYN-
WITTGENSTEIN-BERLEBURG
b. 1934

PRINCESS
BENEDIKTE
b. 1944

PRINCESS
ANNE-MARIE
b. 1946

KING CONSTANTINE II
of GREECE
b. 1940

CROWN PRINCE
FREDERICK
b. 1968

MARY ELIZABETH
DONALDSON
b. 1972

1. ALEXANDRA CHRISTINA
MANLEY
b. 1964 (divorced 2005)

PRINCE
JOACHIM
b. 1969

2. MARIE AGATHE
ODILE CAVALLIER
b. 1976

PRINCE
GUSTAV
b. 1969

PRINCESS
ALEXANDRA
b. 1970

PRINCESS
NATHALIE
b. 1975

PRINCE PAVLOS b. 1967
PRINCESS ALEXIA b. 1965
PRINCE NIKOLAOS b. 1969
PRINCESS THEODORA b. 1983
PRINCE PHILIPPOS b. 1986

PRINCE
CHRISTIAN
b. 2005

PRINCESS
ISABELLE
b. 2007

PRINCE
NIKOLAI
b. 1999

PRINCE
FELIX
b. 2002

COUNT
RICHARD
b. 1999

COUNTESS
INGRID
b. 2003

THE ROYAL HOUSE OF Denmark is the oldest in Europe, able to trace its ancestry back for over 1,000 years to Gorm the Old (d. 958). The monarchy was originally elective, but in practice the succession almost always passed from father to eldest son. This practice ceased during the rule of Frederick III in 1660–1661, when an absolutist hereditary monarchy replaced it. In 1665 a royal decree established the principle of succession based on male primogeniture.

Following political upheaval throughout Europe in 1848, the 'year of revolutions', on 5 June 1849 the Danish monarchy's status changed from absolute to constitutional. The next great change came in 1953 when the Act of Succession allowed for female succession to the Danish throne, thus enabling the current queen to ascend to the throne following the death of her father Frederick IX in 1972.

The direct line of descent was broken in 1448 when King Christoffer III died without issue. The throne was offered to Duke Adolf of Schleswig-Holstein who refused the offer but recommended his nephew, Count Christian of Oldenburg, who was duly crowned King Christian I. The Royal Family of Oldenburg reigned until 1863, when, despite having married three times, the last sovereign of that line, Frederick VII, died in

1863 without producing an heir. The crown passed to a distant cousin, Prince Christian of Glücksburg who acceded to the throne as Christian IX and became the first monarch of the current House of Glücksburg on the Danish throne.

Over time Christian IX was to become known as the 'the father-in-law of Europe': his daughter Princess Alexandra married Edward VII of England, his son William went on to rule Greece as George I, and his grandson Carl became King Haakon VII of Norway. His other children married into the royal families Russia, Hanover and France.

The reigning monarch, Queen Margrethe II — known affectionately by her public as 'Queen Daisy' — was born on 16 April 1940 at Amalienborg Palace in Copenhagen and christened at the naval church in Holmens Kirke on 14 May 1940. The young Margrethe had a wide-ranging education, attending universities in Copenhagen, Cambridge, Aarhus, Paris and London where her studies included political science, economics and archaeology. The queen is a skilled linguist, who speaks French, Swedish, English and German, as well as her native Danish. On 10 June 1967 Princess Margrethe married Henri Marie Jean André Count of Laborde de Monpezat at a ceremony in Holmens Kirke; the couple have two children, Crown Prince Frederick and Prince Joachim. On her accession to the throne on 14 January 1972, Queen Margrethe II became only the second female monarch to rule Denmark.

As well as her royal duties, the queen has long had an active interest in the arts, both as a patron and as an artist in her own right. She has illustrated a Danish edition of J.R.R. Tolkien's *The Lord of The Rings*, and exhibitions of her work have been displayed in Denmark, Sweden, Germany, Japan and Italy.

Right: Fredensborg Palace on the eastern shore of Lake Esrum is often the setting for important royal events such as the wedding of Crown Prince Frederick and Mary Donaldson.

Below: Sumptuous blue silk antique furniture in the Chinese Room at Amalienborg Castle.

Above: The Royal yacht Dannebrog *at anchor at the village of Sandur.*

Below: Crown Prince Frederick, Crown Princess Mary and Prince Christian.

Right: An official portrait of Queen Margrethe taken to celebrate her 65th birthday in 2005.

Left: The imposing front façade of Amalienborg Palace, the winter residence of the Danish monarch.

Below: Tables set ready for the Europa Nostra Gala Dinner 2007, held in the Orangery at Fredensborg Castle.

Below left: Crown Prince Frederick and Crown Princess Mary ready to greet guests at an official function at Amalienborg Palace.

Above and left: Prince Consort Henrik relaxing in his home at Amalienborg Palace in Copenhagen with his two dogs, Evita and Vega. Born in France as Count Henri Andre Marie Jean de Laborede de Monpezat, Prince Henrik has adopted a Danish name and met his wife when he was working as third secretary in the French embassy in London. He became a Danish prince on his marriage, and Prince Consort when his wife became queen in 1972.

Above right: An official portrait of Queen Margrethe taken by the Danish photographer Tine Harden.

Above far right: Queen Margrethe and Prince Consort Henrik with their grandchild Princess Isabella, the daughter of the crown prince born in 2007.

Right: Queen Margrethe and Prince Henrik host a Christmas party for three generations of the Royal Family at Fredensborg Castle.

UNITED KINGDOM
OF GREAT BRITAIN AND NORTHERN IRELAND AND THE COMMONWEALTH REALMS
Queen Elizabeth II

Official title	Queen Elizabeth II
Country ruled	United Kingdom of Great Britain and Northern Ireland and the Commonwealth Realms
Born	21 April 1926
Accession to throne	6 February 1952
Royal house	Windsor
Official residences	Buckingham Palace, Windsor Castle, Palace of Holyrood
Heir	Charles, Prince of Wales (b. 1948, son)

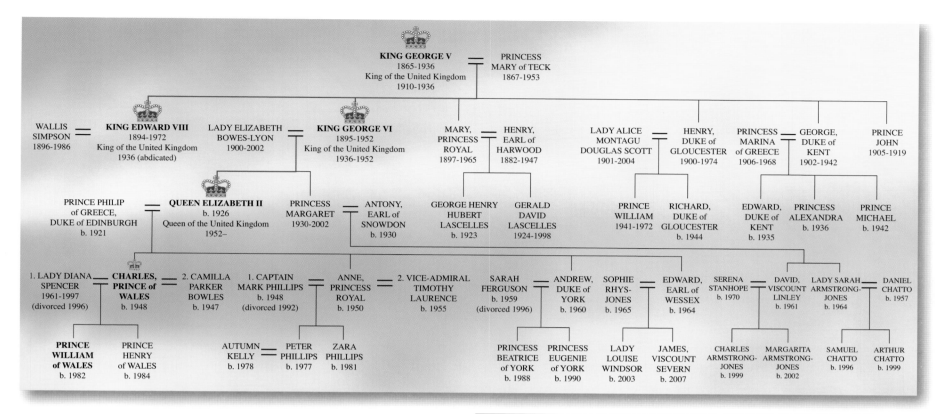

KING GEORGE V
1865-1936
King of the United Kingdom
1910-1936
— PRINCESS MARY of TECK
1867-1953

WALLIS SIMPSON 1896-1986 — KING EDWARD VIII 1894-1972 King of the United Kingdom 1936 (abdicated) — LADY ELIZABETH BOWES-LYON 1900-2002 — KING GEORGE VI 1895-1952 King of the United Kingdom 1936-1952 — MARY, PRINCESS ROYAL 1897-1965 — HENRY, EARL of HARWOOD 1882-1947 — LADY ALICE MONTAGU DOUGLAS SCOTT 1901-2004 — HENRY, DUKE of GLOUCESTER 1900-1974 — PRINCESS MARINA of GREECE 1906-1968 — GEORGE, DUKE of KENT 1902-1942 — PRINCE JOHN 1905-1919

PRINCE PHILIP of GREECE, DUKE of EDINBURGH b. 1921 — QUEEN ELIZABETH II b. 1926 Queen of the United Kingdom 1952– — PRINCESS MARGARET 1930-2002 — ANTONY, EARL of SNOWDON b. 1930 — GEORGE HENRY HUBERT LASCELLES b. 1923 — GERALD DAVID LASCELLES 1924-1998 — PRINCE WILLIAM 1941-1972 — RICHARD, DUKE of GLOUCESTER b. 1944 — EDWARD, DUKE of KENT b. 1935 — PRINCESS ALEXANDRA b. 1936 — PRINCE MICHAEL b. 1942

1. LADY DIANA SPENCER 1961-1997 (divorced 1996) — CHARLES, PRINCE of WALES b. 1948 — 2. CAMILLA PARKER BOWLES b. 1947 — 1. CAPTAIN MARK PHILLIPS b. 1948 (divorced 1992) — ANNE, PRINCESS ROYAL b. 1950 — 2. VICE-ADMIRAL TIMOTHY LAURENCE b. 1955 — SARAH FERGUSON b. 1959 (divorced 1996) — ANDREW, DUKE of YORK b. 1960 — SOPHIE RHYS-JONES b. 1965 — EDWARD, EARL of WESSEX b. 1964 — SERENA STANHOPE b. 1970 — DAVID, VISCOUNT LINLEY b. 1961 — LADY SARAH ARMSTRONG-JONES b. 1964 — DANIEL CHATTO b. 1957

PRINCE WILLIAM of WALES b. 1982 — PRINCE HENRY of WALES b. 1984 — AUTUMN KELLY b. 1978 — PETER PHILLIPS b. 1977 — ZARA PHILLIPS b. 1981 — PRINCESS BEATRICE of YORK b. 1988 — PRINCESS EUGENIE of YORK b. 1990 — LADY LOUISE WINDSOR b. 2003 — JAMES, VISCOUNT SEVERN b. 2007 — CHARLES ARMSTRONG-JONES b. 1999 — MARGARITA ARMSTRONG-JONES b. 2002 — SAMUEL CHATTO b. 1996 — ARTHUR CHATTO b. 1999

Queen Elizabeth II ascended the throne on 6 February 1952 upon the death of her father, King George VI. Her coronation, at Westminster Abbey, followed on 2 June 1953. She is also queen of 16 former British colonies, including Australia, Canada and New Zealand, and head of the Commonwealth, a multi-national body created after the dissolution of the British Empire.

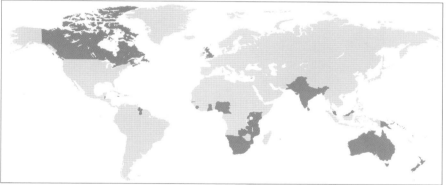

Elizabeth Alexandra Mary was born in London on 21 April 1926, the first child of Prince Albert, Duke of York, the second son of King George V. Third in line to the throne when she was born, it seemed most unlikely that she would become queen.

Elizabeth was educated alongside her younger sister Princess Margaret (1930–2002), with the emphasis on history, religion and languages. When King George V died in 1936, her unmarried uncle acceded to the throne as Edward VIII. Determined, against all advice and the conventions of the time, to marry Wallis Simpson, an American divorcée, he abdicated in favour of his brother, Elizabeth's father in December 1936. Her father became Geroge VI and she became heiress presumptive.

In 1939 when World War II started the sisters were sent to briefly to Balmoral castle in Scotland, then to Sandringham House in Norfolk and finally to Windsor Castle in Berkshire where they lived for five years. In November 1947 Elizabeth married Lieutenant Philip Mountbatten, who was born Prince Philip of Greece and Denmark. Her second cousin once removed, he was a somewhat controversial choice as he had no real royal standing, no fortune, was Greek Orthodox, and had three sisters who married high ranking German noblemen with questionable links to the Nazi regime. He was welcomed by the royal family, however, and given the title Duke of Edinburgh. Their first child, Prince Charles was born in 1948, followed by a daughter Princess Anne, the Princess Royal in 1950 and two further sons, Prince Andrew in 1960 and Prince Edward in 1964.

As her father's health declined Princess Elizabeth took on a greater role in official ceremonies and procedures. In 1951 it became clear that George VI had lung cancer, and his death in

February 1952, was not entirely unexpected. Princess Elizabeth was just 25 years old. Elizabeth and Prince Philip were on safari in Kenya on a royal tour when the news of George VI's death was announced. The tour was abandoned and they returned to Britain. The coronation followed in June 1953, despite the additional death of the Queen's grandmother, the venerable Queen Mary in March 1953.

For more than 50 years, during a period of great social and economic change, Elizabeth II has carried out her political duties as head of state, the ceremonial responsibilities of the sovereign, and an unprecedented programme of visits across the United Kingdom, Commonwealth and many overseas nations. The Queen is a constitutional monarch, and although in theory her powers are vast, in practice (and in accordance with convention) she herself never intervenes in political matters. In the United Kingdom, at least, she is known to take an active interest in the affairs of state, meeting her prime minister once a week and establishing a working relationship with her government ministers. After over 50 years on the throne, she is one of the most experienced statesmen in the world and shows no sign of abdicating.

The British royal family have considerable wealth and live a comfortable, although not overly opulent lifestyle in a great degree of comfort in palaces and castles around the kingdom. Elizabeth II is known for her great love and knowledge of horses and is a keen horsewoman; she is also known to travel wherever possible with her pack of corgi dogs.

The Queen's great-great grandmother, Queen Victoria (1819–1901) reigned as queen of the United Kingdom of Great Britain and Ireland from June 1837, and the first Empress of India from May 1876, until her death on 22 January 1901. Her reign lasted 63 years and seven months, longer than that of any other British monarch to date. She married her first cousin, Prince Albert of Saxe-Coburg-Gotha, on 10 February 1840, and he became not only the queen's companion, but also an important political advisor, replacing Lord Melbourne as the dominant figure in the first half of her life. Together they had nine children and founded a dynasty – among their descendants are the monarchs of Spain, Greece, Sweden, Norway, Denmark,

Left: King George V lying in state in Westminster Hall, London, January 1936. The King's four sons, King Edward VIII, the Duke of York (the future King George VI), Prince Henry, Duke of Gloucester and Prince George, Duke of Kent, mounted the guard at the catafalque on the night before the funeral.

Below left: Her Majesty Queen Elizabeth II wearing the Imperial State Crown and attired in her purple robe of hand woven velvet with white ermin cape and trimming, poses for Cecil Beaton in the throne room at Buckingham Palace London after her coronation 2nd June 1953 In her left hand she holds the orb emblem of sovereign power and in her right the sceptre with cross ensign of kingly power and justice.

Top right: Queen Victoria usurrounded by some of her nine children and 42 grand-children.

Right: Queen Victoria and the Prince Albert entertaine King Louis-Philippe of France inside the royal train. The king visited England in 1844, returning their visits to France, in a personal attempt to repair Anglo-French relations.

and Romania, as well as many more noble and dispossessed royal families, such as the Hohenzollerns and Romanovs.

Queen Victoria was succeeded by her eldest son King Edward VII, and when he died in 1910, his son became George V. Both kings ruled as monarchs of the house of Saxe-Coburg-Gotha, their patrilineal name, but in 1917, when Britain was at war with Germany during World War One, it was deemed to be politically expedient to alter the royal family's name to the far more English name of Windsor. In 1960, the Queen decreed that her descendants would use the surname Mountbatten-Windsor, although the royal dynasty would continue to be called the house of Windsor.

Buckingham Palace in London became the official royal palace of the British monarchs in 1837 when Victoria became queen and has been used as the main royal residence ever since. The Palace of Holyroodhouse has been the main residence of the monarchs of Scotland since the 15th century and the Queen spends early summer there every year. Windsor Castle is even older and has been occupied by almost every English monarch since the Norman Conquest in the 11th century. Additionally, the queen has two privately owned residences, Balmoral Castle in Scotland and Sandringham House in Norfolk.

Above: Holyrood Palace, Edinburgh is the official residence of the monarch in Scotland. The building was founded as a monastery by David I, King of the Scots in 1128, and has served as the principal residence of the monarchs of Scotland since the 15th century.

Right: The Royal Yacht Britannia at anchor off the Cayman Islands 1994. She was built on Clydebank, Scotland in 1953 and commissioned as the royal yacht in 1954. She was decommissioned in 1997 and is now moored in the historic Port of Leith, Edinburgh, Scotland.

Inset: Interconnecting lounges on the Royal Yacht Britannia. c.1980

Right: Sandringham House is the Queen's private estate in Norfolk, England. The house dates from 1870, although earlier buildings occupied the site. When Edward VIII abdicated he still owned both Sandringham and Balmoral as his private properties and George VI had to buy them both from him (rather against Edward's wishes) so they could remain the private retreats of the royal family.

Below: Balmoral Castle in Aberdeenshire was Prince Albert's personal project and was completed in 1855 for Queen Victoria. It is the royal family's home during the summer months.

Above: Queen Elizabeth riding in the Gold State coach from Buckingham Palace to St Paul's Cathedral for a service of Thanksgiving to celebrate to her Golden Jubilee. The coach was built for King George III in 1762, and has only been used by the Queen twice before — for her Coronation and 25 years later for her Silver Jubilee. Later, after lunch at Guildhall in the City of London, she watched a parade and carnival along The Mall. That Monday night more than one million people gathered in central London to hear the Party in the Palace concert, and to watch a spectacular firework display.

Left: Queen Elizabeth II is greeted by well wishers on a walkabout in Durham city centre on the second day of her Golden Jubilee tour of north-east England. While celebrating her 50th year as monarch, Elizabeth together with her husband Prince Philip, made state visits to the Caribbean, Australia, New Zealand, then extensively around the United Kingdom and finally finished her jubilee year in Canada.

Right: Queen Elizabeth the Mother on her 94th Birthday, on 4 August 1994. Always popular with the public, she died in March 2002 when she was 101 years old.

Above: The Princess of Wales was always much in demand for charitable causes and cultural events.

Left: Diana in July 1997.

Right: Prince Charlies and Lady Diana Spencer married at St Paul's Cathedral, London on 29 July 1981. An estimated global audience of 750 million people watched the wedding via television.

Left: Diana with Prince Harry, May 1995.

Below: The Prince and Princess of Wales cycling with Harry (left) and

William on bikes on the isle of Tresco, Scilly Isles, in June 1985.

Above and below: The funeral of Queen Elizabeth

the Queen Mother, March 2002. Her grandchildren mounted guard at the lying-in-state, and were led in the funeral procession by the Duke of Edinburgh.

Left: The official photo of the Royal Silver Wedding, 1977. Back Row, left to right, Earl of Snowdon, Duke of Kent, Prince Michael of Kent, Duke of Edinburgh, Earl of St Andrews, Prince Charles, Prince Andrew, Hon Angus Ogilvy and his son, James Ogilvy. On chairs, left to right, Princess Margaret, the Duchess of Kent (holding Lord Nicholas Windsor, her younger son), Queen Elizabeth the Queen Mother, Queen Elizabeth II, Princess Anne, Marina Ogilvy and her mother, Princess Alexandra. Seated on the floor, left to right, Lady Sarah Armstrong-Jones, Viscount Linley, Prince Edward and Lady Helen Windsor.

Left: Three members of the Highgrove polo team, the Prince of Wales, Prince William and HM the Sultan of Brunei at the Dorchester Polo Trophy match at Cirencester Park Polo Club on 26 June 2004. The team drew 2-2 with Lovelocks.

Below: For many years Prince Philip was a keen competitor in horse-drawn carriage competitions.

Right: Princes William, Harry and Charles compete for their Highgrove polo team at Cirencester Park Polo Club, 15 July 2001.

Below right: Queen Elizabeth II and the Duke of Edinburgh with the Prince of Wales, and his oldest son, Prince William at Clarence House in London before a dinner to mark the 50th anniversary of her coronation.

NETHERLANDS
Queen Beatrix

Official title:	Beatrix, Queen of the Netherlands
Countries ruled:	Netherlands, Dutch Antilles, Aruba
Born	31 January 1938
Accession to throne:	1980
Royal house:	The House of Orange-Nassau
Official residences	The Royal Palace, Amsterdam; Noordeinde Palace, The Hague; and Huis ten Bosch Palace, The Haugue.
Heir:	Crown Prince Willem-Alexander (b.1967, eldest son)

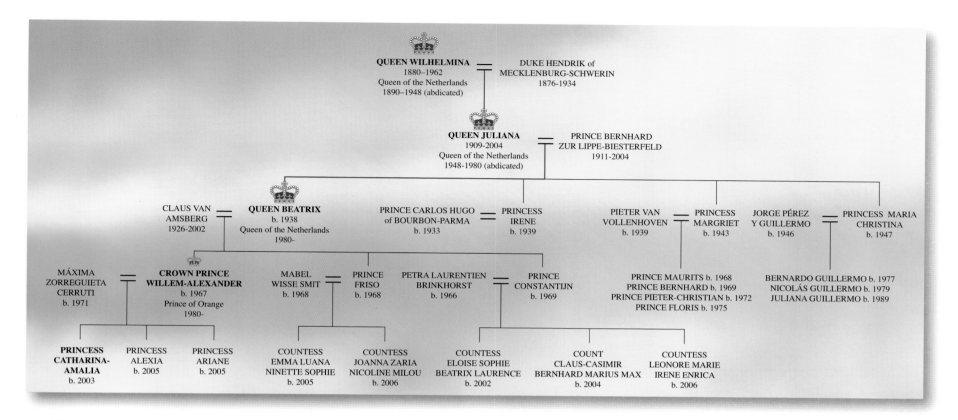

QUEEN WILHELMINA
1880–1962
Queen of the Netherlands
1890–1948 (abdicated)

DUKE HENDRIK of
MECKLENBURG-SCHWERIN
1876-1934

QUEEN JULIANA
1909-2004
Queen of the Netherlands
1948-1980 (abdicated)

PRINCE BERNHARD
ZUR LIPPE-BIESTERFELD
1911-2004

CLAUS VAN
AMSBERG
1926-2002

QUEEN BEATRIX
b. 1938
Queen of the Netherlands
1980-

PRINCE CARLOS HUGO
of BOURBON-PARMA
b. 1933

PRINCESS
IRENE
b. 1939

PIETER VAN
VOLLENHOVEN
b. 1939

PRINCESS
MARGRIET
b. 1943

JORGE PÉREZ
Y GUILLERMO
b. 1946

PRINCESS MARIA
CHRISTINA
b. 1947

MÁXIMA
ZORREGUIETA
CERRUTI
b. 1971

CROWN PRINCE
WILLEM-ALEXANDER
b. 1967
Prince of Orange
1980-

MABEL
WISSE SMIT
b. 1968

PRINCE
FRISO
b. 1968

PETRA LAURENTIEN
BRINKHORST
b. 1966

PRINCE
CONSTANTIJN
b. 1969

PRINCE MAURITS b. 1968
PRINCE BERNHARD b. 1969
PRINCE PIETER-CHRISTIAN b. 1972
PRINCE FLORIS b. 1975

BERNARDO GUILLERMO b. 1977
NICOLÁS GUILLERMO b. 1979
JULIANA GUILLERMO b. 1989

PRINCESS
CATHARINA-
AMALIA
b. 2003

PRINCESS
ALEXIA
b. 2005

PRINCESS
ARIANE
b. 2005

COUNTESS
EMMA LUANA
NINETTE SOPHIE
b. 2005

COUNTESS
JOANNA ZARIA
NICOLINE MILOU
b. 2006

COUNTESS
ELOISE SOPHIE
BEATRIX LAURENCE
b. 2002

COUNT
CLAUS-CASIMIR
BERNHARD MARIUS MAX
b. 2004

COUNTESS
LEONORE MARIE
IRENE ENRICA
b. 2006

Queen Beatrix was born Princess Beatrix Wilhelmina Armgard at Soestdijk Palace on 31 January 1938, the eldest daughter of Crown Princess Juliana of the Netherlands and Bernhard of Lippe-Biessterfeld. During World War II she and her family fled to London and then Canada. Over the years her parents had three further daughters, princesses Irene, Margriet and Christina. The family returned to the Netherlands in August 1945 and in September 1948 her mother became Queen Juliana of the Netherlands on the abdication of Queen Wilhelmina; Beatrix in turn became heir apparent aged ten. As a young princess she was thoroughly educated and attended Leiden University where she studied subjects relevant to her future role as monarch. In July 1961 she passed her law degree.

She first encountered controversy in 1964 when she met and fell in love with a young German aristocrat Claus von Amsberg who had served in the Hitler Youth and Wehrmacht during the Second World War. They wed in Amsterdam on 10 March 1966 amid huge protests and street battles — nevertheless over the years he became the most popular member of the Dutch royal family. Together they had three sons: the heir to the throne, Crown Prince Willem-Alexander, Prince Johan-Friso and Prince Constantijn. Between them, they have given the

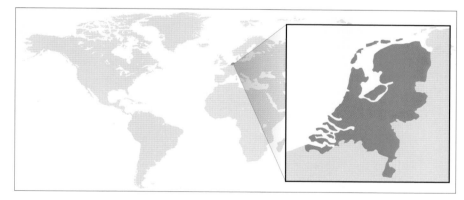

queen eight grandchildren. The first male heir to the Dutch throne for almost a century, Willem-Alexander is married to Princess Máxima and they have three daughters.

Queen Beatrix became queen of the Netherlands in 1980 on the abdication of her mother Queen Juliana, and was invested on 30 April 1980. She is the head of a constitutional monarchy and head of state. On succeeding to the throne, the monarch is publicly sworn in and invested in Amsterdam in front of the Prinsjesdag (parliament). The queen has great influence, but no actual power, although she does wield considerable clout with regard to international relations where her opinions are highly valued.

At one time one of the wealthiest monarchs in the world, Queen Beatrix has sold her royal palaces to the state and placed culturally important royal artifacts such as paintings and antiques into non-personal trusts such as the House of Orange-Nassau Historic Collections Trust, which remains at the disposal of the monarch. Her wealth is now estimated to be around $4.7 billion.

The Kingdom of the Netherlands comprises the Netherlands, the Netherlands (Dutch) Antilles, and Aruba. The crown, sceptre, orb, sword of state and national standard make up the royal regalia and date from 1840 and the reign of King Willem II; however, the monarch is not crowned and never wears the crown.

From the 16th to the 18th centuries, members of the House of Orange-Nassau were *Stadtholders* (governors) of the Dutch Republic. In the early 19th century the Netherlands ceased being a republic and instead became a monarchy under the House of Orange-Nassau. The royal coat of arms dates from 1815 when the kingdom of the Netherlands was founded. It has been changed twice since, and features a golden lion rampant on a blue shield supported by two golden lions rampant.

The House of Orange-Nassau makes use of three state-owned royal palaces, the Royal Palace in Amsterdam, Noordeinde Palace and Huis ten Bosch Palace. Dating from 1533, Noordeinde Palace was originally a medieval farmhouse, and became a royal palace in 1817. Queen Beatrix now uses it as her offices. Since 1981 she has used the 17th-century Huis ten

Bosch in The Hague as her home. Located on Dam Square in Amsterdam, the Royal Palace was originally built as the city hall in 1648. It is now used for royal and state functions and a summer historic or artistic venue when it is open to the public.

Above: Queen Juliana and Prince Bernhard with their four daughters, July 1949.

Above right: Queen Beatrix arrives at Knights Hall with Prince Claus and Prince Willem-Alexander for the opening of Parliament 1993

Left: Queen Beatrix in England in June 2002.

Far left: Princess Beatrix and Prince Claus, Baron Von Amsberg, on their wedding day, 10 March 1966.

Right: Crown Prince Willem-Alexander and Princess Maxima waving from the Royal Palace Noordeinde, 2005.

Left: Huis ten Bosch, also known as Chateau du Bois, as it looked in the late 19th century. It was originally built for Stadholder Frederik Hendrik and called Sael van Oranje — Hall of the Oranges — and used as a summer residence. It became a royal palace in 1815 when Willem I was proclaimed King of the Netherlands. Huis ten Bosch has been Queen Beatrix's home since 1981.

Below left: Originally built in 1648 as the City Hall for Amsterdam, the Royal Palace in Dam Square. It officially became a palace in 1810 for Napoleon's governor of the Netherlands, Charles Lebrun.

Below: Noordeinde Palace is the official residence of the Royal Family in The Hague.

BELGIUM
King Albert II

Official title	Albert II, King of the Belgians
Country ruled	Belgium
Born	6 June 1934
Accession to throne	1993
Royal house	Saxe-Coburg-Gotha
Official residence	Royal Palace of Belgium, Brussels
Heir	Philippe, Duke of Brabant (b. 1960, eldest son)

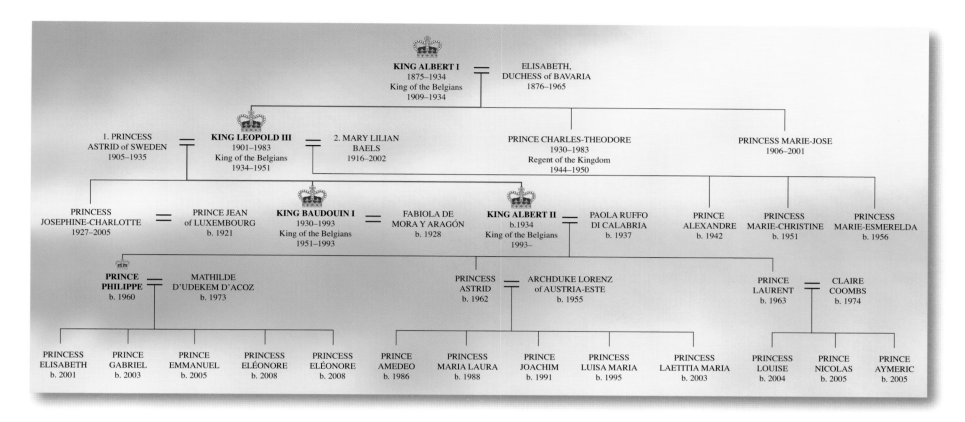

KING ALBERT I
1875–1934
King of the Belgians
1909–1934

ELISABETH,
DUCHESS of BAVARIA
1876–1965

1. PRINCESS
ASTRID of SWEDEN
1905–1935

KING LEOPOLD III
1901–1983
King of the Belgians
1934–1951

2. MARY LILIAN
BAELS
1916–2002

PRINCE CHARLES-THEODORE
1930–1983
Regent of the Kingdom
1944–1950

PRINCESS MARIE-JOSE
1906–2001

PRINCESS
JOSEPHINE-CHARLOTTE
1927–2005

PRINCE JEAN
of LUXEMBOURG
b. 1921

KING BAUDOUIN I
1930–1993
King of the Belgians
1951–1993

FABIOLA DE
MORA Y ARAGÓN
b. 1928

KING ALBERT II
b.1934
King of the Belgians
1993–

PAOLA RUFFO
DI CALABRIA
b. 1937

PRINCE
ALEXANDRE
b. 1942

PRINCESS
MARIE-CHRISTINE
b. 1951

PRINCESS
MARIE-ESMERELDA
b. 1956

PRINCE
PHILIPPE
b. 1960

MATHILDE
D'UDEKEM D'ACOZ
b. 1973

PRINCESS
ASTRID
b. 1962

ARCHDUKE LORENZ
of AUSTRIA-ESTE
b. 1955

PRINCE
LAURENT
b. 1963

CLAIRE
COOMBS
b. 1974

PRINCESS
ELISABETH
b. 2001

PRINCE
GABRIEL
b. 2003

PRINCE
EMMANUEL
b. 2005

PRINCESS
ELÉONORE
b. 2008

PRINCESS
ELÉONORE
b. 2008

PRINCE
AMEDEO
b. 1986

PRINCESS
MARIA LAURA
b. 1988

PRINCE
JOACHIM
b. 1991

PRINCESS
LUISA MARIA
b. 1995

PRINCESS
LAETITIA MARIA
b. 2003

PRINCESS
LOUISE
b. 2004

PRINCE
NICOLAS
b. 2005

PRINCE
AYMERIC
b. 2005

THE COUNTRY THAT WE recognise today as Belgium is generally considered to date from the Belgian revolution of 1830 that ended Belgium's union with the Netherlands. Following the revolution, in 1831, an international conference held in London ended centuries of external rule by recognizing Belgium as an independent nation.

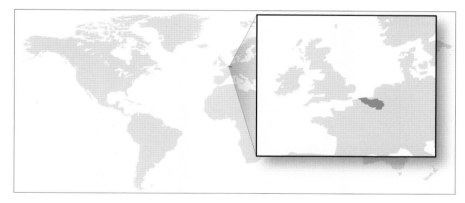

With the advent of independence came the search for a king. The crown was offered to Prince Leopold of Saxe-Coburg, the widower of Princess Charlotte the niece of King William IV of Great Britain. Although he had already decline the throne of Greece, Leopold accepted the offer and he was duly sworn in as the first King of the Belgians on 21 July 1831.

Even though the independence of Belgium had been guaranteed at the London conference, King William I of the Netherlands had not given up hope of reclaiming the land and on 2 August 1831 the Dutch army invaded. Belgium was saved by the intervention of the French army and Leopold spent most of his reign consolidating the position of the nascent nation.

In 1832 Leopold married the daughter of King Louis-Philippe of France, Louise-Marie and the couple went on to have four children. Despite some initial setbacks Belgium slowly began to flourish during Leopold's reign, and highlights included the 1835 opening of the Brussels-Malines line, the first steam passenger line in continental Europe, a project that Leopold had been championing since 1832.

Having worked to nurture the survival of his adopted nation for 34 years, Leopold died on 10 December 1865 and was succeeded, seven days later, by his son Leopold II. Leopold's successors were to face many tribulations, most notably the occupation of Belgium by the Germans during both World Wars. The invasion of Belgium in 1914 led directly to the British involvement in World War I, as it violated the terms of the 1831 treaty. Leopold III was a controversial monarch: although he refused to co-operate with the Nazis during World War II, he was unable to return to the throne at the end of the war and in

1951 he abdicated in favour of his 20-year-old son Baudouin (the brother of the current monarch).

The current monarch, King Albert II, was born in Brussels, at the Chateau of Stuyvenberg, on 6 June 1934, the second son of King Leopold III and his first wife Queen Astrid. In 1953 Prince Albert entered service with the Belgian navy, and in 1962 he was offered the post of Honorary President of the Board of Directors of the Belgian Foreign Trade Office, an office that he held with distinction for over 30 years. In this capacity, the prince travelled extensively throughout the world promoting the interests of Belgian businesses. In recognition of his contribution the Prince Albert Fund was established in 1984 to provide grants for the training of future specialists in foreign trade and international management. Albert also served as the President of the Belgian Red Cross from 1958 to 1993.

On 2 July 1959 Prince Albert married the Italian princess Donna Paola Ruffo di Calabria. King Albert II and Queen Paola have three children: Prince Philippe (b. 15 April 1960), Princess Astrid (b. 5 June 1962) and Prince Laurent (b. 19 October 1963). Following the death of his brother, King Baudouin, Prince Albert was sworn in as the sixth King of the Belgians on 9 August 1993.

As the first in the line of succession to the Belgian throne, Prince Philippe bears the title Duke of Brabant, the traditional title given to the Belgian heir. A trained pilot and commando, Prince Philippe served in the Belgian armed forces and now works to promote Belgian trade interests. He married in 1999 and has three children.

Left: Queen Paola of Belgium at the Tyne Cot War Cemetery, Passchendaele, during a 2007 ceremony to commemorate Commonwealth soldiers of the First World War.

Below left: The official residence of the Belgian monarch, the Royal Palace of Belgium in Brussels.

Above: King Albert II, Queen Fabiola (centre) and Queen Paola waving to the crowds from the balcony of the Royal Palace 1993. Queen Fabiola is the widow of Albert's brother, King Baudouin.

Left: King Albert II salutes the crowd and walks with Queen Paola after he was sworn in as the new King of Belgium, in Brussels on 9 August 1993.

Above: The King and Queen of Belgium pose with their grandchildren for a photograph on the occasion of King Albert's 70th birthday in 2004. Seated left to right: Princess Laetitia Maria, Prince Joachim, Princess Louise, Queen Paola, Princess Elisabeth, Prince Gabriel, King Albert and Princess Maria Laura. Princess Maria Laura and Prince Amadeo are standing behind them.

Above right: Crown Prince Philippe and Princess Mathilde of Belgium at London Waterloo railway station during a visit to the UK.

Right: Princess Mathilde married Prince Philippe, Duke of Brabant in 1999 and the couple now have four children.

Far right: King Albert II of Belgium inspecting the guard of honour at the official residence of the President of Ireland during a three-day visit in 2007.

LUXEMBOURG
Grand Duke Henri

Official title	Henri, Grand Duke of Luxembourg, Duke of Nassau
Country ruled	Luxembourg
Born	16 April 1955
Accession to throne	2000
Royal house	House of Luxembourg-Nassau
Official residence	Grand Ducal Palace, City of Luxembourg; Fischbach Castle; Berg Castle
Heir	Hereditary Grand Duke Guillaume (b. 1981, son)

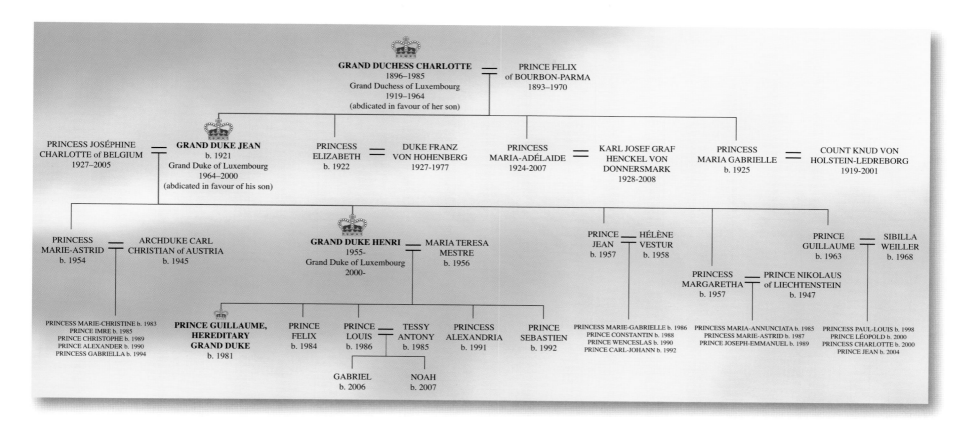

GRAND DUCHESS CHARLOTTE
1896–1985
Grand Duchess of Luxembourg
1919–1964
(abdicated in favour of her son)

PRINCE FELIX
of BOURBON-PARMA
1893–1970

PRINCESS JOSÉPHINE
CHARLOTTE of BELGIUM
1927–2005

GRAND DUKE JEAN
b. 1921
Grand Duke of Luxembourg
1964–2000
(abdicated in favour of his son)

PRINCESS
ELIZABETH
b. 1922

DUKE FRANZ
VON HOHENBERG
1927-1977

PRINCESS
MARIA-ADÉLAIDE
1924-2007

KARL JOSEF GRAF
HENCKEL VON
DONNERSMARK
1928-2008

PRINCESS
MARIA GABRIELLE
b. 1925

COUNT KNUD VON
HOLSTEIN-LEDREBORG
1919-2001

PRINCESS
MARIE-ASTRID
b. 1954

ARCHDUKE CARL
CHRISTIAN of AUSTRIA
b. 1945

GRAND DUKE HENRI
1955-
Grand Duke of Luxembourg
2000-

MARIA TERESA
MESTRE
b. 1956

PRINCE
JEAN
b. 1957

HÉLÈNE
VESTUR
b. 1958

PRINCE
GUILLAUME
b. 1963

SIBILLA
WEILLER
b. 1968

PRINCESS
MARGARETHA
b. 1957

PRINCE NIKOLAUS
of LIECHTENSTEIN
b. 1947

PRINCESS MARIE-CHRISTINE b. 1983
PRINCE IMRE b. 1985
PRINCE CHRISTOPHE b. 1989
PRINCE ALEXANDER b. 1990
PRINCESS GABRIELLA b. 1994

PRINCE GUILLAUME,
HEREDITARY
GRAND DUKE
b. 1981

PRINCE
FELIX
b. 1984

PRINCE
LOUIS
b. 1986

TESSY
ANTONY
b. 1985

PRINCESS
ALEXANDRIA
b. 1991

PRINCE
SEBASTIEN
b. 1992

PRINCESS MARIE-GABRIELLE b. 1986
PRINCE CONSTANTIN b. 1988
PRINCE WENCESLAS b. 1990
PRINCE CARL-JOHANN b. 1992

PRINCESS MARIA-ANNUNCIATA b. 1985
PRINCESS MARIE-ASTRID b. 1987
PRINCE JOSEPH-EMMANUEL b. 1989

PRINCESS PAUL-LOUIS b. 1998
PRINCE LÉOPOLD b. 2000
PRINCESS CHARLOTTE b. 2000
PRINCE JEAN b. 2004

GABRIEL
b. 2006

NOAH
b. 2007

THE RECORDED HISTORY OF Luxembourg is generally agreed to begin in 963 with the building of a castle, called Lucilinburhuc ('Little Fortress'), by Siegfried, Count of Ardennes who had traded his lands for the site. Through a mixture of conquest, diplomacy and marriage, Siegfried's heirs expanded their domain, and by around 1060 Count Conrad had become the first person to bear the title Count of Luxembourg. The house of Luxembourg that Conrad founded went on to provide four emperors of the Holy Roman Empire.

With the death of the Luxembourgois Emperor Sigismund in 1437, the lands passed through his only child, Elizabeth to the Habsburgs (she had married Albert of Habsburg in 1421). For the next four centuries Luxembourg was dominated by various European nations, until in 1815 it was raised in status to a grand duchy and, under the terms of the Congress of Vienna, placed under the rule of the prince of Orange-Nassau and king of the Netherlands.

King William I proved to be a heavy-handed and unpopular ruler, and much of the country joined in the Belgian Revolution against William in 1830. The following year the Great Powers (France, Britain, Prussia, Russia, and Austria) intervened and divided Luxembourg in two. The French-speaking part of the

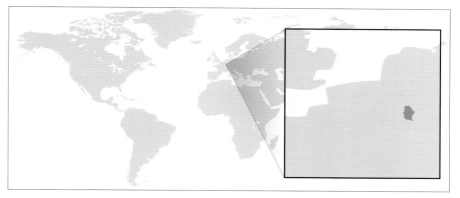

duchy was given to Belgium, while William retained control of the Luxembourgish-speaking portion. Finally on 11 May 1867 the grand duchy gained its independence, with its neutrality guaranteed by the Great Powers. At that time the Dutch king, William III, still retained nominal authority as grand duke. When William died in 1890 without a male heir, the crown passed to Adolf, Duke of Nassau, from whom the current royal family are descended.

The current grand duke, Henri, was born on 16 April 1955 at Betzdorf Castle in Luxembourg. His secondary education was in Luxembourg and France, where he successfully gained his baccalaureate in 1974. He then went on to study in Britain, the USA and Switzerland, where he studied political science at the

University of Geneva, graduating in 1980. It was while studying in Geneva that he met fellow political science student, Maria Teresa Mestre, who he married 1981.

Grand Duke Henri ascended to the throne on 7 October 2000 when his father, Grand Duke Jean abdicated in his favour after 36 years as ruler of Luxembourg. Henri is the sixth grand duke to rule Luxembourg since Adolf. The Luxembourgian monarchy is constitutional in nature and the grand duke's role is mostly symbolic, but he does have the constitutional power to appoint the prime minister and his government, to dissolve the Chamber of Deputies, and to promulgate laws and to accredit ambassadors.

In December 2008 Henri provoked a constitutional crisis when he let it be known that he would oppose a parliamentary bill to permit euthanasia in Luxembourg. The government responded by proposing a constitutional amendment that would remove the need for the grand duke to approve new laws. The only other time that a sovereign had blocked a law was in 1912, when the Grand Duchess Marie-Adelaide refused to sign an education bill.

Above: A portrait of Princess Margaretha of Luxembourg taken in 1982.

Left: Prince Jean of Luxembourg and Princess Josephine Charlotte of Belgium were married in 1953.

Above right: Prince Henri, the second son of Grand Duke Jean of Luxembourg, with his wife Princess Maria Teresa.

Right: A formal family portrait of the Royal Family of Luxembourg.

Above: Prince Guillaume of Luxembourg sharing a smile with his wife Princess Sibilla at their wedding at Versailles in September 1994. The couple have four children.

*Left: (From right to left):
Grand Duke Henri of
Luxembourg, the Russian
president's wife Lyudmila,
Russian President Vladimir
Putin and Grand Duchess
Maria Teresa.*

*Below: Grand Duchess
Josephine Charlotte and
Grand Duke Jean of
Luxemburg on the balcony
of the Grand Ducal Palace
with their son Henri and his
wife Princess Maria Teresa.
Grand Duke Jean abdicated
in favour of Henri in 2000.*

Right: A statue of William II stands proudly in front of the Grand Ducal Palace in Luxembourg.

Below: Berg Castle in the town of Colmar-Berg has been the official the home of the Grand Duke of Luxembourg since 1948.

FRANCE
Pretenders to the French throne

Official title	Prince Henri VII d'Orléans, Comte de Paris, Duc de France	Prince Louis XX, Duc d'Anjou, Bourbon et Touraine	Jean-Christophe Napoléon, Prince Napoléon
Pretender to	King of France	King of France	Emperor of France
Born	14 June 1933	25 April 1974	11 July 1986
Pretence from	1999	1989	1997
Royal house	Orléans	Bourbon	Bonaparte
Official residences	Private residence, Paris	Private residences, Caracas and Madrid	Private residence, Paris
Heir	Dauphin, Jean d'Orléans, Duc de Vendôme (b. 1961, son)	King Juan Carlos of Spain (b. 1938, cousin)	None

Henri VII, Comte de Paris.

Prince Louis de Bourbon, Duc d'Anjou.

Charles Napoléon (father of Prince Napoléon).

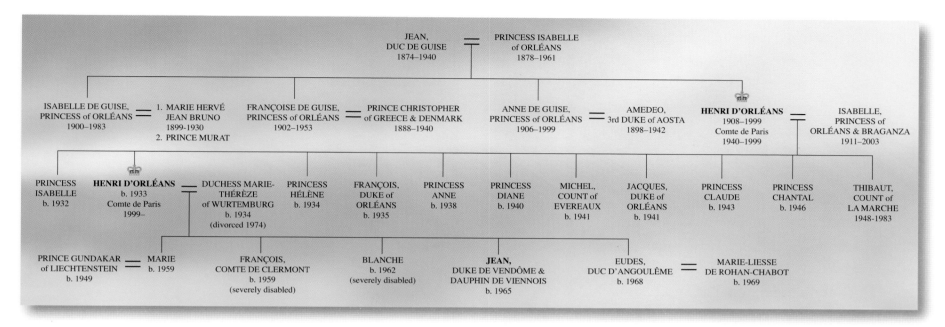

In 1789 the storming of the Bastille marked the beginning of the end for the French monarchy, and the execution of King Louis XVI in 1793 sent out a clear signal that republican rule was more to French taste than despotic monarchy. In spite of this, over 200 years later, three families lay claim to the long-defunct French throne: the Orléanist descendants of King Louis Philippe (reigned 1830–1848); the Bourbon descendants of the great 17th century 'Sun King', Louis XIV (1643–1715); and the descendants of Emperor Napoléon Bonaparte (reigned 1804–1815).

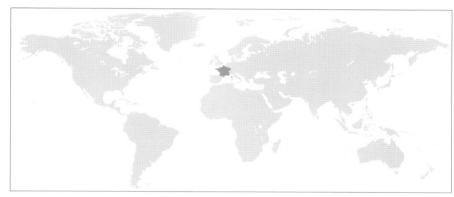

COUNTS OF PARIS

A descendant of the Bourbon 'Citizen King' Louis Philippe (1773–1850), the Comte de Paris would be Henri VII of France were the throne to be restored as the monarchist Orleanist supporters wish. Louis Philippe, Duke of Orelans, became king in 1830, propelled to the throne because of his liberal tendencies in place of the absolutist Charles X from the senior branch of the house of Bourbon.

The family were famously quarrelsome and the current count's father (Henri VI, 1908–1999) disinherited several of his children over the years. When Comte Henri VI sold some family jewels, including those belonging to Louis' Philippe's queen, his children went to court to prevent the sale. The current count, Henri VII, disinherited in 1984 because his father disapproved of his second marriage, finally inherited the title in 1999, and

restored his siblings to the line of succession. Once fabulously wealthy, the family's riches declined in the middle years of the 20th century when the current count's father lived like a king, with an extravagant lifestyle centred on the Ritz Hotel in Paris.

In a separate dispute with his distant cousins, the Spanish Bourbon successors of the house of Anjou, the Comte de Paris challenged their right to use an undifferentiated coat of arms. The case was thrown out of the French courts, which asserted that they did not have the jurisdiction to judge such a case. Such haughty indifference to what is basically a family quarrel contrasts with the interest shown in the pretender's family by the French public. The Comte de Paris and his relations frequently appear in the pages of *Paris Match* and *Point de Vue*, while every few years the question of restoration is debated in the more serious newspapers. President de Gaulle toyed with the idea of proposing Comte Henri VI as his successor as president, but nothing ever came of it.

Until 1950 the French Law of Exile prevented claimants to the French throne from living in France, and the present count was born in Belgium. He lived in exile in Morocco, Spain and Portugal until the Law of Exile was abolished and the family returned to France. The Comte de Paris stood for election in the European elections of 2004 and his son, Prince Jean, Dauphin and Duc de Vendôme runs as association called Gens de France, which aims to promote French cultural heritage.

The count and his family live privately in Paris, but the family owns and maintains the Chateau d'Amboise on the River Loire, as well as the Chapelle Royale at Dreux in the Ile de France, the traditional burial place of the house of Orléans.

HOUSE OF BOURBON

The claim of the man who would be King Louis XX of France begins further back in French history. In 1700, France laid claim to the throne of Spain, and King Louis XIV despatched his grandson Philip, Duc d'Anjou to take up the post as Philip V of Spain. Philip renounced his right of succession to the French throne, and the Treaty of Utrecht, which ended the War of Spanish Succession in 1713, further reinforced this.

As the French Bourbon monarchy died out during the Revolutionary years, the Bourbon claim to the throne split between the 'junior' and 'senior' branches of the family. King Louis Philippe and his descendants represented the claims of a junior branch of the house of Bourbon, while the senior branch – the Spanish royal family as descended from Philip V – maintained their claim to be kings of France.

Today, what is known as minority support for the legitimist claim, rests with Louis Alphonse de Bourbon, Duc d'Anjou and a cousin of Juan Carlos, King of Spain. Descended from both the Spanish royal family and General Franco, Louis was brought up in Spain and now divides his time between Venezuela, his wife's homeland, and Spain, where he has a magnificent apartment in Madrid. A keen sportsman, he is an international polo player, who enjoys sailing and ice hockey. He also devotes a considerable amount of time to commemorative royal duties as head of the house of Bourbon.

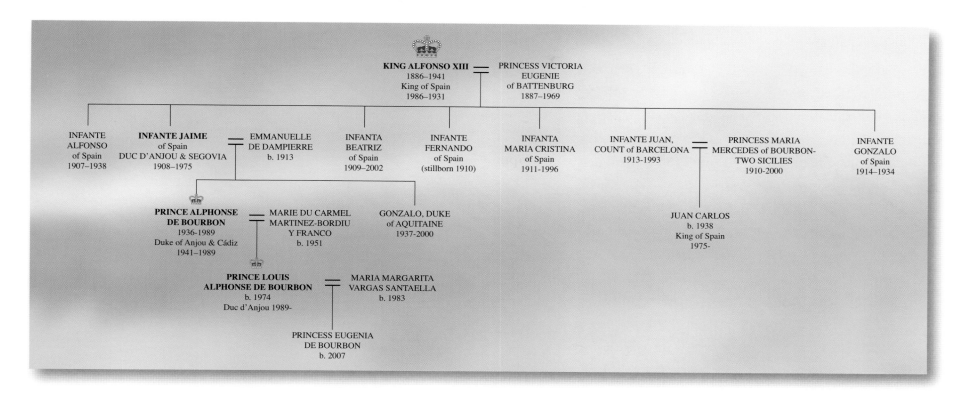

KING ALFONSO XIII
1886–1941
King of Spain
1986–1931

PRINCESS VICTORIA
EUGENIE
of BATTENBURG
1887–1969

INFANTE
ALFONSO
of Spain
1907–1938

INFANTE JAIME
of Spain
DUC D'ANJOU & SEGOVIA
1908–1975

EMMANUELLE
DE DAMPIERRE
b. 1913

INFANTA
BEATRIZ
of Spain
1909–2002

INFANTE
FERNANDO
of Spain
(stillborn 1910)

INFANTA
MARIA CRISTINA
of Spain
1911–1996

INFANTE JUAN,
COUNT of BARCELONA
1913–1993

PRINCESS MARIA
MERCEDES of BOURBON-
TWO SICILIES
1910–2000

INFANTE
GONZALO
of Spain
1914–1934

PRINCE ALPHONSE
DE BOURBON
1936–1989
Duke of Anjou & Cádiz
1941–1989

MARIE DU CARMEL
MARTINEZ-BORDIU
Y FRANCO
b. 1951

GONZALO, DUKE
of AQUITAINE
1937–2000

JUAN CARLOS
b. 1938
King of Spain
1975-

PRINCE LOUIS
ALPHONSE DE BOURBON
b. 1974
Duc d'Anjou 1989-

MARIA MARGARITA
VARGAS SANTAELLA
b. 1983

PRINCESS EUGENIA
DE BOURBON
b. 2007

Above left: The Comte and Comtesse de Paris attend the wedding of their son, the Dauphin, Jean, Duc de Vendôme, 2009.

Middle left: Jean, Duc de Vendôme married Princess Philomena in 2009 at Senlis Cathedral, France.

Left: Prince Louis Alphonse, Duc d'Orléans represents the Bourbon claim to the French throne.

Above: Louis Philippe, the 'Citizen King' ruled France 1830–1848, abdicating and fleeing to London when he was deposed by the revolution of 1848. He is the ancestor of the current Comte de Paris.

Above: Louis XIV, the 'Sun King' is the ancestor of both the Bourbon and Orléanist families.

THE BONAPARTES

Neither Napoléon I (1869–1821) nor his nephew Napoléon III (1808–1873) left legitimate sons to carry on the Bonapartist claim to the French throne. Today, the Imperial claim rests with the descendants of Napoléon Bonaparte's youngest brother, Jerome, King of Westphalia (1784–1860).

Currently, father and son dispute the title. Prince Louis Napoléon VI (1914–1997) disinherited his son Charles Napoléon because he disapproved of his son's republican views, and he decreed that the title would pass to his grandson, Jean-Christophe. Charles Napoléon was born and grew up in France, and is now a successful businessman with a doctorate in economics from the Sorbonne. Based in Corsica, his famous ancestor's birthplace, he is a former mayor of Ajaccio, and stood for election to the European parliament in 2007. He uses the title Prince Imperial, and although he believes that his father had no right to disinherit him, he has publicly vowed that he will not dispute his son's use of the title of Prince Napoléon.

Below: Charles Napoléon with his children in Corsica, 2000. His son Jean Christophe (left) is the current Prince Napoléon.

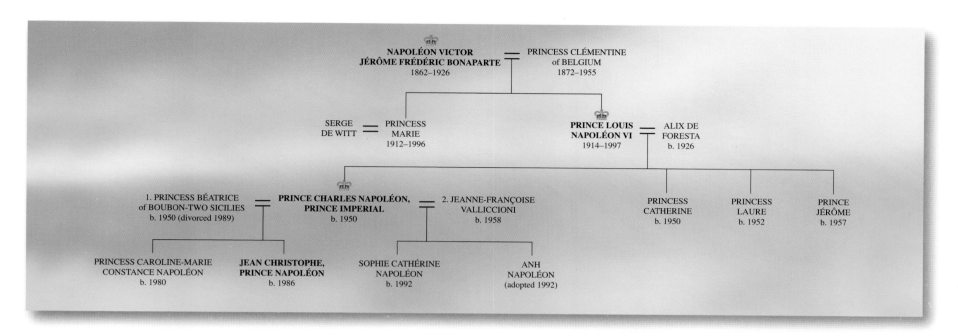

NAPOLÉON VICTOR
JÉRÔME FRÉDÉRIC BONAPARTE
1862–1926 — PRINCESS CLÉMENTINE
of BELGIUM
1872–1955

SERGE
DE WITT — PRINCESS
MARIE
1912–1996

PRINCE LOUIS
NAPOLÉON VI
1914–1997 — ALIX DE
FORESTA
b. 1926

1. PRINCESS BÉATRICE
of BOUBON-TWO SICILIES
b. 1950 (divorced 1989) — PRINCE CHARLES NAPOLÉON,
PRINCE IMPERIAL
b. 1950 — 2. JEANNE-FRANÇOISE
VALLICCIONI
b. 1958

PRINCESS
CATHERINE
b. 1950

PRINCESS
LAURE
b. 1952

PRINCE
JÉRÔME
b. 1957

PRINCESS CAROLINE-MARIE
CONSTANCE NAPOLÉON
b. 1980

JEAN CHRISTOPHE,
PRINCE NAPOLÉON
b. 1986

SOPHIE CATHÉRINE
NAPOLÉON
b. 1992

ANH
NAPOLÉON
(adopted 1992)

Left: The Bonaparte family in the 1960s. Prince Louis Napoléon VI stands in front of a portrait of their most famous ancestor, with from left Princess Catherine, Princess Napoleon Prince Napoleon, Prince Jerome, Princess Laure, and Prince Charles.

Right: The Emperor Napoléon III, was elected president of the French republic in 1848 and became emperor of the Second Empire, 1853–1870.

Far right: Napoléon Bonaparte crowned himself emperor in 1804. He left no heirs and the current Bonaparte family are descended from his brother Jerome.

MONACO
Prince Albert II

Official title	Albert II, Sovereign Prince of Monaco
Country ruled	Monaco
Born	14 March 1958
Accession to throne	6 April 2005
Royal house	House of Grimaldi
Official residences	Palais de Monaco, Monaco
Heir	Princess Caroline, the. Princess of Hanover (b. 1957, older sister)

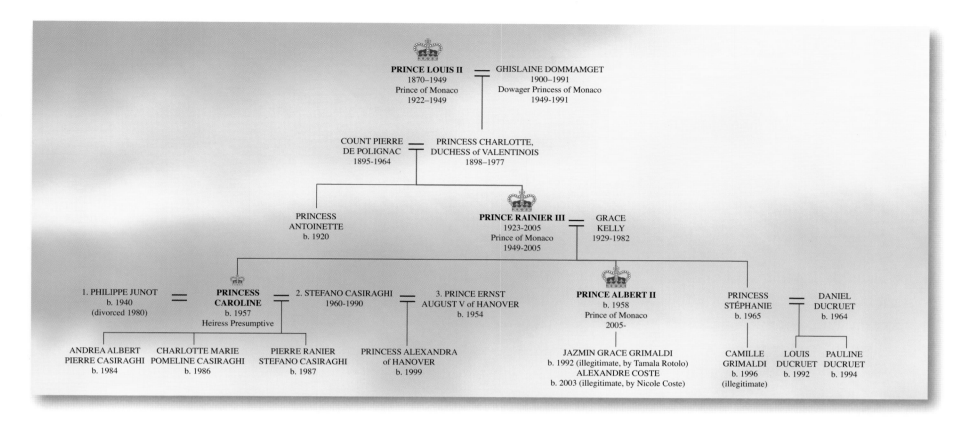

MONACO BECAME A PRINCIPALITY in 1612 and is a tiny independent sovereign state sandwiched between France and Italy on the Côte d'Azur. It has been the possession of the Grimaldi family for over 700 years, making them the most longstanding ruling royal family in Europe. Under their recent guidance a substantial proportion of land has been reclaimed from the sea, yet Monaco still only comprises an area of under one square mile.

Monaco only became a prosperous country following the opening of the Monte Carlo Casino in the late 19th century. Soon the tiny country had the reputation of being the decadent playground of the rich and disreputable. Prince Rainier III inherited a dilapidated palace in 1949 and set about restoring both it and Monaco to become a thriving principality, earning its wealth from its position as an exclusive resort and tax haven.

The head of the house of Grimaldi is His Serene Highness Prince Albert Alexandre Louis Pierre. Born in the Palais de Monaco in 1958, he was the second child and only son of Rainier III, Prince of Monaco and Princess Grace, formerly the Hollywood actress Grace Kelly. His birth was announced to the people of Monaco with a 101-gun fusillade. Albert was educated locally until attending Amherst College in

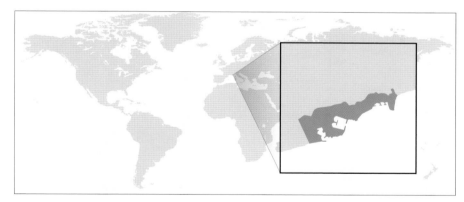

Massachusetts and then Bristol University in England. Throughout his youth as well as in later life he has participated in a wide range of sports including swimming, sailing, skiing and fencing, and competed in the bobsled events at five Winter Olympics. In 1985 he became a member of the International Olympic Committee, a position he continues to occupy.

In September 1982 the world was stunned when his mother Princess Grace suffered a stroke while driving on the mountainside above Monaco and crashed her car. She died the following day at Monaco Hospital, aged only 52.

On 7 March 2005, aged 47, the Crown Council of Monaco appointed Albert regent while his 81 year old father was seriously ill in hospital. Prince Rainier died within a few weeks on 6 April 2005 and Albert became the Sovereign Prince of Monaco. Under his care Monaco has remained a wealthy enclave on the north Mediterranean coast.

Prince Albert is unmarried, although he has two acknowledged illegitimate children with two different mothers: a son, Alexandre Coste (b. 2003), and a daughter, Jazmin Grimaldi (b. 1992). They are not included in the line of succession and until he has legitimate children, Albert's successor remains his older sister Caroline, Princess of Hanover, and then her son Andrea Casiraghi.

The Palais de Monaco (or the Palais de Prince) is the official residence of the Grimaldi family who have owned it since the last years of the 13th century. With land in Monaco being so limited, the princely family has built and rebuilt the palace over the centuries, while other monarchs simply constructed new buildings in new locations. The front facade of the palace shows a pink Renaissance-style building that conceals its original purpose as a fortress. The Grimaldi family has not occupied the palace continually, because at various points in history they have

been exiled from Monaco, most notably during the years of the French Revolution when Monaco was incorporated into the French Republic. The palace became a hospital and poor house until the 1815 Treaty of Paris restored the Grimaldis to Monaco.

Above: Princess Grace, lying in state. She was buried in the Grimaldi family vault on 18 September 1982, following a requiem mass in Saint Nicholas Cathedral.

Right: Prince Rainier, Prince Albert, Princess Stephanie, Princess Caroline and her second husband, Stefano Casiraghi.

Above left: Prince Rainier III hands the flag of office to the colonel of his army in a ceremony outside the Palais de Monaco on 13 April 1950, the day he became ruler of the principality.

Far left: 19 April 1956, Prince Rainier and film star Grace Kelly during their marriage ceremony at Monaco Cathedral.

Left: Prince Rainier and Princess Grace with their children, Albert, 8, Caroline, 9 and Stephanie, 15 months, 1966.

Left and below: The Palais Royal was founded in 1191 as a Genoese fortress and still retains much of its martial purpose behind its pink facade. The Grimaldi family seized the fortress by subterfuge in the very last years of the 13th century and have lived almost continuously in the stronghold over the next 700 years. Prince Albert is the current incumbent. Unable to expand the palace for lack of space — or build another in its stead elswhere for the same reason — the palace has been adapted and remodelled over the centuries and comprises a unique mixture of architectural styles.

Left: Princess Caroline's elder son Andrea Casiraghi, is currently third in line of succession after his mother.

Below: Princess Caroline of Monaco and her brother Prince Albert arriving at a state banquet to celebrate the 50th birthday of King Carl Gustav of Sweden in July 1996. Princess Caroline is heiress presumptive and will inherit the throne from her brother should he predecease her without producing legitimate offspring.

Below: Princess Caroline with her second husband Stefano Casiraghi at the 1987 Milan Fashion Show. Casiraghi was a wealthy Italian sportsman who died in a speed boat accident three years later. Caroline subsequently married for a third time, to Ernst August V, Prince of Hanover. giving her the title of Princess of Hanover.

ANDORRA
Co-Princes

Joint Rulers	Joan-Enric Vives i Sicília, Bishop of Urgell	Nicolas Sarkozy, President of the French Republic
Official title	Episcopal Co-Prince of Andorra	French Co-Prince of Andorra
Country ruled	Andorra	Andorra
Born	July 24 1949	28 January 1955
Accession to throne	May 12 2003	16 May 2007
Royal house	N/A	N/A
Official residences	Palau Episcopal, Barcelona	Élysée Palace, Paris
Heir	N/A	N/A

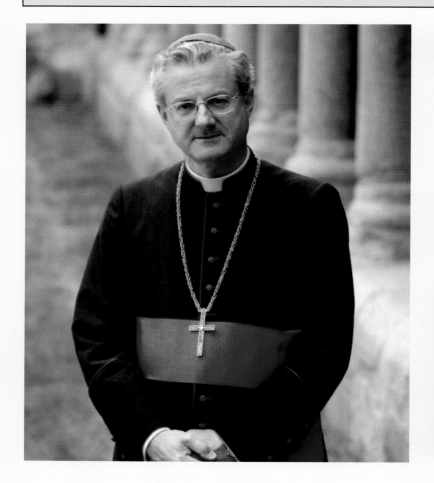

Joan-Enric Vives i Sicilia, Bishop of Urgell.

Nicholas Sarkozy, President of France.

Bishops of Urgell		Presidents of the French Republic	
		Chairmen of the Provisional Government	
		CHARLES DE GAULLE	1944-1946
		FÉLIX GOUIN	1946
		GEORGES BIDAULT	1946-1947
RAMON IGLESIAS I NAVARRI	1943-1969		
		Presidents of the French Fourth Republic	
		VINCENT AURIOL	1947-1954
		RENÉ COTY	1954-1959
		Presidents of the French Fifth Republic	
		CHARLES DE GAULLE	1959-1969
RAMÓN MALLA CALL (acting)	1969-1971	GEORGES POMPIDOU	1969-1973
		VALÉRY GISCARD D'ESTANG	1974-1981
JOAN MARTI ALANIS	1971-2003	FRANÇOIS MITTERAND	1981-1995
		JACQUES CHIRAC	1995-2007
JOAN-ERIC VIVES I SICILIA	2003-	NICOLAS SARKOZY	2007-

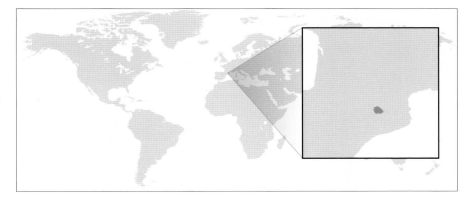

THE SMALL PYRÉENEAN KINGDOM of Andorra is a parliamentary co-principality ruled jointly by France and the Spanish Bishop of Urgell. The ties between Andorra and Urgell, in the Catalan region of Spain, stretch back to the 9th century when the area was given to Count Sunifred I of Cerdagne-Urgell under the terms of a charter issued by the Holy Roman Emperor Charles II. In the 12th century Sunifred's descendant, Ermengol VI gave the lands to the diocese of Urgell. However, the fraught political climate of the time meant that the bishops soon needed to forge an alliance with a powerful noble family in order to preserve their sovereignty over the area. To this end, a treaty was signed in 1159 between the Bishop of Urgell and the House of Caboet.

By the 13th century the rights to the fiefdom of Andorra had passed from the House of Caboet to the House of Foix. Rising tensions between the Bishop of Urgell and the Count of Foix led to the intercession of King Peter II of Catalonia-Aragon, backed by a number of Catalonian nobles. A court of arbitration was established and this issued two judgements, known as the first (in 1278) and second (in 1288) Paréages. These judgements were accepted by both the Bishop of Urgell and the Count of Foix and settled the disputes between the two sides as well as establishing the principles of the system of co-principality in Andorra that has lasted for over 700 years.

Through a series of marriages, the title of co-prince passed from the counts of Foix to the viscounts of Béarn and then to the French head of state when Henry de Bourbon, King of Navarre (1553–1610), acceded to the French throne in 1589 as Henri IV. In 1607 he issued an edict establishing the French head of state and the Bishop of Urgell as co-princes of Andorra.

In 1993 Andorra adopted its first written constitution, thus establishing a parliamentary co-principality and greatly reducing the power of the co-princes whose roles are now largely honorary in nature.

The tiny, landlocked country of Andorra has been ruled jointly by France and the Bishops of Urgell for over a thousand years. Legislative power is exercised by the democratically elected prime minister and the General Council, the Andorran parliament. The country is prosperous and derives its income from tourism and its status as a tax haven.

The Andorran coat of arms carved on to the parliament building in Andorra La Vella. The country's motto is 'Strength United is Stronger' - an apt phrase for a country with two heads of state.

SPAIN
King Juan Carlos I

Official title	Juan Carlos I, King of Spain
Country ruled	Spain
Born	5 January 1938
Accession to throne	1975
Royal house	House of Bourbon
Official residences	Palacio de la Zarzuela, Madrid; La Almudaina Majorca;
Heir	Felipe, Prince of Asturias (b. 1968, son)

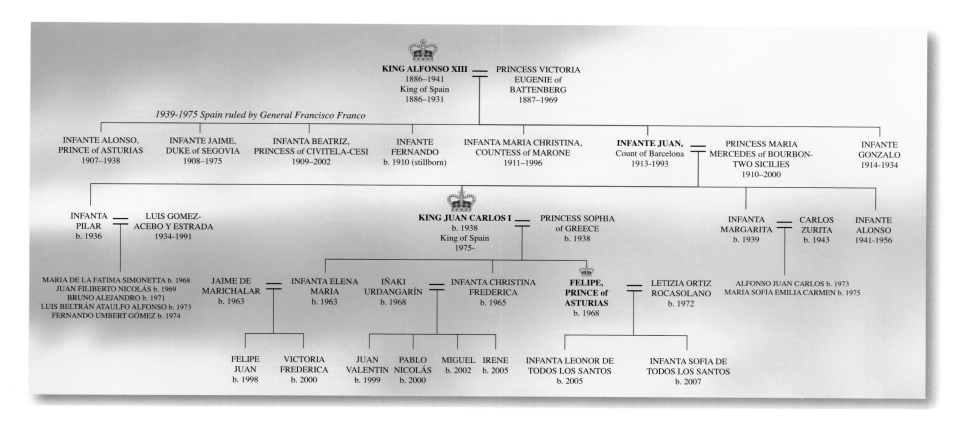

KING ALFONSO XIII
1886–1941
King of Spain
1886–1931

PRINCESS VICTORIA
EUGENIE of
BATTENBERG
1887–1969

1939-1975 Spain ruled by General Francisco Franco

INFANTE ALONSO,
PRINCE of ASTURIAS
1907–1938

INFANTE JAIME,
DUKE of SEGOVIA
1908–1975

INFANTA BEATRIZ,
PRINCESS of CIVITELA-CESI
1909–2002

INFANTE
FERNANDO
b. 1910 (stillborn)

INFANTA MARIA CHRISTINA,
COUNTESS of MARONE
1911–1996

INFANTE JUAN,
Count of Barcelona
1913-1993

PRINCESS MARIA
MERCEDES of BOURBON-
TWO SICILIES
1910–2000

INFANTE
GONZALO
1914-1934

INFANTA
PILAR
b. 1936

LUIS GOMEZ-
ACEBO Y ESTRADA
1934-1991

KING JUAN CARLOS I
b. 1938
King of Spain
1975-

PRINCESS SOPHIA
of GREECE
b. 1938

INFANTA
MARGARITA
b. 1939

CARLOS
ZURITA
b. 1943

INFANTE
ALONSO
1941-1956

MARIA DE LA FATIMA SIMONETTA b. 1968
JUAN FILIBERTO NICOLÁS b. 1969
BRUNO ALEJANDRO b. 1971
LUIS BELTRÁN ATAULFO ALFONSO b. 1973
FERNANDO UMBERT GÓMEZ b. 1974

JAIME DE
MARICHALAR
b. 1963

INFANTA ELENA
MARIA
b. 1963

IÑAKI
URDANGARÍN
b. 1968

INFANTA CHRISTINA
FREDERICA
b. 1965

FELIPE,
PRINCE of
ASTURIAS
b. 1968

LETIZIA ORTIZ
ROCASOLANO
b. 1972

ALFONSO JUAN CARLOS b. 1973
MARIA SOFIA EMILIA CARMEN b. 1975

FELIPE
JUAN
b. 1998

VICTORIA
FREDERICA
b. 2000

JUAN
VALENTIN
b. 1999

PABLO
NICOLÁS
b. 2000

MIGUEL
b. 2002

IRENE
b. 2005

INFANTA LEONOR DE
TODOS LOS SANTOS
b. 2005

INFANTA SOFIA DE
TODOS LOS SANTOS
b. 2007

Juan Carlos Alfonso Victor María de Borbón y Borbón-Dos Sicilias, more usually called Juan Carlos I, became king of Spain in November 1975, two days after the death of the Spanish dictator Francisco Franco (1892–1975) ended his 30-year dictatorship. Juan Carlos enthusiastically took on the job of reuniting and restoring his battered country to parliamentary democracy.

Juan Carlos was born while his family were in exile in Rome during the Second Spanish Republic and it was not generally expected that he would have the opportunity to inherit his throne. However, his father, Juan de Borbón, Count of Barcelona (1913–1993), persuaded General Franco to allow his son to be educated in Spain, initially in San Sebastián, then later in Madrid. On completing his education, Juan Carlos spent two years between 1955 and 1957 at the Military Academy of Zaragoza and then a further year at naval school, followed by a year with the air force.

Juan Carlos's future role was still uncertain, General Franco was reluctant to appoint a successor and his supporters all lobbied their various opinions, predominantly for an absolutist monarchy. Franco regarded the natural heir, the Count of Barcelona (Juan Carlos's father), as too liberal and seemed to

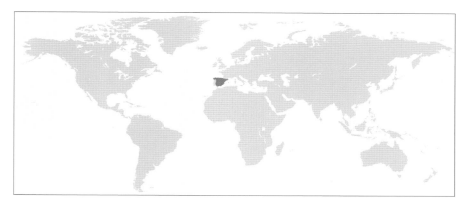

favor instead his cousin (and soon to be son-in-law) Alfonso, Duke of Anjou and Cádiz. Franco's ultimate decision was to sideline both claimants and instead opt for the young Prince Juan Carlos who he intended to mould to his hardline politics. This became official policy in 1969 when Juan Carlos was officially named and given the title Prince of Spain and swore loyalty to Franco's values and ideals.

From then on Juan Carlos frequently accompanied General Franco at official and state functions, but in time he secretly communicated with his father and other liberals and reformers. When Franco died in October 1975 the Cortes Generales proclaimed Juan Carlos King of Spain. Almost immediately he set about dismantling the fascist structures and instituting liberal reforms — much to the fury of Franco's supporters. In May 1977 the Count of Barcelona formally renounced his claim to the throne and recognised his son as rightful heir. The first democratic elections were held in June 1977 and in 1978 the new Spanish constitution proclaimed Juan Carlos the rightful historic heir rather than the dictator's appointment, and the king relinquished absolute power to become a constitutional monarch. None of this was achieved without opposition from the extreme right (particularly from the armed forces),which launched an abortive coup in 1981, but Juan Carlos overcame the opposition to become a popular and much loved king, whose position has been undisputed for over 25 years.

Juan Carlos married Princess Sophia of Greece and Denmark in Athens in 1962. They have three children, heir apparent Felipe, and the *infantas* Elena and Cristina. The royal family lives a modestly opulent lifestyle with the king, in particular, being a keen sailor and huntsman.

The official residence of the king and queen of Spain is Palacio de la Zarzuela (Palace of Zarzuela) located in the outskirts of Madrid. It is one of seven royal palaces now owned by the state, and was built as a royal hunting lodge during the 17th century on the orders of King Philip IV. King Juan Carlos and Queen Sophia have lived there since 1962; they refused to move into General Franco's residence El Pardo after his death and have remained at Zarzuela. The state-owned former official royal residence, Palacio Real de Madrid is located in the centre of Madrid and is used for state occasions and important ceremonies. It is the largest royal palace in western Europe and had its origin as a 10th century fortress. On the island of Majorca is the royal summer official residence of La Almudaina. Originally built by the Moors as a citadel in the 13th century, it overlooks Palma Bay and was converted to become a fortified palace in the early years of the 14th century.

Left: On 14 May 1962 Princess Sophia of Greece married Don Juan Carlos in Athens, at the time when he was the Pretender to the Spanish throne. On the bride's right is her mother, Queen Frederika and on the groom's left is his mother, the Countess of Barcelona. The bride's younger brother, Crown Prince Constantine is to her right. The bride and groom were distantly related through their ancestor Queen Victoria of Great Britain. Over 150 members of Europe's royal families attended the wedding making it, at the time, the largest gathering of royalty since before World War I.

C.N.M.

Above: King Juan Carlos (red hat, second right) sailing his yacht Bribon in the race around the Isle of Wight, for the America's Cup Jubilee in June 2001. The king is a keen sailor who started sailing at the age of 12 and regularly competes in sailing competitions.

Above right: King Juan Carlos walking to St George's Chapel, Windsor, to attend the Order of the Garter ceremony.

Right: Queen Sophia and Juan Carlos I at the Ernst Happel Stadium in Vienna for the quarter-final football match between Spain and Italy (4:2) during Euro 2008.

Left: The wedding of Crown Prince Felipe, Prince of Asturias to Letizia Ortiz Rocasolano was held on 22 May 2004 at the Cathedral Santa María la Real de la Almudena in Madrid.

Below left: His Royal Highness the Prince of Asturias, Felipe de Borbon y Grecia, heir to the Spanish throne.

Below: Crown Prince Felipe with his sister Dona Cristina at the 1995 Wimbledon Tennis Championships.

Right: The Prince and Princess of Wales were frequent holiday companions of the Spanish royal family. Here they are on board King Juan Carlos' yacht off Majorca. From left to right, Queen Anne-Marie and King Constantine of Greece and their daughter Princess Theodora, Prince Charles and Diana, Princess of Wales, Infanta Cristina, King Juan Carlos, Princes Harry and William of Wales, and Queen Sophia.

Left: The royal family's summer holiday home, Marivent Palace on Palma de Mallorca. The palace was built in 1923 on a high rocky promontery overlooking the city of Palma by the architect Guillem Fortesa. It was originally intended to be an art gallery and museum but in more recent times the government of the Balaeric Islands has given the palace over to royal use.

Above: The Royal Palace at Aranjuez is also called the 'Spanish Versailles'. In 1561 King Philip II declared the area a royal site and it became the royal family's spring residence. Work on the palace was started by Philip II and completed by Charles III and the result is a wide variety of architectural styles.

Left: The rococo-decorated Gasperini Salon in the Royal Palace.

Top: Horseguards at the Palacio Real — Royal Palace of Madrid.

Top right: The audience chamber in the Palacio Real. Everthing in the room is carefully balanced to be arranged like a mirror image.

Right: The front facade of the Palacio Real. The palace is the official residence of the royal family, although, these days it is only used for official ceremonies. The royal family live on the outskirts of Madrid in the Palacio de la Zarzuela.

PORTUGAL
Duke of Braganza

Official title	Dom Duarte Pio, Duke of Braganza
Pretender to	Throne of Portugal
Born	15 May 1945
Pretendency	1976–
Royal house	House of Braganza
Residence	Sintra, Portugal
Heir	Afonso, Prince of Beira (b. 1996, elder son)

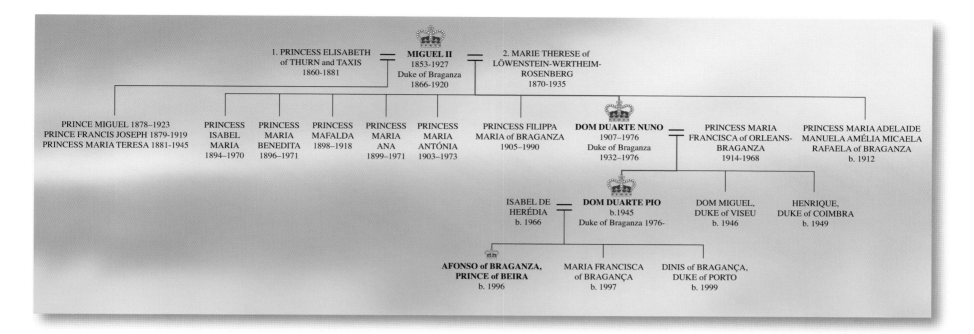

Family tree:

1. PRINCESS ELISABETH of THURN and TAXIS 1860-1881 — **MIGUEL II** 1853-1927 Duke of Braganza 1866-1920 — 2. MARIE THERESE of LÖWENSTEIN-WERTHEIM-ROSENBERG 1870-1935

PRINCE MIGUEL 1878–1923
PRINCE FRANCIS JOSEPH 1879-1919
PRINCESS MARIA TERESA 1881-1945

PRINCESS ISABEL MARIA 1894–1970

PRINCESS MARIA BENEDITA 1896–1971

PRINCESS MAFALDA 1898–1918

PRINCESS MARIA ANA 1899–1971

PRINCESS MARIA ANTÓNIA 1903–1973

PRINCESS FILIPPA MARIA of BRAGANZA 1905–1990

DOM DUARTE NUNO 1907–1976 Duke of Braganza 1932–1976 — PRINCESS MARIA FRANCISCA of ORLEANS-BRAGANZA 1914-1968

PRINCESS MARIA ADELAIDE MANUELA AMÉLIA MICAELA RAFAELA of BRAGANZA b. 1912

ISABEL DE HERÉDIA b. 1966 — **DOM DUARTE PIO** b.1945 Duke of Braganza 1976-

DOM MIGUEL, DUKE of VISEU b. 1946

HENRIQUE, DUKE of COIMBRA b. 1949

AFONSO of BRAGANZA, PRINCE of BEIRA b. 1996

MARIA FRANCISCA of BRAGANÇA b. 1997

DINIS of BRAGANÇA, DUKE of PORTO b. 1999

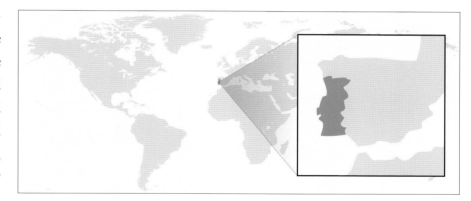

IN 1908 KING CARLOS I of Portugal (1863–1908) was assassinated alongside his son Luis Philippe in Lisbon, and the death of the king and the heir to the throne threw the country into chaos. The younger son of Carlos was declared king as Manuel II two days after the death of his father and brother, but republican influence was growing within Portugal and the 1910 revolution drove the royal family into exile, forcing them to flee to Gibraltar aboard the royal yacht. They moved to Britain where Manuel married, but had no children. He died suddenly in 1932, but had nominated as his heir his cousin Dom Duarte Nuno (1907–1976), the descendant of a rival branch of the family. Several other family members claimed the title of pretender, the most colourful being Maria Pia of Saxe-Coburg-and-Gotha-Braganza (1907–1995), who alleged that she was an illegitimate daughter of Carlos I and called herself Duchess of Braganza.

Duarte Nuno married his distant cousin Princess Maria Francisca of Orléans-Braganza in 1942, and their marriage united two rival lines of the prolific Braganza family. They had three sons, the eldest being Dom Duarte Pio, the current Duke of Braganza (the honorific title accorded to the eldest son of the Portuguese king) who was born in 1945 in Switzerland where his family was in exile. In 1950 Portugal rescinded the Ban Law that had excluded the royal family from the country, and Dom Duarte Nuno returned to Portugal in 1952.

Dom Duarte Pio has lived in Portugal ever since. He served in the Portuguese air force during the Angolan war, 1968–71, and although the 'Carnation Revolution' of 1974 began the move to democracy within Portugal, there was no suggestion of restoring the monarchy. Duke of Braganza since his father's death in 1976, Dom Duarte Pio and his family attract a good deal of popular attention in a country where he is regarded as an entirely benevolent link with Portugal's past. His wedding to businesswoman Isabel de Herédia in 1995 was attended by the president and prime minister of Portugal, and the subsequent births of his children were occasions of national celebration. The Duke of Braganza carries out a variety of honorific and quasi-diplomatic duties and he is also internationally respected for his humanitarian work on behalf of the people of East Timor, a former Portuguese colony in Indonesia, long before the country's plight came to international attention.

Below: A gathering of European royalty at a dinner party given by the
Pretender to the Spanish throne, the Count of Barcelona Juan de Bourbon, at
the Villa Giralda in Estoril , Portugal , 4 May 1967 to celebrate the wedding
of his daughter , Pilar de Bourbon, to Luis Gomes Acebo, Duke of Estrada.
The guests are left to right: Carolina of Liechtenstein; Archduchess of
Habsburg; Umberto of Savoy, ex-king of Italy ; Queen Victoria Eugenie,
widow of King Alfonso XIII, last King of Spain ; the Pretender to the
Portuguese throne, Duarte Nuno de Braganza; the French Countess of
Rambuteau and the Count of Paris.

Right: Dom Duarte Nuno , with his wife Maria Francisca of Orléans-Braganza and their children Dom Pio (right) aged 12 and Dom Miguel and Dom Henrique, 1957.

Below right: Dom Duarte Pio and his wife Isabel on their wedding day in 1995. The couple now have three children, Afonso of Braganza, Prince of Beira, Princess Maria Francisca and Prince Dinis of Braganza, Duke of Porto

ITALY
Prince of Naples

Official title	Vittorio Emanuele, Prince of Naples
Pretender to	Throne of Italy
Born	12 February 1937
Pretendence	1983
Royal house	Savoy
Residence	Geneva
Heir	Emanuele Filiberto, Prince of Venice (b. 1972, son)

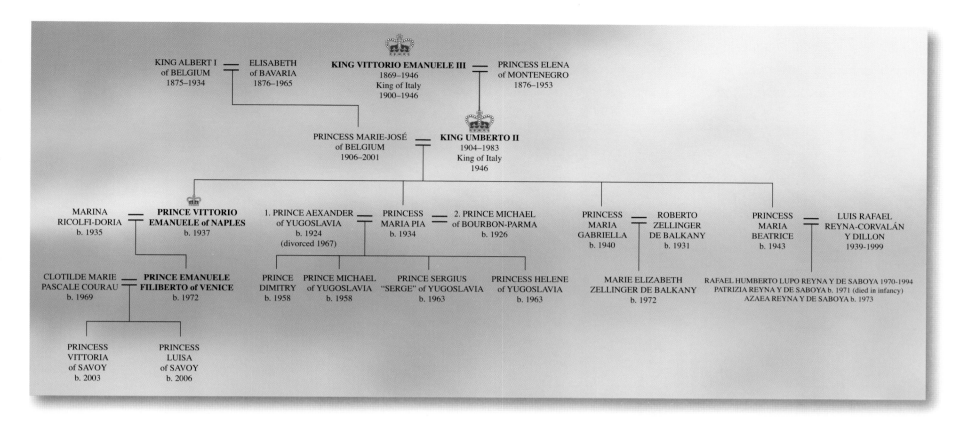

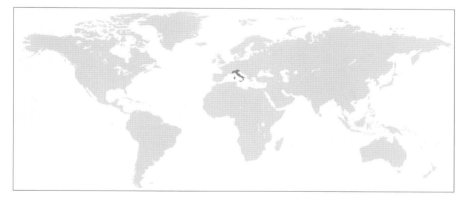

THERE IS A DELIGHTFUL irony in the fate of the man who was exiled from his native country for over 50 years, only to find that a mere three years after his return, he was barred from leaving while the authorities investigated corruption charges against him. Vittorio Emanuele, Prince of Naples and head of the house of Savoy, is one of Europe's more colourful royal pretenders.

The Italian monarchy was abolished in 1946 after a public referendum, the people of Italy perhaps disenchanted with their royal family's links with the fascist dictator Mussolini and their backing for Italy's wartime anti-Jewish laws. The last king of Italy, Umberto II, reigned for only a month before he and his family were exiled, and in 1948 Italy passed a law forbidding any male members of the house of Savoy from setting foot in Italy.

Umberto and his family settled in Switzerland, and on his death in 1983, his son Vittorio Emanuele, Prince of Naples became head of the family and the man who would be king of Italy. Umberto has worked as a financier, arms dealer and aircraft salesman, but has struggled to maintain his claim to the throne with dignity. In 1991 he was acquitted for manslaughter after the accidental shooting of a German tourist in Corsica, and in 2005 a family row with the Duke of Aosta became physical when he punched his rival for the headship of the house of Savoy in the face at a dinner held by King Juan Carlos of Spain.

Vittorio Emanuele lobbied the Italian authorities and the European Court of Human Rights for permission to return to his native land, and his wish was finally granted in 2002. He has renounced any claim to the Italian throne (thus alienating many monarchist supporters), while the republicans simply regard him as an irrelevance. His formal request for damages from the state of Italy to compensate his family for their confiscated lands and property has done little to endear him to the majority of the Italian people.

Prince Emanuele Filibert, the Prince of Venice and Vittorio's only child, accompanied his father on the Italian homecoming in

2002 and is a well-known figure. A hedge fund manager, he starred in a television commercial for olives, and has appeared on a reality-TV dancing show. His marriage in Rome to the popular French actress Clotilde Courau in 2003 attracted widespread publicity, as did the birth of his two daughters in subsequent years.

Above: Vittorio Emanuele of Savoy and his wife Princess Marina attend the premiere of the play Mrs. Warren's Profession, *Paris, 2004, with their son Emanuele Filiberto of Savoy and his wife Princess Clotilde Courau.*

Left: Prince Umberto married Princess Marie-José of Belgium in 1930. After the marriage ceremony they were recived by the Pope in the Vatican.

Above right: Prince Emanuele Filiberto, Prince of Venice, the only child of the Prince of Savoy married French actress Clotilde Courau in 2003.

Right: Vittorio Emanuele, Prince of Naples with his wife Princess Marina at their home in Gstaad.

Far left: Ex-King of Italy Umberto of Savoy with his wife Marie-José and their children, Maria Beatrice, Vittorio Emanuele, Maria Gabriella and Maria Pia, 1946.

Left: Benito Mussolini and Adolf Hitler give the fascist salute at a military parade for Hitler's official visit to Italy. King Vittorio Emanuele III and Queen Helen are to Hitler's left.

VATICAN
Pope Benedict XVI

Official title	Bishop of Rome, Vicar of Christ, Successor of the Prince of the Apostles, Supreme Pontiff of the Universal Church, Primate of Italy, Archbishop and Metropolitan of the Roman Province, Sovereign of the State of the Vatican City, Servant of the Servants of God
Country ruled	Vatican City State
Born	16 April 1927
Accession to throne	2005
Royal house	n/a
Official residence	The Vatican
Heir	Unknown (elective office)

Pontificate	English Name	Regnal (Latin) Name	Personal Name	Place of Birth
1903-1914	POPE PIUS X	Papa Pius Decimus	Giuseppe Melchiorre Sarto	Riese, Italy
1914-1922	POPE BENEDICT XV	Papa Benedictus Quintus Decimus	Giacomo Della Chiesa	Genoa, Italy
1922-1939	POPE PIUS XI	Papa Pius Unecimus	Achille Ambrogio Damiano	Desio, Italy
1939-1958	POPE PIUS XII	Papa Pius Duodecimus	Eugenio Maria Giuseppe Giovanni Pacelli	Rome, Italy
1958-1963	POPE JOHN XXIII	Papa Ioannes Vicesimus Tertius	Angelo Giuseppe Roncalli	Sotto il Monte, Italy
1963-1978	POPE PAUL VI	Papa Paulus Sextus	Giovanni Battista Enrico Antonio Maria Montini	Concesio, Italy
1978	POPE JOHN PAUL I	Papa Ioannes Paulus Primus	Albino Luciani	Forno di Canale (now Canale d'Agordo), Italy
1978-2005	POPE JOHN PAUL II	Papa Ioannes Paulus Secundes	Karol Józef Wojtyla	Wadowice, Poland
2005-	POPE BENEDICT XVI	Papa Benedictus Sextus Decimus	Joseph Alois Ratzinger	Marktl am Inn, Germany

THE CURRENT POPE, BENEDICT XVI, was born at Marktl am Inn, in the Diocese of Passau in Germany on 16 April 1927, he was baptised the same day and christened Joseph Alois Ratzinger. His father, Joseph Ratzinger Sr., was a policeman and his mother, Maria, had worked as a cook in a number of hotels prior to her marriage.

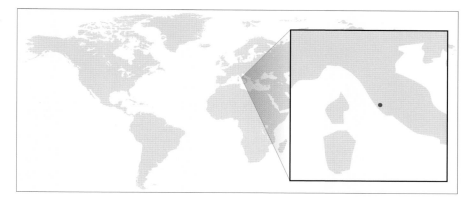

The young Joseph's early life was overshadowed by World War II, and his father's outspoken criticism of the Nazis made life even harder for the family. Following the war he enrolled in the Higher School of Philosophy and Theology of Freising and at the University of Munich, where he studied philosophy and theology. Following his graduation he was ordainded as a priest in June 1951. In the ensuing years he had a distinguished career as a university theologian, until his appointment as Archbishop of Munich-Freising in May 1977; two months later Pope Paul VI elevated him to cardinal. In November 1981 Pope John Paul II named him Prefect for the Congregation for the Doctrine of the Faith, and the following year he resigned as Archbishop of Munich-Freising.

In April 2005, following four ballots of the Conclave, Cardinal Joseph Ratzinger was elected to the papacy at the age of 78. He was the oldest cardinal to become pope since Clement XII was elected in 1730. Aside from his spiritual duties, Pope Benedict XVI is known for his love of both classical music, the work of Mozart in particular, and cats.

Left: Pope Benedict XVI celebrates the "Via Crucis," the Way of the Cross, at the Colosseum in Rome.

Overleaf: An aerial view of the majestic Vatican Palace surrounded by its lush gardens.

GERMANY
Prince of Prussia

Official title	Georg Friedrich, Prince of Prussia
Pretender to	Imperial throne of Germany
Born	10 June 1976
Pretendence	1994
Royal house	Hohenzollern
Official residences	Hohenzollern Castle, Sigmaringen Castle
Heir	Prince Christian-Sigismund of Prussia (b. 1946, uncle)

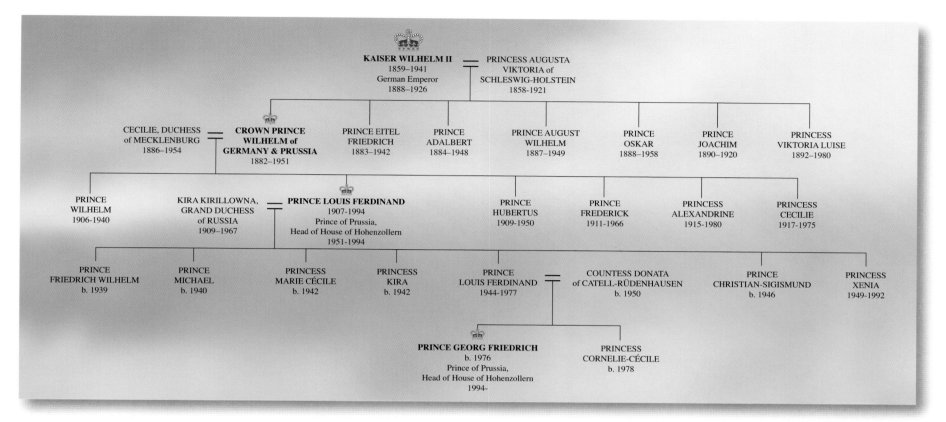

KAISER WILHELM II
1859–1941
German Emperor
1888–1926

PRINCESS AUGUSTA
VIKTORIA of
SCHLESWIG-HOLSTEIN
1858-1921

CECILIE, DUCHESS
of MECKLENBURG
1886–1954

CROWN PRINCE
WILHELM of
GERMANY & PRUSSIA
1882–1951

PRINCE EITEL
FRIEDRICH
1883–1942

PRINCE
ADALBERT
1884–1948

PRINCE AUGUST
WILHELM
1887–1949

PRINCE
OSKAR
1888–1958

PRINCE
JOACHIM
1890–1920

PRINCESS
VIKTORIA LUISE
1892–1980

PRINCE
WILHELM
1906-1940

KIRA KIRILLOWNA,
GRAND DUCHESS
of RUSSIA
1909–1967

PRINCE LOUIS FERDINAND
1907-1994
Prince of Prussia,
Head of House of Hohenzollern
1951-1994

PRINCE
HUBERTUS
1909-1950

PRINCE
FREDERICK
1911-1966

PRINCESS
ALEXANDRINE
1915-1980

PRINCESS
CECILIE
1917-1975

PRINCE
FRIEDRICH WILHELM
b. 1939

PRINCE
MICHAEL
b. 1940

PRINCESS
MARIE CÉCILE
b. 1942

PRINCESS
KIRA
b. 1942

PRINCE
LOUIS FERDINAND
1944-1977

COUNTESS DONATA
of CATELL-RÜDENHAUSEN
b. 1950

PRINCE
CHRISTIAN-SIGISMUND
b. 1946

PRINCESS
XENIA
1949-1992

PRINCE GEORG FRIEDRICH
b. 1976
Prince of Prussia,
Head of House of Hohenzollern
1994-

PRINCESS
CORNELIE-CÉCILE
b. 1978

THE HOHENZOLLERN FAMILY WHO ruled Prussia and Germany for so long were nothing if not prolific. Related to every ruling family in Europe, as well as most of the uncrowned heads, members of Germany's former imperial family are scattered throughout Europe. Kaiser Wilhelm II (reigned 1888–1918), who abdicated after the First World War, spent his remaining years in exile in Holland, but many of his relatives remained in Germany, and some even hung on to their family estates after the devastation of the Second World War and the division of Germany itself.

Prince Georg Friedrich, the head of the family since his grandfather's death in 1994, takes the title Prince of Prussia and is the Kaiser's great-great grandson. His grandfather, Prince Louis Ferdinand (1907–94) named him as his successor, by-passing a generation, mainly because two of his sons had renounced their claims to the title by marrying commoners. Prince Georg's uncles Prince Friedrich Wilhelm (b. 1939) and Prince Michael (b. 1940) have challenged their rights in the federal German courts, which finally ruled in Prince's Georg's favour with regard to the title, but decreed that the children of Prince Louis Ferdinand were entitled to a share of the imperial Prussian inheritance.

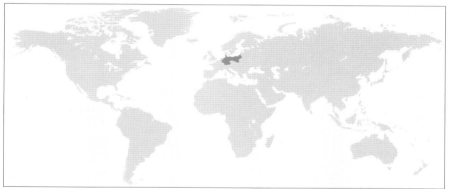

Prince Georg Friederich was born in Bremen in 1976, but his father Prince Louis Ferdinand jr. (1944–77) died when he was barely a year old from injuries sustained during a military training exercise. He was educated in Germany and Scotland, and after two years of military service, attended university in Freiberg, where he studied business and economics. He takes his responsibilities as head of the family seriously, working to maintain the family traditions and uphold memories of Prussia's imperial past.

At its height, the Hohenzollern Empire spread across half of Europe, and while most of the surviving palaces and castles, such as Schloss Charlottenburg in Berlin, are now in the hands of the German state, the family still own two. The family's spiritual home is Schloss Hohenzollern, a romantic 19th century castle 50 miles south of Stuttgart, and the burial place of the kaiser's eldest son Crown Prince Wilhelm (1882–1951) and his son Prince Louis Ferdinand. Only 40 miles away on a cliff overlooking the River Danube stands Schloss Sigmaringen, one of the largest European royal palaces still in private hands, and the ancestral castle of the Hohenzollerns since 1535. None of the family live there today, but they maintain it as a museum to provide a glimpse into the past lives of one of Europe's most venerable ruling dynasties.

Above: The wedding of Louis Ferdinand, Prince of Prussia in 1938 to Princess Kira, Grand Duchess of Russia. The prince wears the uniform of a Luftwaffe officer. Behind him are his grandfather, the former kaiser, Wilhelm II and his father, the former crown prince Wilhelm.

Top right: Prince Louis Ferdinand was head of the house of Hohenzollern from 1951 until his death in 1994. He outlived his eldest eligible son, and so the title skipped a generation to Prince Georg.

Right: After World War I the German royal family lived in exile in Doorn, Holland. This 1927 photograph shows the Kaiser with his son and grandson.

Far right: Schloss Hohenzollern, the family seat 50 miles south of Stuttgart.

HANOVER
Prince Ernst August

Official title	Ernst August, Prince of Hanover, Duke of Brunswick and Lunenburg, (Prince of Great Britain and Ireland)
Pretender to	Principality of Hanover
Born	26 February 1954
Pretendence	1987
Royal house	Hanover
Official residence	Marienburg Castle, Hanover
Heir	Prince Ernst August (b. 1983, elder son)

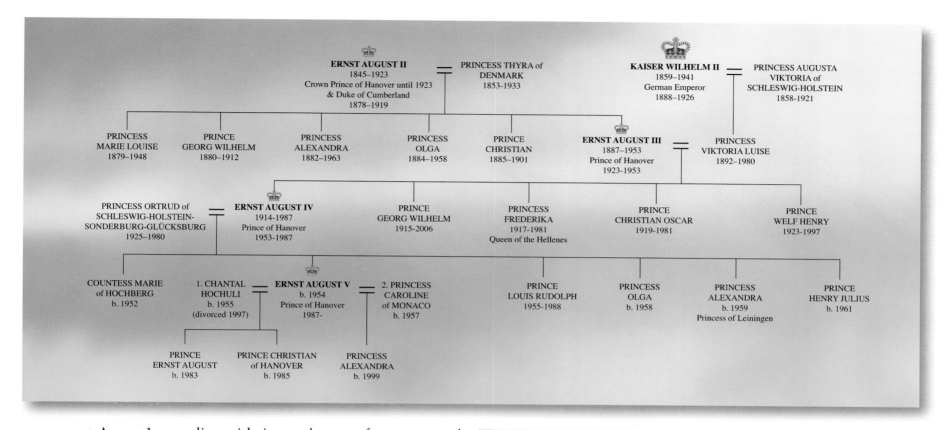

Ernst August's grandiose title is purely one of courtesy and is not recognised under modern law in Britain, Germany or Ireland, but nevertheless, he is heir to a remarkable inheritance. Prince Ernst is extremely well-connected: first cousin to Queen Sofia of Spain and ex-King Constantine of Greece, and a great-grandson of Kaiser Wilhelm II of Germany, he is also a male-line descendant of George III of Britain, and, until his marriage to the Catholic Princess Caroline of Monaco, was in the line of succession for the British crown. Great Britain and Hanover shared the same king from 1714 until the accession of Queen Victoria in 1837. Salic law within Hanover forbad the accession of a woman to the Hanoverian throne, so the crown passed to Victoria's uncle, Prince Ernest, Duke of Cumberland, and the current Prince Ernst is descended from him.

Prince Ernst was born in 1954 and brought up at Marienburg Castle and the family estate near Hanover in northern Germany. The eldest of six children, he attended university in Canada, as well as the Royal Agricultural College, Cirencester, England, and acquired a reputation as a playboy in his youth. He married the Swiss pharmaceutical heiress Chantal Hochuli in 1981 and the couple had two sons before their divorce in 1997. During the 1980s Ernst took over management of his family's extensive estates in Germany, Austria and Kenya, and his marriage to Princess Caroline of Monaco in 1999 ensured that the couple are among Europe's wealthiest royals.

Prince Ernst is known for his fiery temperament and has delighted the tabloids with tales of assaulting bar owners and his struggle with pancreatitis. More seriously, he was severely ill in a coma in the week that his father-in-law Prince Rainier of Monaco died in 2005.

As head of the house of Hanover, Prince Ernst has custody of a number of castles and palaces. The family seat at Marienburg is still used by the family, although it is also open to the public at certain times of the year. His sister Princess Olga lives in Schloss

Calenburg, and Herrenhausen, formerly the family's summer palace, which was badly damaged during World War II, is now in the hands of the City of Hanover and awaits restoration. When they married, Prince Ernst and Princess Caroline individually had large property portfolios, with residences in Germany, Austria, France, Monaco, Kenya and London. They spend most time at the Manoir de Mée, Foutnainbleu, outside Paris, the private house they bought when they married. They are also especially fond of the hunting lodge in Auerbach, Austria, where their daughter Alexandra was christened in 1999, and where Ernst's younger brother Louis is buried.

Left: Prince Ernst married his second wife, Princess Caroline of Monaco, in 1999. Old friends, they resisted their families' attempts at matchmaking when they were younger. The couple have one daughter, Princess Alexandra, born in 1999.

Right: Schloss Marienburg, the ancestral home of the princes of Hanover.

LIECHTENSTEIN
Reigning Prince Hans-Adam II

Official title	Reigning Prince of Liechtenstein, Duke of Troppau and Jägerndorf, Count of Rietberg, Sovereign of the House of Liechtenstein
Country ruled	Liechtenstein
Born	14 February 1945
Accession to throne	1989
Royal house	Princely House of Liechtenstein
Official residences	Schloss Vaduz (Vaduz Castle)
Heir	Hereditary Prince Alois (b. 1968, son)

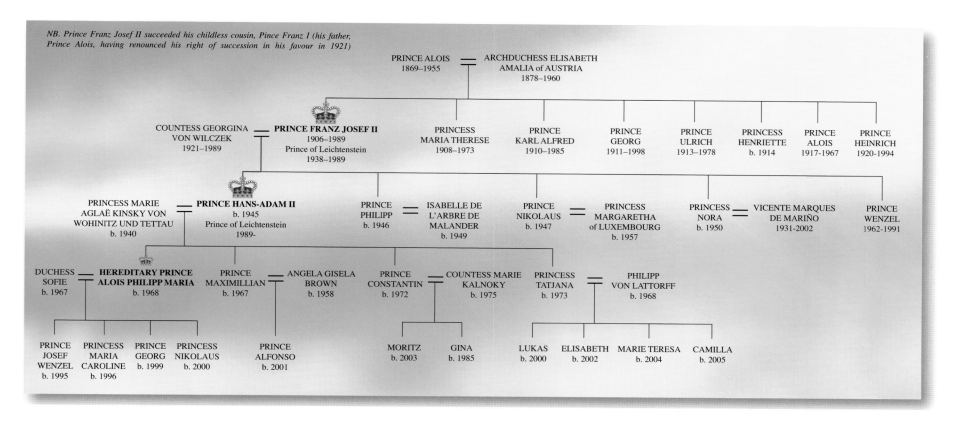

NB. Prince Franz Josef II succeeded his childless cousin, Pince Franz I (his father, Prince Alois, having renounced his right of succession in his favour in 1921)

PRINCE ALOIS 1869–1955 — ARCHDUCHESS ELISABETH AMALIA of AUSTRIA 1878–1960

COUNTESS GEORGINA VON WILCZEK 1921–1989 — **PRINCE FRANZ JOSEF II** 1906–1989 Prince of Leichtenstein 1938–1989

PRINCESS MARIA THERESE 1908–1973

PRINCE KARL ALFRED 1910–1985

PRINCE GEORG 1911–1998

PRINCE ULRICH 1913–1978

PRINCESS HENRIETTE b. 1914

PRINCE ALOIS 1917-1967

PRINCE HEINRICH 1920-1994

PRINCESS MARIE AGLAË KINSKY VON WOHINITZ UND TETTAU b. 1940 — **PRINCE HANS-ADAM II** b. 1945 Prince of Leichtenstein 1989-

PRINCE PHILIPP b. 1946 — ISABELLE DE L'ARBRE DE MALANDER b. 1949

PRINCE NIKOLAUS b. 1947 — PRINCESS MARGARETHA of LUXEMBOURG b. 1957

PRINCESS NORA b. 1950 — VICENTE MARQUES DE MARIÑO 1931-2002

PRINCE WENZEL 1962-1991

DUCHESS SOFIE b. 1967 — **HEREDITARY PRINCE ALOIS PHILIPP MARIA** b. 1968

PRINCE MAXIMILLIAN b. 1967 — ANGELA GISELA BROWN b. 1958

PRINCE CONSTANTIN b. 1972 — COUNTESS MARIE KALNOKY b. 1975

PRINCESS TATJANA b. 1973 — PHILIPP VON LATTORFF b. 1968

PRINCE JOSEF WENZEL b. 1995

PRINCESS MARIA CAROLINE b. 1996

PRINCE GEORG b. 1999

PRINCESS NIKOLAUS b. 2000

PRINCE ALFONSO b. 2001

MORITZ b. 2003

GINA b. 1985

LUKAS b. 2000

ELISABETH b. 2002

MARIE TERESA b. 2004

CAMILLA b. 2005

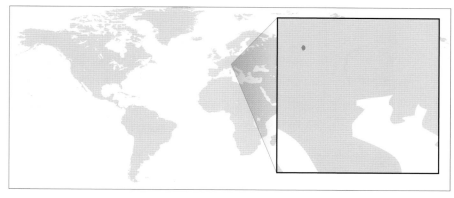

T HE PRINCELY HOUSE OF Liechtenstein can claim to be one of the oldest noble families in Europe, with the first mention occurring in 1136—one Hugo of Liechtenstein owned properties in the surrounding area and named himself after Liechtenstein Castle, located to the south of Vienna.

The modern history of Liechtenstein begins in January 1719 with a decree by the Holy Roman Emperor Charles VI that created of the Imperial Principality of Liechtenstein. This new sovereign member state of the Holy Roman Empire was formed by the amalgamation of the territories of Schellenberg and Vaduz that had been purchased in 1699 and 1712 respectively by Prince Johan Adam I, known to his contemporaries as Hans Adam the Rich, and constitutes the principality as it stands today. Johan's direct line of male descent died with him in 1712 and the current family is descended from Prince Johan I, who ruled from 1805 to 1836.

From 1806 to 1813, during the reign of Prince Johann I, Liechtenstein was a member of the Confederation of the Rhine set up by Napoleon Bonaparte. Two years later, in 1815, the country was included in the German Confederation. In 1866, during the reign of Prince Johann II (r. 1858–1929), the country gained full independence. In 1921 the country adopted a modern constitution that saw Liechtenstein become a constitutional monarchy; although unlike in many modern constitutional monarchies, the Prince exercises real rather than symbolic power.

Unusually, the princes of Liechtenstein did not reside in the country itself until the 20th century, indeed Prince Alois II (reigned 1836–1858) was the first prince to actually visit the country (in 1842 and 1847). During the 18th and 19th centuries they lived mainly in Feldsberg (in what is now the Czech Republic) and Vienna, and it was only in 1938 that Prince Franz Josef II moved his permanent residence to Vaduz Castle, where the family seat remains today. Prior to the arrival of the princely family, major renovation work was carried out on the castle in the early 20th century during the reign of Prince Johan II, that was overseen by Johan's brother, the future Prince Franz I.

The current reigning prince, Hans-Adam II, was born in 1945, the eldest son of Prince Franz Joseph II of Liechtenstein. His name harks back to the founder of the principality Prince Johan (Hans) Adam I. Hans-Adam grew up in the family home at Vaduz Castle and began his primary education in Vaduz, before following in his father's footsteps and attending the Schottengymnasium in Vienna, followed by the Grammar School at Zuoz, Switzerland. In 1965 he began studies in Business and Economics at the University of St Gallen, Switzerland, graduating in 1969. During Prince Hans-Adam II's reign, Liechtenstein became a member of the United Nations (in 1990), the European Free Trade Association (in 1991), and the World Trade Organization (in 1995), although he has declined to put the country forward for membership of the European Union.

On 15 August 2004 Hans-Adam handed over the reigns of power to his son Hereditary Prince Alois who has carried out the duties of head of state since. Hans-Adam still retains the title of Reigning Prince.

Over the centuries the princes have built up a world-famous art collection that includes the work of many of the outstanding 17th-century Dutch and Flemish painters. Much of the collection is exhibited in the Engländerhaus in the centre of Vaduz.

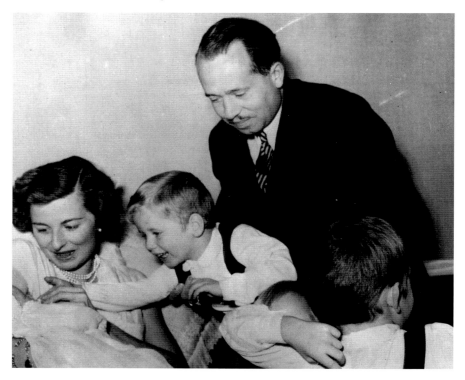

Left: Reigning Prince Hans Adam II, pictured in 1993 with his wife Princess Marie.

Far left: Prince Franz Joseph II and Princess Georgina playing with their children (from left to right: the newborn Princess Nora, Prince Hans-Adam, Prince Philipp and Prince Nikolaus).

Bottom left: A 1959 family portrait of Prince Franz Josef II with his wife Georgina, Prince Hans-Adam, Prince Philipp, Prince Nikolaus and Princess Nora Elizabeth.

Right: Among her many interests Princess Marie is President of the Liechtenstein Red Cross and Honoury President of the Society for Orthopaedic Aid.

Right: Vaduz Castle, the official residence of the Prince of Liechtenstein. The castle overlooks Vaduz, the capital of Liechtenstein, and takes its name from the town. It is an ancient castle, with parts dating back to the 12th century, and although it has been owned by the royal family of Liechtenstein since 1712, the family only took up permanent residence in 1938. Between 1905 and 1920 Hereditary Prince Johann II began extensive restoration work, which Prince Franz Joseph II continued during the early 1930s.

Below: Hereditary Prince Alois of Liechtenstein with his bride Princess Sophie after their wedding in Vaduz on 3 July 1993. The eldest daughter of Prince Max, Duke of Bavaria, Princess Sophie will eventually inherit her father's position as head of the house of Stuart, the Jacobite pretenders to the British throne. Prince Alois and Princess Sophie have four children. In 2004 Prince Aloes assumed responsibility for day-to-day governmental decisions, acting on advice from the prime minister, as 'prince-regent', while his father Prince Hans-Adam II remained head of state.

AUSTRIA-HUNGARY
Crown Prince Otto

Official title	Otto, Crown Prince of Austria, Hungary, Croatia and Bohemia
Pretender to	Austro-Hungarian Empire
Born	20 November 1912
Pretendence	1922–
Royal house	Habsburg
Residence	Villa Austria, Bavaria, Germany
Heir	Archduke Karl von Habsburg (b. 1961, eldest son)

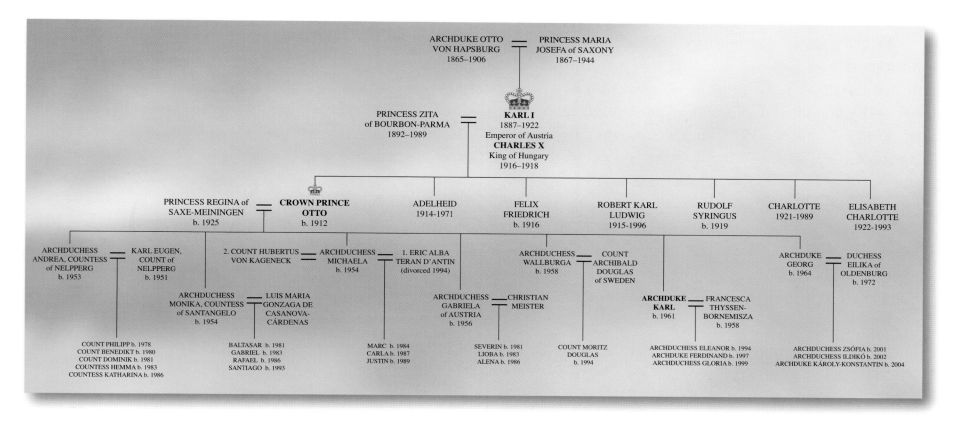

ARCHDUKE OTTO VON HAPSBURG 1865–1906 — PRINCESS MARIA JOSEFA of SAXONY 1867–1944

PRINCESS ZITA of BOURBON-PARMA 1892–1989 — **KARL I** 1887–1922 Emperor of Austria **CHARLES X** King of Hungary 1916–1918

PRINCESS REGINA of SAXE-MEININGEN b. 1925 — **CROWN PRINCE OTTO** b. 1912 | ADELHEID 1914–1971 | FELIX FRIEDRICH b. 1916 | ROBERT KARL LUDWIG 1915–1996 | RUDOLF SYRINGUS b. 1919 | CHARLOTTE 1921–1989 | ELISABETH CHARLOTTE 1922–1993

ARCHDUCHESS ANDREA, COUNTESS of NELPPERG b. 1953 — KARL EUGEN, COUNT of NELPPERG b. 1951 | 2. COUNT HUBERTUS VON KAGENECK — ARCHDUCHESS MICHAELA b. 1954 — 1. ERIC ALBA TERAN D'ANTIN (divorced 1994) | ARCHDUCHESS WALLBURGA b. 1958 — COUNT ARCHIBALD DOUGLAS of SWEDEN | ARCHDUKE GEORG b. 1964 — DUCHESS EILIKA of OLDENBURG b. 1972

ARCHDUCHESS MONIKA, COUNTESS of SANTANGELO b. 1954 — LUIS MARIA GONZAGA DE CASANOVA-CÁRDENAS | ARCHDUCHESS GABRIELA of AUSTRIA b. 1956 — CHRISTIAN MEISTER | **ARCHDUKE KARL** b. 1961 — FRANCESCA THYSSEN-BORNEMISZA b. 1958

COUNT PHILIPP b. 1978 COUNT BENEDIKT b. 1980 COUNT DOMINIK b. 1981 COUNTESS HEMMA b. 1983 COUNTESS KATHARINA b. 1986 | BALTASAR b. 1981 GABRIEL b. 1983 RAFAEL b. 1986 SANTIAGO b. 1993 | MARC b. 1984 CARLA b. 1987 JUSTIN b. 1989 | SEVERIN b. 1981 LIOBA b. 1983 ALENA b. 1986 | COUNT MORITZ DOUGLAS b. 1994 | ARCHDUCHESS ELEANOR b. 1994 ARCHDUKE FERDINAND b. 1997 ARCHDUCHESS GLORIA b. 1999 | ARCHDUCHESS ZSÓFIA b. 2001 ARCHDUCHESS ILDIKÓ b. 2002 ARCHDUKE KÁROLY-KONSTANTIN b. 2004

D R OTTO VON HABSBURG, Crown Prince of Austria-Hungary, is the son of the last emperor of the Austro-Hungarian Empire, Karl I (also known as Karl IV of Hungary). When the Emperor Franz-Joseph died in 1916 after a 68-year reign, he was succeeded by his grand-nephew, Archduke Karl, Otto's father.

Born in 1912 in the twilight years of the empire, Prince Otto's inheritance fractured around him in the early years of his life. It was the assassination of his great-uncle Archduke Franz Ferdinand in Sarajevo in 1914 that precipitated the First World War and his father's accession as emperor, and in 1919 as the empire broke up into independent republics, the Austrian parliament expelled the Habsburg family and confiscated their estates and possessions. Emperor Karl I took his family into exile in Switzerland and Madeira, having issued a careful proclamation in which he 'renounced participation' in affairs of state, but did not abdicate. Rather like Britain's Charles I three centuries earlier, he believed that his oath of kingship would only end with his death.

Otto himself has been similarly circumspect. With his father's death in Madeira in 1922, Otto became titular head of

the house of Habsburg at the age of ten. The Habsburg Law of 1919 expelled the imperial family and confiscated the family properties. At the same time, the nobility was abolished and between the wars, the Prince Otto and his family were effectively refugees without money or support. For a short period Otto worked as a fisherman in Spain to support his family. An Austrian patriot who opposed the Nazi Anschluss of 1938, Otto lived in Belgium and spent the war years with his brothers in the USA, where President Roosevelt used him as a focus for anti-Nazi resistance. After the war, and especially in the light of Nazi excesses, the Habsburg family were regarded more favourably in Austria, although they were still not allowed to return to their native country.

In 1961 Crown Prince Otto renounced all claims to the Austrian throne, and was rewarded five years later, with and Austrian passport and permission to re-enter his homeland. He has an abiding interest in a unified Europe and served for 20 years, from 1979 to 1999, in the European parliament at Strasbourg, representing Bavaria.

Otto met his wife, Regina, herself a dispossessed German princess, while she was working in a refugee camp after World War II. They married in 1951 and their long marriage has produced seven children and 22 grandchildren. In 2007 Otto passed on the position as head of the house of Habsburg to his eldest son, Archduke Karl, who, like his father, was elected to the European parliament in 1996. Karl Habsburg – Austria is a republic that does not recognise noble titles – has lived in Salzburg, Austria since 1981 and has three children.

Prince Otto has large extended family with relatives scattered across Europe (and beyond) and it is entirely fitting that this man, the head of a family which once ruled such wide tracts of Europe, should have worked so hard throughout his long life to bring about European unity. The divisions and rifts of two world wars, and the polarization of the Cold War had a brutally direct effect on his life and family, but he has striven to mend the wounds and answers questions about his nationality with the reply, 'I am a European'.

Above: Crown Prince Otto with his siblings, 1918

Left: Young Prince Otto at his father's coronation, 1917.

Above: Crown Prince Otto with his wife Princess Regina and their seven children, at their Bavarian home,1965.

Left: Crown Prince Otto became head of the house of Habsburg on his father's death in 1922.

Above: Francesca Von Thyssen Bornemisza and Karl Habsburg Lothringen, before their wedding ceremony in Mariazell Cathedral, January1993.

Right: A replica of the imperial crown of the Holy Roman Empire surmounts the the arms of the Habsburgs on the exterior of the Hofburg Palace, Vienna.

Right: Crown Prince Otto has lived in 'Villa Austria' Pöcking, Bavaria, Germany for many years and represented Pöcking as member of the European Parliament.

Below: The christening of Karl von Habsburg's son Ferdinand in Zagred, Croatia. 1997. Ferdinand has two sisters, the Archduchess Eleanore, born in 1994 and the Archduchess Gloria born in 1999.

ROMANIA
King Michael

Official title	Michael, King of the Romanians
Pretender to	Throne of Romania
Born	25 October 1921
Accession to throne	1927–1930; 1940–1947 (deposed)
Royal house	Hohenzollern
Official residences	Elisabeta Palace, Bucharest; Savarsin Castle Romania
Heir	Princess Margarita, Crown Princess of Romania (b. 1949, eldest daughter)

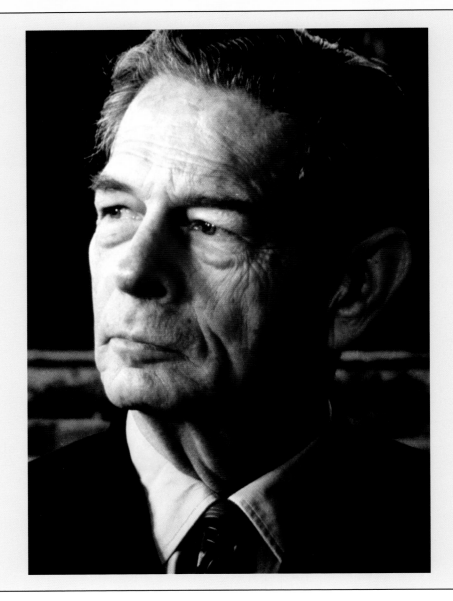

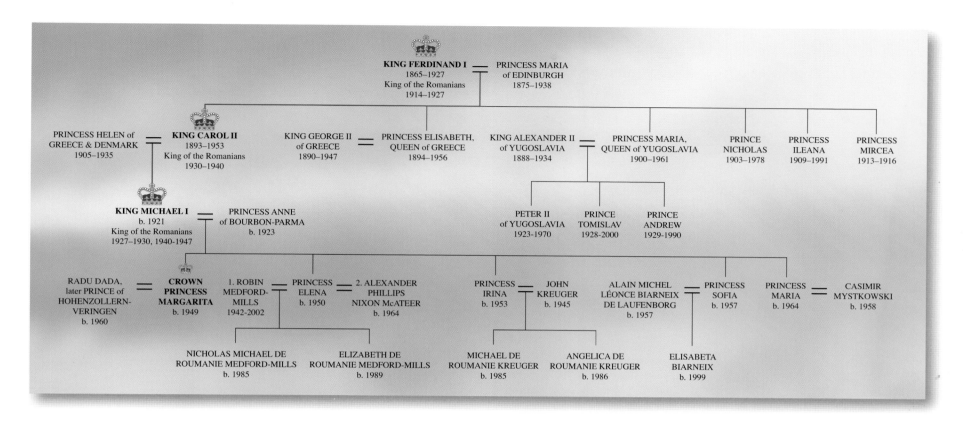

KING FERDINAND I
1865–1927
King of the Romanians
1914–1927
—— PRINCESS MARIA
of EDINBURGH
1875–1938

PRINCESS HELEN of
GREECE & DENMARK
1905–1935
—— KING CAROL II
1893–1953
King of the Romanians
1930–1940

KING GEORGE II
of GREECE
1890–1947
—— PRINCESS ELISABETH,
QUEEN of GREECE
1894–1956

KING ALEXANDER II
of YUGOSLAVIA
1888–1934
—— PRINCESS MARIA,
QUEEN of YUGOSLAVIA
1900–1961

PRINCE
NICHOLAS
1903–1978

PRINCESS
ILEANA
1909–1991

PRINCESS
MIRCEA
1913–1916

KING MICHAEL I
b. 1921
King of the Romanians
1927–1930, 1940-1947
—— PRINCESS ANNE
of BOURBON-PARMA
b. 1923

PETER II
of YUGOSLAVIA
1923-1970

PRINCE
TOMISLAV
1928-2000

PRINCE
ANDREW
1929-1990

RADU DADA,
later PRINCE of
HOHENZOLLERN-
VERINGEN
b. 1960
—— CROWN
PRINCESS
MARGARITA
b. 1949

1. ROBIN
MEDFORD-
MILLS
1942-2002
—— PRINCESS
ELENA
b. 1950
—— 2. ALEXANDER
PHILLIPS
NIXON McATEER
b. 1964

PRINCESS
IRINA
b. 1953
—— JOHN
KREUGER
b. 1945

ALAIN MICHEL
LÉONCE BIARNEIX
DE LAUFENBORG
b. 1957
—— PRINCESS
SOFIA
b. 1957

PRINCESS
MARIA
b. 1964
—— CASIMIR
MYSTKOWSKI
b. 1958

NICHOLAS MICHAEL DE
ROUMANIE MEDFORD-MILLS
b. 1985

ELIZABETH DE
ROUMANIE MEDFORD-MILLS
b. 1989

MICHAEL DE
ROUMANIE KREUGER
b. 1985

ANGELICA DE
ROUMANIE KREUGER
b. 1986

ELISABETA
BIARNEIX
b. 1999

W ITH HIS COUSIN KING Simeon of Bulgaria, King Michael of Romania is the last surviving monarch to have reigned during the Second World War. The Romanian royal family have, in recent years, been models of decorum, but the same cannot be said of their forebears. In the early years of the 20th century, Romanian royalty was a byword for louche living and scandal. In 1936, when Britain's Queen Mary heard about her eldest son's dilemma over whether to marry a divorcée or abdicate, her immediate response was 'Really! This might be Romania!' King Michael's parents divorced acrimoniously in 1928 after his father, Crown Prince Carol, had run off with an actress and forfeited his place in the line of succession. Even before that, Carol's mother, the infamous and beautiful Queen Marie of Romania, had scandalized Europe with her unconventional antics.

Michael inherited the throne from his grandfather King Ferdinand in 1927 at the age of six, but his father reappeared in 1930 and ruled as King Carol II before being forced to abdicate in 1940. Michael resumed his reign, but he was little more than a puppet, having no choice but to sign the decrees issued by the Fascist dictator Ion Antonescu. King Michael is still widely respected for his actions in leading the coup against Antonescu

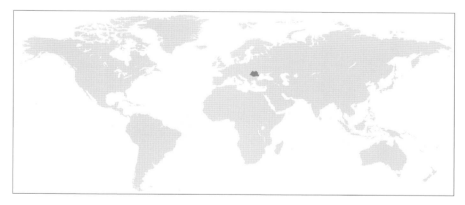

and freeing Romania from its links to Nazi Germany in August 1944. It was unfortunate that the USA and Britain were unable to prevent the Soviet Union from absorbing Romania in 1945, and King Michael reportedly still feels angry about the events of that time to this day.

Caught between the twin evils of Fascism and Communism, King Michael was forced to abdicate at gunpoint in 1947. He led his family into exile in Britain and married Princess Anne of Bourbon-Parma in 1948. Fascinated by engines of all sorts, he took up a job as a pilot and settled in Switzerland for 30 years. The downfall of Romania's Communist regime in 1989 propelled the country's former king back into the limelight. 'If the people want me to come back, of course, I will come back,' he said in 1990. 'Romanians have had enough suffering imposed on them to have the right to be consulted on their future'.

King Michael and his family returned to Bucharest for several short visits in the 1990s, before being formally invited back to live in the Elisabeta Palace in 1997. He now divides his time between Romania and Switzerland, working alongside the Romanian government in a quasi-diplomatic role.

In 2007, on the 60th anniversary of his abdication, King Michael designated Princess Margarita, the eldest of his five daughters, heir to the throne, despite Romania's adherence to Salic law, which forbids the accession of female heirs. At the same time, he asked the Romanian parliament to consider removing the strictures of Salic Law, should the monarchy ever be fully restored. Crown Princess Margarita was apparently once the girlfriend of British prime minister Gordon Brown when they were students together at Edinburgh University. She spent several years working for the United Nations. Today, she is married to Radu Duda, Prince of Hohenzollern-Veringen and runs the Princess Margarita Foundation, a charity established to carry out humanitarian work in Romania.

Far left: King Michael, Queen Anne and Crown Princess Margarita at their home in Switzerland.

Left: King Michael's grandfather, King Ferdinand of Romania (reigned 1914–27). His wife was the flamboyant Queen Marie, a great-granddaughter of both the Queen of England and the Tsar of Russia. Kaiser Wilhelm II felt that Ferdinand 'betrayed' his Hohenzollern roots by supporting the Triple Entente of Britain, France and Russia during the First World War.

Right: The young king of Romania on board a BMW motorcycle, 1943.

Below: Pelisor Palace, Sinaia, Prahova Valley, Transylvania, Romania was built by Carol I. The Romanian state has decreed that the royal family can repossess it.

BULGARIA
Simeon II

Official title	Simeon II, Tsar of Bulgaria
Pretender to	Throne of Bulgaria
Born	16 June 1937
Reigned	1943–1946
Royal house	Saxe-Coburg-Gotha
Official residences	Vrana Palace, Sofia, Bulgaria
Heir	Kardam, Prince of Turnovo (b. 1962, eldest son)

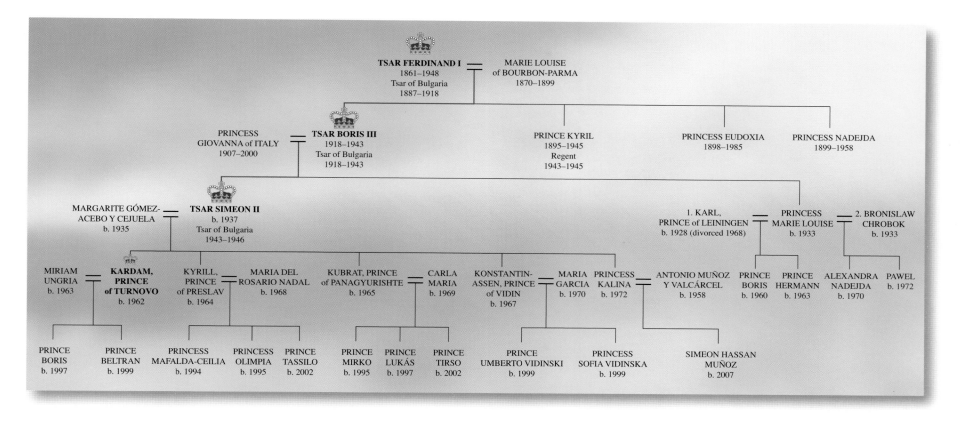

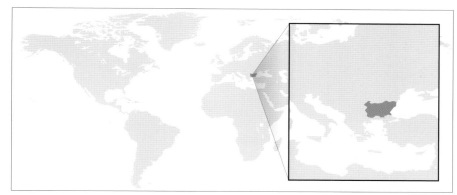

S IMEON SAXE-COBURG-GOTHA, or Simeon Borisov Sakskoburggotski, as he is now known in Bulgaria, was prime minister of Bulgaria from 2001 until 2005, the first exiled monarch to return to his homeland as a democratically elected leader. Born in 1937, the son of King Boris III, Simeon became Tsar of Bulgaria aged six in 1943.

Having become a principality of the Ottoman Empire in 1878, Bulgaria needed a ruler. Simeon's grandfather Ferdinand, the son of Prince August of Saxe-Coburg, (and a cousin of Queen Victoria) was offered the throne in 1887 with the title of Prince Regnant of Bulgaria. When the country won its independence from the Ottoman Empire in 1908, Ferdinand became Tsar of the Bulgarians. Bulgaria fared badly in the Balkan Wars and the First World War, and with his army in tatters, Ferdinand abdicated in favour of his son Boris in 1918. Boris survived the turbulent inter-war years, as well as two assassination attempts, although his power was diminished. He was a reluctant ally of the Axis Powers in World War II, but refused to send any Bulgarian Jews to Poland, or any troops to support Germany on the Russian front. In 1943, Boris died in questionable circumstances and was succeeded by his young son Simeon. Prince

Kyril, Boris's younger brother, acted as Regent, until he was executed by the invading Soviet forces in 1945. Simeon and his mother Queen Giovanna were forced into exile in 1948, fleeing first to Cairo where his grandfather, Vittorio Emanuele III, the former king of Italy, was living.

They eventually settled in Spain in 1951, and Simeon completed his education in Britain and the USA, where he attended the Valley Forge Military Academy. He enjoyed a tranquil life in Spain, where he met his wife, worked as a businessman, and became a good friend of King Juan Carlos. After the collapse of Communism in Eastern Europe in 1990, Simeon returned to Bulgaria in 1996, where he was greeted by rapturous crowds. The Bulgarian people rejected a return to monarchical rule, but in an extraordinary move, Simeon founded a political party, the Movement for Stability and Progress or NDSV and was elected prime minister in 2001.

"I am very proud to be king, also to be prime minister, but having an elected title is much more important than one which is inherited," he said. He initiated economic reforms and worked for Bulgaria's admission to NATO and the EU. He left office in 2005 when his party lost the election.

Right: When King Ferdinand was offered the throne of Bulgaria in 1887, some of his relatives expressed their surprise. 'He is totally unfit . . . delicate, eccentric and effeminate', wrote his cousin Queen Victoria. However, Ferdinand confounded his critics and was a successful tsar, until forced to abdicate in 1918. He retired to Coburg, pleased that his son was able to inherit the Bulgarian throne, and equally relieved that he had managed to salvage some of the family fortune, which enabled him to live in a suitably regal style.

Below: King Boris III was a reluctant ally of the Axis powers during the Second World War. At a meeting in 1943 Hitler tried to force him to commit Bulgaria more fully to the Nazi war effort, but Boris refused, only allowing German troops within Bulgaria to guard the railway line that traversed the country to Greece.

Left: Sitnyakovo Villa, Bulgaria. Built by King Ferdinand this has been restored to Tsar Simeon since the fall of the Communist regime.

Below left: King Boris III and his wife, Queen Giovanna married in 1930 and their first child, Princess Maria Louisa was born in 1933, followed by Prince Simeon in 1937.

Below: Crown Prince Kardam of Bulgaria and his wife, Miriam de Ungria Lopez.

SERBIA
Crown Prince Alexander

Official title	Crown Prince Alexander
Pretender to	Throne of Serbia
Born	17 July 1945
Pretendence	1970–
Royal house	Karadjordjevic
Official residences	Palaces of Dedinje, Belgrade
Heir	Hereditary Prince Peter (b. 1980, eldest son)

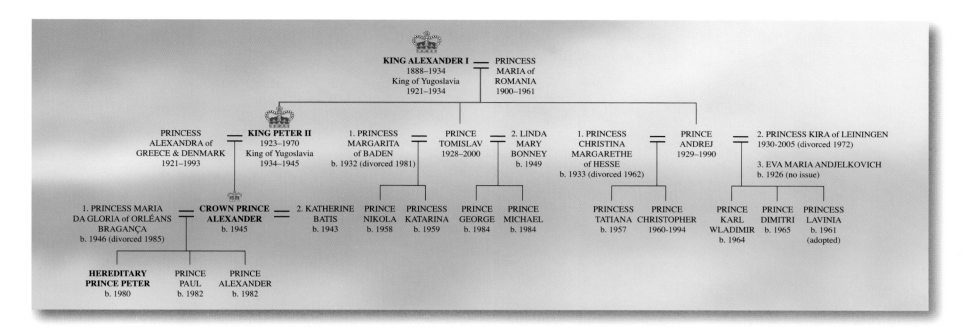

KING ALEXANDER I
1888–1934
King of Yugoslavia
1921–1934

PRINCESS
MARIA of
ROMANIA
1900–1961

PRINCESS
ALEXANDRA of
GREECE & DENMARK
1921–1993

KING PETER II
1923–1970
King of Yugoslavia
1934–1945

1. PRINCESS
MARGARITA
of BADEN
b. 1932 (divorced 1981)

PRINCE
TOMISLAV
1928–2000

2. LINDA
MARY
BONNEY
b. 1949

1. PRINCESS
CHRISTINA
MARGARETHE
of HESSE
b. 1933 (divorced 1962)

PRINCE
ANDREJ
1929–1990

2. PRINCESS KIRA of LEININGEN
1930-2005 (divorced 1972)

3. EVA MARIA ANDJELKOVICH
b. 1926 (no issue)

1. PRINCESS MARIA
DA GLORIA of ORLÉANS
BRAGANÇA
b. 1946 (divorced 1985)

**CROWN PRINCE
ALEXANDER**
b. 1945

2. KATHERINE
BATIS
b. 1943

PRINCE
NIKOLA
b. 1958

PRINCESS
KATARINA
b. 1959

PRINCE
GEORGE
b. 1984

PRINCE
MICHAEL
b. 1984

PRINCESS
TATIANA
b. 1957

PRINCE
CHRISTOPHER
1960-1994

PRINCE
KARL
WLADIMIR
b. 1964

PRINCE
DIMITRI
b. 1965

PRINCESS
LAVINIA
b. 1961
(adopted)

**HEREDITARY
PRINCE PETER**
b. 1980

PRINCE
PAUL
b. 1982

PRINCE
ALEXANDER
b. 1982

B ORN IN EXILE IN Claridges Hotel in London in 1945, Crown Prince Alexander of Yugoslavia spent the early part of his life at odds with the Communist regime that deprived his family of their nationality and property. His father, King Peter II left Yugoslavia in 1941 when the Germans invaded, to form a government in exile in London. Yugoslavia was split between the Fascists and the Communists, and at the end of the war the Allies supported the Communist partisans under Marshal Tito. The royal family were unceremoniously dismissed. King Peter did not abdicate his throne, firmly maintaining his family's claim throughout his life, but nor did he ever return to his homeland.

The Karadjordjevic family have always had strong relationships with their royal cousins throughout Europe. Prince Paul of Yugoslavia, who ruled as regent for his young cousin King Peter in the 1930s, was an Oxford-educated Anglophile, whose best man at his wedding in 1923 was the Duke of York (the future George VI). He married Princess Olga of Greece and Denmark, the sister of Princess Marina who later married Britain's Duke of Kent. Crown Prince Alexander's godmother is Queen Elizabeth II, and these associations undoubtedly eased the suffering of the Yugoslav royal family during their early years in exile.

Crown Prince Alexander was educated in Britain, Switzerland and the USA, and he served as an officer in the British army during the 1960s and early 1970s. His father King

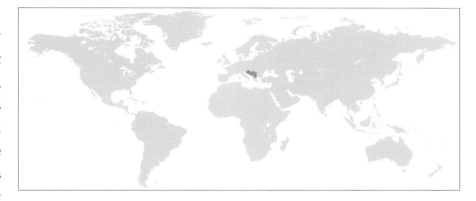

Peter died of cirrhosis of the liver in 1970, but Alexander has preferred to retain his title of crown prince, sensibly understanding that the title of king has very little meaning for an exiled monarch.

The Balkan wars of the 1990s, and the disintegration of the state of Yugoslavia into its constituent parts, resulted in a useful accommodation between the house of Karadjordjevic and the new Serbian regime. Opposed to the worst excesses of Serbian nationalism, Crown Prince Alexander nevertheless accepts that he and his family are figureheads of Serbia's past, and representatives of an age when Serbia was an independent state – as indeed the country is again now. Alexander paid his first visit to Yugoslavia in 1991 and supported democratic forces against the despotic regime of Slobodan Miloseviç during the troubled 1990s. After the fall of Miloseviç in 2001, the royal family was invited to return to their palaces in Belgrade, an invitation they accepted.

The crown prince is an advocate of constitutional monarchy and believes that this form of government would provide continuity and stability for Serbia, a country that has suffered more than its share of upheaval in recent years. The crown prince works for a number of humanitarian causes, and although he has a high public profile within Serbia, he is not politically active, acknowledging that a return to the throne can only come about as a result of the democratic process.

Above: Crown Prince Alexander in 1959 at the Culver Military Academy. He subsequently attended the Royal Military College, Sandhurst, England and served as an officer in the British army.

Above: King Peter II of Yugoslavia, in front of his cousin, the Regent Prince Paul. Peter acceded to the Yugoslav throne at the age of 11 when his father was assassinated in 1934. Deposed in 1945, he refused to abdicate, but settled in the USA, where he died in 1970.

Right: The Old Palace, Belgrade, which has been restored to the royal family Built in the 1920s by King Alexander I, it is now home to Crown Prince Alexander and his family.

Below: Crown Prince Alexander, with his wife Princess Katherine and his younger sons Alexander and Philip at a ceremony to present Certificates of Citizenship to the family in 2001, restoring both their citizenship of Yugoslavia and their right to claim private property, both of which had been illegally confiscated in 1947 by the ruling Communist Party.

MONTENEGRO
Crown Prince Nicholas

Official title	Crown Prince Nicholas of Montenegro
Born	7 July 1944
Pretendence	1986–
Royal house	House of Petrovic-Njegos
Residence	Paris
Heir	Hereditary Prince Boris (b. 1980, son)

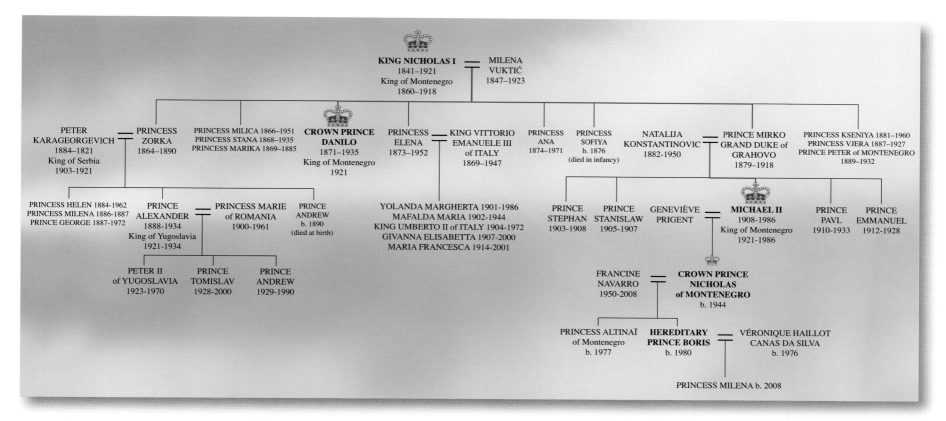

KING NICHOLAS I
1841–1921
King of Montenegro
1860–1918
— MILENA VUKTIĆ
1847–1923

PETER KARAGEORGEVICH
1884–1821
King of Serbia
1903-1921

PRINCESS ZORKA
1864–1890

PRINCESS MILICA 1866–1951
PRINCESS STANA 1868–1935
PRINCESS MARIKA 1869–1885

CROWN PRINCE DANILO
1871–1935
King of Montenegro
1921

PRINCESS ELENA
1873–1952

KING VITTORIO EMANUELE III
of ITALY
1869–1947

PRINCESS ANA
1874–1971

PRINCESS SOFIYA
b. 1876
(died in infancy)

NATALIJA KONSTANTINOVIC
1882-1950

PRINCE MIRKO GRAND DUKE of GRAHOVO
1879–1918

PRINCESS KSENIYA 1881–1960
PRINCESS VJERA 1887–1927
PRINCE PETER of MONTENEGRO
1889–1932

PRINCESS HELEN 1884-1962
PRINCESS MILENA 1886-1887
PRINCE GEORGE 1887-1972

PRINCE ALEXANDER
1888-1934
King of Yugoslavia
1921-1934

PRINCESS MARIE of ROMANIA
1900-1961

PRINCE ANDREW
b. 1890
(died at birth)

YOLANDA MARGHERTA 1901-1986
MAFALDA MARIA 1902-1944
KING UMBERTO II of ITALY 1904-1972
GIVANNA ELISABETTA 1907-2000
MARIA FRANCESCA 1914-2001

PRINCE STEPHAN
1903-1908

PRINCE STANISLAW
1905-1907

GENEVIÈVE PRIGENT

MICHAEL II
1908-1986
King of Montenegro
1921-1986

PRINCE PAVL
1910-1933

PRINCE EMMANUEL
1912-1928

PETER II of YUGOSLAVIA
1923-1970

PRINCE TOMISLAV
1928-2000

PRINCE ANDREW
1929-1990

FRANCINE NAVARRO
1950-2008

CROWN PRINCE NICHOLAS of MONTENEGRO
b. 1944

PRINCESS ALTINAÏ
of Montenegro
b. 1977

HEREDITARY PRINCE BORIS
b. 1980

VÉRONIQUE HAILLOT CANAS DA SILVA
b. 1976

PRINCESS MILENA b. 2008

I N 1915 DURING THE First World War the Austro-Hungarian army defeated the forces of Montenegro, prompting the annexation of the kingdom and the exile of the royal family at the end of the war in 1918. King Nicholas I, the last king of Montenegro, fled to Paris, where he died in 1921. At the end of the war the kingdom of Serbia absorbed Montenegro, and the Petrovic-Njegos dynasty was officially deposed. It was an ignoble end to the reign of a man generally regarded as a skilled statesman and progressive monarch. King Nicholas had done much to modernise Montenegro, introducing judicial reforms and giving the country its first constitution in 1905.

King Nicholas was succeeded by his son Danilo II, who promptly abdicated in favour of his nephew King Michael I after only a week on the throne. No one is absolutely sure why Danilo followed this course of action, but nevertheless, Michael's reign began as a regency, which lasted until 1929, when he celebrated his 21st birthday and declared his allegiance to the throne of Yugoslavia, which rewarded him with an allowance from the civil list.

King Michael spent all of his reign in exile, much of it in France, where he was arrested by the Nazis in 1941 shortly after his marriage and imprisoned. When he refused to become a

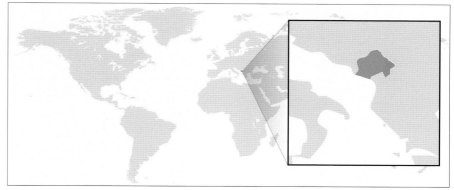

puppet monarch for the Nazis, he and his wife were sent to a concentration camp. His son Prince Nicholas was born in 1944. After the war, Michael worked briefly for Marshal Tito as Head of Protocol in Yugoslavia, but returned to exile in France in 1948.

Crown Prince Nicholas is based in France, where he was educated and brought up his family. He trained as an architect and has undertaken the restoration of a number of public buildings. He continues to promote the cause of Montenegro and advocated the separation of Montenegro from the republic of Serbia prior to the 2006 referendum. He has said that he would like to return to the Montenegrin throne if that is the wish of the people. Montenegro is now an independent republic that aims to promote itself as a tourist destination and full member of the EU.

The heir to the title is Hereditary Prince Boris, a graduate of the École Nationale Supérieure des Arts Décoratif and a typographic designer. He married Véronique Haillot Canas da Silva in 2007 and they have one daughter, Princess Miléna Petrovic-Njegos of Montenegro.

Above: Nicholas I, King of Montenegro was nicknamed the 'father-in-law of Europe', as his children married into the royal families of Russia, Italy and Yugoslavia.

Left: Danilo II married Duchess Jutta of Mecklenburg in 1899, but the marriage was childless.

Left: A postcard from World War One showing the allied heads of state of the Entente Powers. From left: Russian Tsar Nicholas II, British King George V, Albert, King of the Belgians, French President Poincaré, King Peter of Serbia, King Nicholas of Montenegro, and Emperor Taisho of Japan.

Above: A festive procession leaving the royal palace in Cetinje, the capital of Montenegro on the occasion of the marriage of Prince Mirko to Natalija Konstantinovic in 1902. Prince Mirko (1879–1918), a younger son of King Nicholas I, is the grandfather of the current crown prince. Built by Nicholas I, the royal palace is now the National Museum of Montenegro (see right).

ALBANIA
King Leka

Official title	Leka, King of the Albanians
Pretender to	Throne of Albania
Born	5 April 1939
Pretendence	1961–
Royal house	Zogu
Residence	Private residence, Tirana, Albania
Heir	Crown Prince Leka (b. 1982, son)

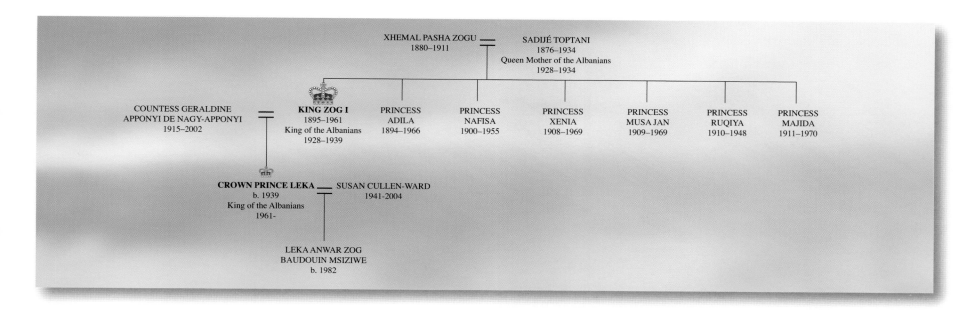

XHEMAL PASHA ZOGU
1880–1911

SADIJÉ TOPTANI
1876–1934
Queen Mother of the Albanians
1928–1934

COUNTESS GERALDINE
APPONYI DE NAGY-APPONYI
1915–2002

KING ZOG I
1895–1961
King of the Albanians
1928–1939

PRINCESS
ADILA
1894–1966

PRINCESS
NAFISA
1900–1955

PRINCESS
XENIA
1908–1969

PRINCESS
MUSA JAN
1909–1969

PRINCESS
RUQIYA
1910–1948

PRINCESS
MAJIDA
1911–1970

CROWN PRINCE LEKA
b. 1939
King of the Albanians
1961-

SUSAN CULLEN-WARD
1941-2004

LEKA ANWAR ZOG
BAUDOUIN MSIZIWE
b. 1982

ORCED TO FLEE HIS homeland when only two days old, King Leka of Albania has spent most of his life in exile. The Albanian royal family is one of Europe's more recent and some might say Ruritanian dynasties. Leka's father, King Zog, proclaimed himself king in 1928, having ruled from 1922, first as prime minister and then as president, 1925–28. King Zog was born Ahmet Muhtar Bey Zogolli into a landowning family in Mati, Albania and claimed descent from the great Balkan hero Skanderbeg. His wife, Geraldine, was the daughter of an impoverished Hungarian count and an American heiress. They married in 1938, with Musssolini's ambassador Count Ciano as a witness, and a drove off to their honeymoon in an open-topped Mercedes sent by Hitler.

King Zog established a constitutional monarchy in Albania, which he based on that in Italy. Indeed, political links with the Italians were so close that by 1939 Mussolini effectively controlled Albania's economy and army. Despite his efforts to weaken the Italian grip on Albania, Zog was forced into exile in April 1939 when Mussolini made Albania an Italian 'protectorate'. After the Second World War, the Communists under Enver Hoxha gained power and Zog's dreams of returning to rule his homeland were shattered. He abdicated in 1946.

The only child of King Zog and Queen Geraldine, Prince Leka began his long years of exile in the Ritz Hotel, London. Interestingly, he was consecrated King of the Albanians in another grand hotel, the Hotel Bristol in Paris in 1961 after his

father's death. King Zog and his family were certainly not impoverished exiles, apparently arriving in London in 1939 with suitcases full of bullion and jewels. Leka was educated in England, studied at the Sorbonne and gained a commission in the British Army after training at the Royal Military Academy, Sandhurst.

A some-time commodity broker, King Leka's well-known interest in firearms may stem from the fact that his father survived over 50 assassination attempts during his 11-year reign. However, "Mr Zogu" as he was known in exile, was arrested in South Africa in 1999 for the possession of an extensive arms cache, and he was expelled from France and Spain when the French authorities took exception to his penchant for carrying personal weapons, and the Spanish disapproved of his alleged links with arms dealers.

King Leka married Susan Cullen-Ward, an Australian, in Biarritz in 1975. 'I normally wear two pistols but not even I could carry guns at my wedding reception,' said the king on his wedding day. Their only child, Crown Prince Leka Anwar Zog Reza Baudouin Msiziwe, was born in South Africa in 1982; his names reflect the king's gratitude to those who had befriended him – Anwar Sadat, the Shah of Iran, King Badouin of Belgium, and the South African nation. Crown Prince Leka II, like his father a talented linguist and graduate of the Royal Military Academy, Sandhurst, works for the Albanian foreign ministry.

At several points since the fall of the Berlin Wall and the Balkan wars of the 1990s, King Leka has made headlines as commentators speculated about the restoration of the Albanian monarchy. Having made his first visit to his homeland in 1993, Leka returned to Albania in 1997, where a referendum rejected a return to monarchist rule. Leka and his followers refused to accept the result and he fled the country after a botched attempt to storm the building where the voting papers were stored. He returned in 2002 at the invitation of parliament, and now lives in Tirana, where his wife died in 2004. His father's Art Deco summer palace in Durres near Tirana has been redeveloped as timeshare holiday apartments, and King Leka retains the penthouse suite.

Right: President Ahmed Bey Zogu with his bodyguards in 1927, the year before he proclaimed himself king of Albania.

Below: The marriage of King Zog and Queen Geraldine, 1938 at the Royal Palace, Tirana.

Above: The accession of King Leka is proclaimed at the Hotel Bristol, Paris in 1961.

Left: Crown Prince Leka accepts the Mother Teresa medal on behalf of his late grandmother Queen Geraldine, in memory of her philanthropic work.

Below: King Leka, Queen Susan and Prince Leka at their home in South Africa during the 1990s.

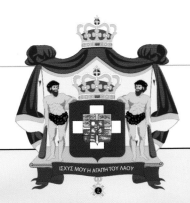

GREECE
Constantine II

Official title	Constantine II, King of the Hellenes
Pretender to	Throne of Greece
Born	2 June 1940
Accession to throne	1964; deposed 1974
Royal house	House of Glücksburg
Residence	Private residence, Hampstead Heath, London
Heir	Pavlos, Crown Prince of the Hellenes (b. 1967, eldest son)

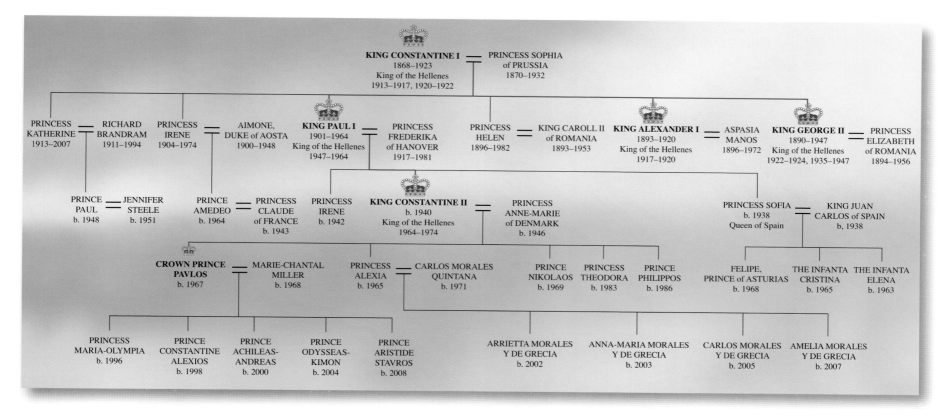

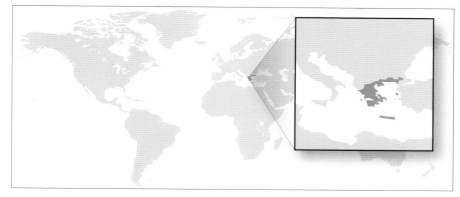

I N 1863 THE THRONE of Greece was offered to a number of European princes. Prince William of Denmark, a younger son of the Danish royal family, willingly adopted the title of King George I of the Hellenes and devoted his life to bringing stability to the fragmented country. His successors struggled to impose order on Greece, with varying degrees of success, and the Greek throne was something of a byword for instability throughout the 20th century.

Born in Athens in 1940, the son of Crown Prince Paul and Princess Frederika, Constantine was evacuated with his family from Athens and spent his early years in exile in Egypt and Cape Town during World War II. In 1946 the Greek people voted to restore the monarchy and the royal family returned. Constantine was educated in Greece and studied law at Athens University. He acceded to the Hellenic throne on the death of his father King Paul in 1964 and inherited a bitter political struggle between the Communists and monarchists that had been fermenting since 1945. He married his third cousin, Princess Anne-Marie of Denmark in the same year, and the couple have five children.

After the Colonels' Coup in Greece in 1967 the Greek royal family went into exile in Rome, then stayed with their Danish cousins in the Amalienborg Palace in Copenhagen, before settling in London. The 1974 referendum in Greece ended the king's hope of returning to the throne of Greece.

As a male line descendant of King Christian IX of Denmark, King Constantine II's only undisputed title is Prince of Denmark. A great-grandson of George I of the Hellenes, he is generally known as 'the former King' within Greece, and like several former monarchs, he is now free to visit the country of his birth. That he is permitted to do so must be due in part to his pragmatic attitude to the events surrounding his overthrow: he advised his supporters to accept the results of the 1974 plebiscite, although he has never enjoyed a particularly easy relationship with any Greek government.

Although he spent the early years of his adult life embroiled in Greek politics, Constantine also demonstrated a great love of sports, in particular sailing, winning a gold medal for Greece at the 1960 Olympics. In his later years he has worked with the International Olympic Committee, as well as devoting a great deal of his time to education and charitable work. He founded the Hellenic College of London in 1980, and is chairman of the Round Square Schools, an educational organisation that aims to promote international understanding between young people.

Above: King Paul and Queen Frederika, shortly after the restoration of the Greek monarchy in 1946.

Above left: Some 40 European royals rub shoulders at King Paul's 60th birthday party. Among them are Princess Marina of Kent, Crown Prince Constantine, Prince Juan Carlos of Spain, and Princess Beatrix of the Netherlands.

Left: The young King Constantine with the National Government of Greece in 1967.

Above: Queen Frederika and King Paul driving to Salonika Cathedral on the 45th anniversary of the liberation of the city from the Turks. Prince Paul proposed to Princess Frederika of Hanover when he was in Berlin to attend the 1936 Olympics. They married in 1938.

Above right: Crown Prince Constantine helms the yacht Ivanhoe off Corfu, 1963. Extreme right in sunglasses is Prince Juan Carlos of Spain, his brother-in-law.

Right: The Tatoi Palace, Athens, home of the Greek royal family.

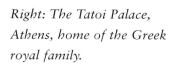

Above: Queen Anne Marie of Greece is the Queen of Denmark's younger sister and the families reman close. When the Greek royal family was driven into exile in 1968, they spent several *months staying with their Danish relations in Copenhagen.*

Right: The christening of Crown Prince Pavlos's second child Prince *Constantine Alexios in 1998. Among the godparents were Pavlos's first cousin, Prince Felipe of Spain (back row, second right) and Prince William of Wales (front row, right).*

RUSSIA
Prince Nicholas Romanov

Official title	Nicholas Romanov, Prince of Russia
Pretender to	Imperial throne of Russia
Born	26 September 1922
Pretendence	1992
Royal house	Romanov
Residence	Rougmont, Switzerland, and Italy
Heir	Prince Dimitri Romanov (b. 1926, brother)

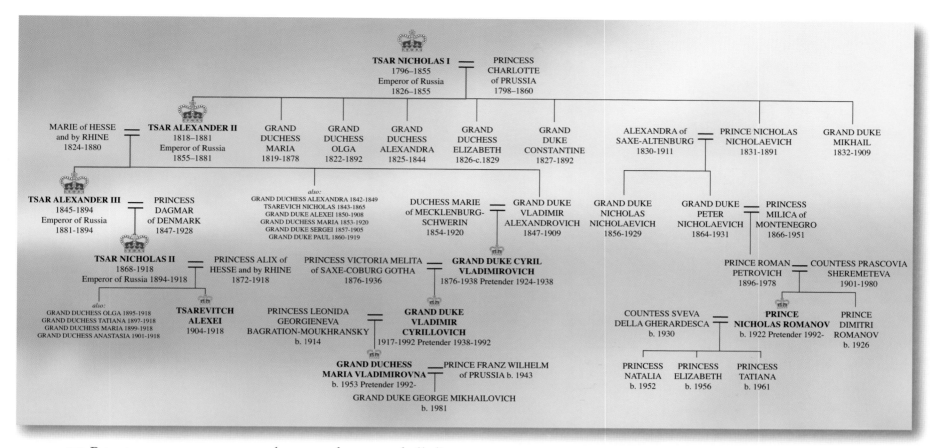

TSAR NICHOLAS I
1796–1855
Emperor of Russia
1826–1855
— PRINCESS
CHARLOTTE
of PRUSSIA
1798-1860

MARIE of HESSE and by RHINE
1824-1880
— **TSAR ALEXANDER II**
1818–1881
Emperor of Russia
1855–1881

GRAND DUCHESS MARIA
1819-1878

GRAND DUCHESS OLGA
1822-1892

GRAND DUCHESS ALEXANDRA
1825-1844

GRAND DUCHESS ELIZABETH
1826-c.1829

GRAND DUKE CONSTANTINE
1827-1892

ALEXANDRA of SAXE-ALTENBURG
1830-1911
— PRINCE NICHOLAS NICHOLAEVICH
1831-1891

GRAND DUKE MIKHAIL
1832-1909

TSAR ALEXANDER III
1845-1894
Emperor of Russia
1881-1894
— PRINCESS DAGMAR of DENMARK
1847-1928

also:
GRAND DUCHESS ALEXANDRA 1842-1849
TSAREVICH NICHOLAS 1843-1865
GRAND DUKE ALEXEI 1850-1908
GRAND DUCHESS MARIA 1853-1920
GRAND DUKE SERGEI 1857-1905
GRAND DUKE PAUL 1860-1919

DUCHESS MARIE of MECKLENBURG-SCHWERIN
1854-1920
— GRAND DUKE VLADIMIR ALEXANDROVICH
1847-1909

GRAND DUKE NICHOLAS NICHOLAEVICH
1856-1929

GRAND DUKE PETER NICHOLAEVICH
1864-1931
— PRINCESS MILICA of MONTENEGRO
1866-1951

TSAR NICHOLAS II
1868-1918
Emperor of Russia 1894-1918
— PRINCESS ALIX of HESSE and by RHINE
1872-1918

PRINCESS VICTORIA MELITA of SAXE-COBURG GOTHA
1876-1936
— **GRAND DUKE CYRIL VLADIMIROVICH**
1876-1938 Pretender 1924-1938

PRINCE ROMAN PETROVICH
1896-1978
— COUNTESS PRASCOVIA SHEREMETEVA
1901-1980

also:
GRAND DUCHESS OLGA 1895-1918
GRAND DUCHESS TATIANA 1897-1918
GRAND DUCHESS MARIA 1899-1918
GRAND DUCHESS ANASTASIA 1901-1918

TSAREVITCH ALEXEI
1904-1918

PRINCESS LEONIDA GEORGIENEVA BAGRATION-MOUKHRANSKY
b. 1914
— **GRAND DUKE VLADIMIR CYRILLOVICH**
1917-1992 Pretender 1938-1992

COUNTESS SVEVA DELLA GHERARDESCA
b. 1930
— **PRINCE NICHOLAS ROMANOV**
b. 1922 Pretender 1992-

PRINCE DIMITRI ROMANOV
b. 1926

GRAND DUCHESS MARIA VLADIMIROVNA
b. 1953 Pretender 1992-
— PRINCE FRANZ WILHELM of PRUSSIA b. 1943

PRINCESS NATALIA
b. 1952

PRINCESS ELIZABETH
b. 1956

PRINCESS TATIANA
b. 1961

GRAND DUKE GEORGE MIKHAILOVICH
b. 1981

THE ROMANOVS ARE PROBABLY the most famous of all dispossessed royal families, cruelly deprived of their lives, as well as their palaces and titles, during the Russian Revolution. Although Tsar Nicholas II, his wife and children were all murdered at Yekaterinburg in 1918, the descendants of the wider family live on, and two branches of the family claim the title of head of the House of Romanov. For many years the fate of at least one of Nicholas's daughters, Grand Duchess Anastasia, was uncertain and caught the public imagination, with several books and films produced about her fate.

In 1886 Tsar Alexander III (1845–1894) decreed that the children and grandchildren of a tsar should be titled Grand Duke or Grand Duchess of Russia, with the style Imperial Highness; all other descendants were titled Prince or Princess of Russia, with the rank of Highness or Serene Highness. Furthermore, the Russian line of succession was clearly laid down by Tsar Paul I (1754–1801) in 1797 and codified last by Nicholas II in 1911. The crown passed down the male line of succession by primogeniture, only devolving to the female line when male heirs had been exhausted. And these rules, which were designed to prevent conflicting claims to the throne, should also apply to pretenders to the throne. Unfortunately, the changing fortunes of the Romanov family, as well as many other royal houses, have meant that dynastic marriages are not as common as they once were, and some family members have entered into marriages that have not been deemed 'dynastic', that is with a person of equal social stature. The children of such marriages may lose their place in the line of succession, which complicates the already complex line of succession.

Over 90 years since the revolution, the Romanovs have largely come to terms with the fact that blood is thicker than water and have most of them have banded together to form the Romanov Association, with the intention of maintaining their family ties, upholding the memory of the Russia's imperial past, and carrying out acts of benevolence within Russia itself, as permitted by the ruling authorities. Most of the Romanovs now agree that restoration of the monarchy will only come about by democratic vote, and so inter-family arguments about precedence are fairly pointless.

In 1998 the remains of the murdered last tsar and his family were re-buried in St Petersburg, and over 50 relatives of the imperial family, who had travelled from all over Europe and beyond, attended the Orthodox service. It was an extraordinary ceremony, as the last Romanov tsar was mourned by relatives born (in the main) many years after his death, by successors of the regime that killed him, and by the diplomatic corps of ambassadors. The controversy over whether any of the tsar's children survived the massacre in 1918 came to a definitive end in 2008, when DNA tests revealed that human remains found a short distance from the main burial site, were indeed those of the tsarvitch and his one of his sisters.

The current head of the family, as recognized by the majority of the Romanov clan, is Prince Nicholas Romanov, a great-great-grandson of Tsar Nicholas I (1796–1855). He believes that he inherited the title on the death of his cousin Grand Duke Vladimir Cyrillovich (1938–1992), as he was the next surviving male dynast. Unfortunately, Vladimir's daughter and only child, Grand Duchess Maria Vladimirovna (b. 1953) does not agree, alleging that Nicholas, like many of his male cousins, was disinherited because of his parents' unequal marriage. The claim of Grand Duchess Maria and her son, Grand Duke George Mikhailovich (b. 1981) is supported only by a minority of Russian royalists.

Born in exile in Cap d'Antibes in 1922, Prince Nicholas was a successful businessman for many years. He assumed the duties of head of the family in 1992, leading the Romanovs in mourning at the reburial of the remains of the last tsar, and at the funeral of the tsar's mother the Dowager Empress Maria Feodorovna when her remains were re-interred in Russia in 2006. He has no interest in reclaiming the Russian throne, recognising that Russia is still learning to deal with democracy and not wishing to cause controversy.

Left: Tsar Nicholas II, Tsarina Alexandra and their five children. The Imperial family was wiped out by revolutionaries in 1918.

Below: Grand Duchess Marie Vladmirovna, her mother Princess Leonida and her son Prince George, who claims the title of head of the Romanov family.

Below left: Prince Dimitri Romanov, the younger brother of Prince Nicholas, and the Princess Dorrit. opening a museum dedicated to theEmpress Maria Feodorovna in Copenhagen.

Left: The Empress Maria Feodorovna, the mother of Tsar Nicholas II, survived the Russian Revolution and spent her last days in her native land of Denmark, where she was buried on her death in 1928. In 2006, her remains were transported amid great ceremony, to Russia from Denmark to be buried in St Petersburg alongside her husband Tsar Alexander III.

Since the fall of Communism, the imperial apartments and palaces have been restored to their former glory, although today they are merely used as historical sites. The Rococo Catherine Palace in Tsarskoye Selo (Pushkin), 25 km southeast of St. Petersburg, was destroyed during the Second World War but has undergone extensive renovation.
The throne room (above) is in the Winter Palace, the tsars' official residence.

Below: An inlaid Fabergé cigar box with miniature portraits of Tsar Nicholas II and the Tsarina Alexandra inlaid within a heraldic Russian eagle.

ASIA

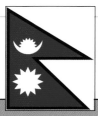

NEPAL
King Gyanendra Bir Bikram Shah Dev

Official title	King of Nepal
Country ruled	Nepal
Born	7 July 1947
Accession to throne	2001-2008 (deposed)
Royal house	Shah Dynasty
Official residence	Narayanhiti Palace, Katmandu
Heir	Crown Prince Paras (b. 1971, son)

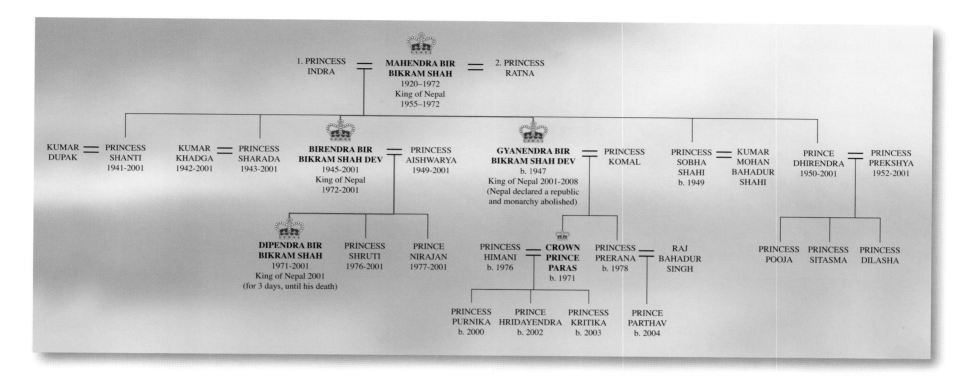

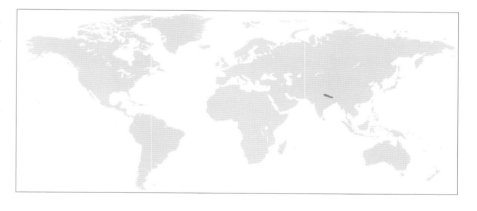

THE STORY OF THE Shah dynasty begins in the 16th century with Jagdeva Khan who conquered the principality of Kaski (now a part of Gandaki Zone and one of the 75 districts of Nepal) and secured the title of Shah from the Emperor of India. King Dravya Shah, the great-grandson of Jagdeva, founded the Kingdom of Gurkha, the seat of the Shah Dynasty, in 1559. In 1768 Dravya's descendant, Prithvi Narayan Shah, managed to bring the six principalities of Makawanpur, Kathmandu, Patan, Bhaktapur, Chaudandi and Bijayapur under his rule, thus laying the foundations of the modern Nepalese nation. Successive generations of rulers expanded the borders of Nepal and continued the work of unifying the country.

In 1814, however, a territorial dispute with the British East India Company led to the Gurkha War, and by the end, in 1816, Nepal had lost one third of its territory. Despite being beaten by the British, the remarkable fighting abilities of the Gurkha soldiers won them huge admiration from their conquerors, and this began the long association between the British armed forces and the Gurkhas.

The aftermath of the Kot Massacre on 14 September 1846 saw Jang Bahadur Kunwar Ranaji, become prime minister, a title that became hereditary within his family for the next 104 years. During this period the kings were reduced to little more than figureheads while the Rana dynasty effectively ruled the country through hereditary government positions.

The Rana hegemony came to an end in 1951, when India sponsored both King Tribhuvan as Nepal's new ruler, and a new, more democratic, government. However, it took until 1959 for a constitution to be approved, after which elections were held for a national assembly. Within a year, though, the constant disagreements between the assembly and King Mahendra saw him dismiss the government and imprison many of its leaders; in 1962 Mahendra abolished the 1959 constitution and replaced it with one that established the king as the real holder of power in Nepal.

In 1990 Mahendra's successor, King Birendra, reversed much of this policy, turning Nepal into a constitutional monarchy and restoring a measure of democracy to the country. On 1 June 2001 the Nepalese royal family was plunged into crisis when King Birendra, his wife and their two younger children, as well as five other members of the Royal Family, were killed by the Crown Prince Dipendra, in the Narayanhiti Palace. In the aftermath of this tragic event King Gyanendra, the surviving brother of Birendra, succeeded to the throne.

Gyanendra was born in Kathmandu, Nepal, on 7 July1947. He was educated at St Joseph's College in Darjeeling, India, and graduated in 1969 from Tribhuvan University in Kathmandu.

As the younger son of King Mahendra, Gyanendra was not directly involved in politics during the reigns of his father or brother, but his short reign was to prove no less controversial. Twice between 2002 and 2005 he dismissed the government and assumed control himself. The second time was to prove his undoing, as weeks of demonstrations by hundreds of thousands of Nepalese in 2006 forced him to reinstate parliament. By May 2008 parliament had overwhelmingly voted in favour of a bill that abolished royal rule in Nepal, thus ending King Gyanendra's reign and with it that of the Shah dynasty.

Above: Prince Dhirendra (aged ten) leaving a Vickers Valiant V bomber by the circular door during a visit to Weybridge in England.

Above: Crown Prince Birendra on his way to attend Eton College, England, as a new pupil in 1959.

Left: King Mahendra and Queen Ratna arriving at the Nepalese Embassy in London to attend a dinner given by them for members of the British Royal Family in 1960.

Below left: King Gyanendra and Queen Komal attending a religious ceremony in Durbar Square, Kathmandu in 2005.

Below: Crown Prince Dipendra Bir Bikram Shah Dev shot and killed his parents, King Birendra and Queen Aishwarya, and as many as nine other members of his family, before turning the gun on himself at the royal palace in Kathmandu on 1 June 2001 after a reported argument over Dipendra''s choice of a bride.

Left: King Birendra and Queen Aaishwarya entertain the Prince of Wales in Pokara, Nepal during a 2001 visit.

Below: King Gyanendra and Queen Komal (left) with their family. From left to right: Princess Purnica, five-year-old Prince Hridayendra, Princess Kritika, Crown Princess Himani, and Crown Prince Paras.

Right: Narayanhiti, the royal palace of Nepal in Kathmandu: the towered throne room can be seen behind the prominent front window.

BHUTAN
King Jigme Khesar Namgyel Wangchuck

Official title	Druk Gyalpo (Dragon King) of Bhutan
Country ruled	Bhutan
Born	21 February 1980
Accession to throne	2006
Royal house	Wangchuck Dynasty
Official residence	Samteling Palace, Thimphu
Heir	Prince Jigyel Ugyen Wangchuck (b. 1984, half-brother)

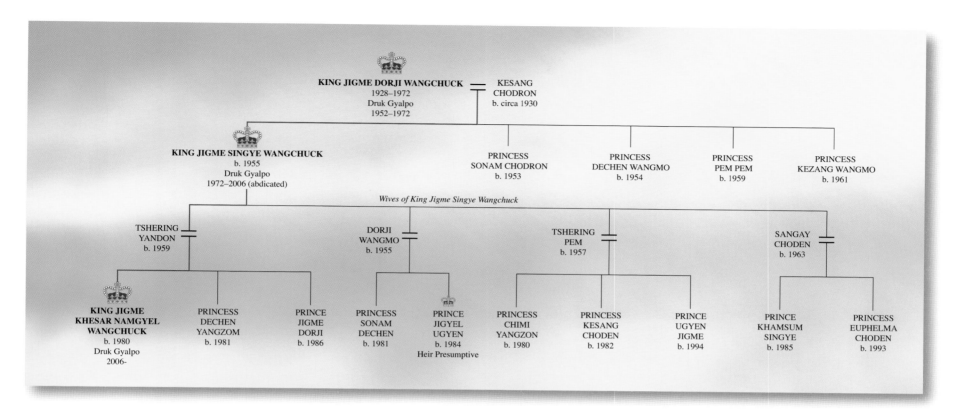

KING JIGME DORJI WANGCHUCK
1928–1972
Druk Gyalpo
1952–1972

KESANG
CHODRON
b. circa 1930

KING JIGME SINGYE WANGCHUCK
b. 1955
Druk Gyalpo
1972–2006 (abdicated)

PRINCESS
SONAM CHODRON
b. 1953

PRINCESS
DECHEN WANGMO
b. 1954

PRINCESS
PEM PEM
b. 1959

PRINCESS
KEZANG WANGMO
b. 1961

Wives of King Jigme Singye Wangchuck

TSHERING
YANDON
b. 1959

DORJI
WANGMO
b. 1955

TSHERING
PEM
b. 1957

SANGAY
CHODEN
b. 1963

KING JIGME
KHESAR NAMGYEL
WANGCHUCK
b. 1980
Druk Gyalpo
2006-

PRINCESS
DECHEN
YANGZOM
b. 1981

PRINCE
JIGME
DORJI
b. 1986

PRINCESS
SONAM
DECHEN
b. 1981

PRINCE
JIGYEL
UGYEN
b. 1984
Heir Presumptive

PRINCESS
CHIMI
YANGZON
b. 1980

PRINCESS
KESANG
CHODEN
b. 1982

PRINCE
UGYEN
JIGME
b. 1994

PRINCE
KHAMSUM
SINGYE
b. 1985

PRINCESS
EUPHELMA
CHODEN
b. 1993

THE KINGDOM OF BHUTAN, called *Druk Yul* (Land of the Thunder Dragon) by its people, lies in the eastern Himalayas and is surrounded by mountains. This geographical remoteness led to an almost complete isolation from the outside world that was actively encouraged by its rulers until well into the 20th century.

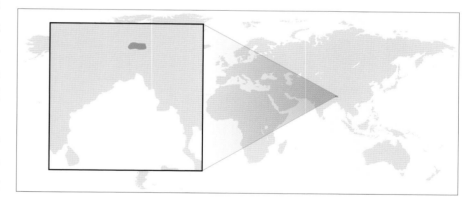

The early history of Bhutan remains obscure. Until the early 17th century it was little more than a collection of frequently warring fiefdoms. The consolidation of Bhutan began in 1616 when the Tibetan monk Ngawang Namgyal united the various competing factions. During his reign Ngawang Namgyal repulsed three Tibetan invasions and put in place a dual system of government that lasted until 1907.

The current ruling family of Bhutan, the Wangchuck dynasty, came to power in 1907 when an assembly of leading Buddhist monks, government officials, and heads of important families elected Ugyen Wangchuck as the hereditary ruler and gave him the title of *Druk Gyalpo* (Dragon King). Until his election to the throne Ugyen had been the *ponlop* (governor) of the Tongsa region and had spent the previous 30 years consolidating his powerbase within the country. The British government, keen for stability in the area, was quick to recognise the new monarchy, and in 1910 they signed the Treaty of Punakha, the terms of which granted an annual subsidy to Bhutan and guaranteed British non-intervention in the internal affairs of the country in return for an acceptance of British advice on its external affairs. The gradual process of modernization in Bhutan began with King Ugyen, most notably through his introduction of a western-style system of education.

Following the death of Ugyen in 1926, his son Jigme Wangchuck became the next ruler. During Jigme's reign Bhutan became one of the first countries to recognize India's new-found independence in 1947 and friendly relations between the two nations were formalized on 8 August 1949 with the signing of the Indo-Bhutan Friendship Treaty.

Bhutan slowly began to forsake its self-imposed isolation from the outside world during the reign of Jigme's successor,

King Jigme Dorji Wangchuck. In 1971 the country was admitted to the United Nations and during King Jigme's reign, he significantly restructured the country's administration, introducing a national assembly (the *Tshogdu*) and thereby taking the first steps away from an absolute monarchy, towards a more democratic form of government.

In 1972 Jigme Singye Wangchuck ascended to the throne following the sudden death of his father Jigme Dorji Wangchuck from a heart attack. At just 17 he became the youngest serving monarch in the world. The fourth king continued his father's policies of the gradual modernization of Bhutan and reformation of the country's government. Most significantly, he gave up the majority of his administrative powers and granted the *Tshodgu* the power to impeach the king via a two-thirds majority vote. Aside from the political reforms that he introduced, King Jigme Singye Wangchuck is internationally renowned for his theory of 'Gross National Happiness', that places a strong emphasis on a communal striving for the well-being and happiness of all citizens.

On 14 December 2006 King Jigme Singye Wangchuck abdicated, passing the throne to his son Jigme Khesar Namgyel Wangchuck who was officially crowned on 6 November 2008. King Jigme Khesar Namgyel Wangchuck's father was keen to ensure that his son would be ready for the challenges of ruling his country, and to this end he attended a university preparatory school, the Phillips Academy, in the United States, followed by higher education at the Cushing Academy, the Wheaton College in Massachusetts, and Oxford University. Since his ascension to throne King Jigme Khesar Namgyel Wangchuck has travelled extensively throughout Bhutan promoting the democratic process set in motion by his father. Reflecting his nation's entry into the 21st century, the new king even has his own Facebook page.

Right: The mausoleum of King Jigme Dorji Wangchuk: his mother commissioned the mausoleum in 1974 as a memorial to the life and work of the late third king.

Left: King Jigme Singye Wangchuck talking with the Prince of Wales at the Tashichho Dzong in the capital Thimphu.

Left and below: King Jigme Khesar Namgyel Wangchuck during his coronation ceremony at the Tashichho Dzong Palace in Thimphu on 6 November 2008. The fifth Dragon King of Bhutan, King Jigme was well-prepared for his position as monarch. He studied in the USA before attending Magdalen College, Oxford University where he gained an MPhil in Politics. The coronation was a lavish three-day event, a mixture of Buddhist and traditional Bhutanese ceremonies, culminating in the crowning of the new king with the Raven Crown of Bhutan (below).

Right: King Jigme Khesar Namgyel Wangchuck prepares to take part in a demonstration of archery, the national game, during his coronation celebrations. Bhutanese archery contests take place over a longer course and feature a smaller target than their European equivalents.

Below: Built in the 17th century, Tashichho Dzong is the home of the Bhutanese government, the royal palace and a religious centre, in Thimpu, the capital city.

BURMA
King Taw Phaya

Official title	Taw Phaya, King of Burma
Pretender to	Throne of Burma
Born	22 March 1924
Pretendence	1936–
Royal house	Konbaung
Residence	Private home, Pyin U Lwin, Burma
Heir	Richard Taw Phaya Myat Gyi (b. 1945, son)

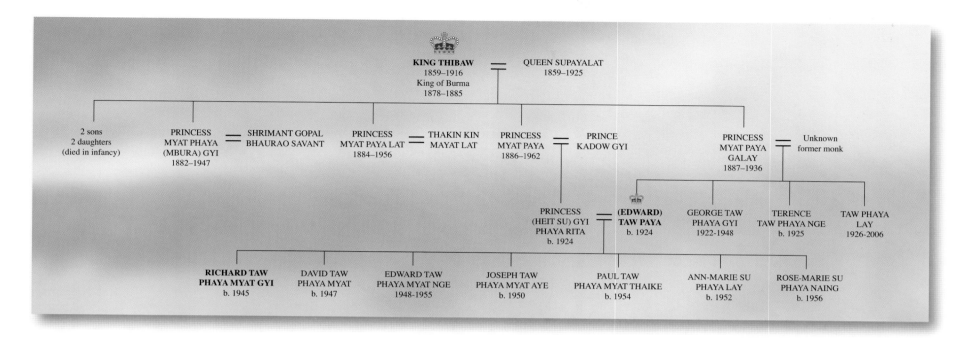

KING THIBAW
1859–1916
King of Burma
1878–1885

QUEEN SUPAYALAT
1859–1925

2 sons
2 daughters
(died in infancy)

PRINCESS
MYAT PHAYA
(MBURA) GYI
1882–1947

SHRIMANT GOPAL
BHAURAO SAVANT

PRINCESS
MYAT PAYA LAT
1884–1956

THAKIN KIN
MAYAT LAT

PRINCESS
MYAT PAYA
1886–1962

PRINCE
KADOW GYI

PRINCESS
MYAT PAYA
GALAY
1887–1936

Unknown
former monk

PRINCESS
(HEIT SU) GYI
PHAYA RITA
b. 1924

(EDWARD)
TAW PAYA
b. 1924

GEORGE TAW
PHAYA GYI
1922-1948

TERENCE
TAW PHAYA NGE
b. 1925

TAW PHAYA
LAY
1926-2006

RICHARD TAW
PHAYA MYAT GYI
b. 1945

DAVID TAW
PHAYA MYAT
b. 1947

EDWARD TAW
PHAYA MYAT NGE
1948-1955

JOSEPH TAW
PHAYA MYAT AYE
b. 1950

PAUL TAW
PHAYA MYAT THAIKE
b. 1954

ANN-MARIE SU
PHAYA LAY
b. 1952

ROSE-MARIE SU
PHAYA NAING
b. 1956

THE RECENT HISTORY OF Myanmar, or Burma is not a peaceful story, and the history of its royal dynasties is similarly fraught. The Konbaung dynasty ruled Burma from 1752 to 1886, when the reign of the last king Thibaw Min, was abruptly ended by the British, who invaded Upper Burma on the pretext of preventing the king from recovering Lower Burma from the colonial invaders. Driven from his capital at Mandalay, Thibaw Min, 'Golden-footed Lord of the White Elephant, Master of a Thousand Gold Umbrellas, Owner of the Royal Peacocks, Lord of the Sea and of the World, Whose face is like the Sun', was driven into exile with his wife and children, and died in India in 1916.

Thibaw Min was survived by four daughters, and the royal line continues to thrive through the descendants of his youngest daughter, Princess Mayat Phaya Galay (1887–1936). Her second son, Taw Paya, is the current head of the royal house and the only surviving grandson of King Thibaw Min. He lives a modest life in Pyin U Lwin, a hill station 50 miles from Mandalay, once favoured by the British to escape the oppressive heat of Burma's central plains. Now in his 80s, Taw Paya has survived immense political changes, and has seen two of his brother die at the hands of the country's rulers. He has four sons and two daughters, but has no political ambitions, saying, 'I'd be mad to want to become a king now'.

In the immediate aftermath of independence, Burma was a

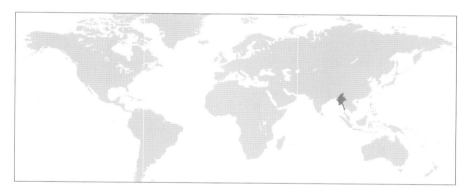

democratic republic, but in 1962 Ne Win, the Communist prime minister, launched a military coup. He led a one-party state under his Burma Socialist Programme Party until his resignation in 1988, ruthlessly suppressing political dissent and isolating the country economically and politically from the rest of the world. The situation continues today under the military rule of his successors.

In Britain, a man known as Crown Prince Shwebomin (b. 1942) also claims descent from the Konbaung Dynasty through his maternal grandmother, although his detractors say he has never submitted material proof of his paternity. What is clear is that there is no prospect of Burma returning to monarchical rule any time soon. Protests against the ruling military junta are harshly suppressed, and the world's most famous political prisoner, Aung San Suu Kyi, has been under house arrest for nearly 20 years. The Burmese are more concerned with returning their country to democracy that restoring the last scion of a distant royal dynasty to his throne – whoever he may be.

Above: A photograph of King Thibaw, Queen Supayalat and her sister Princess Supayaji, at the Royal Palace, Mandalay, in 1885.

Right: The royal palace at Mandalay was built by King Mindon in 1857, but when the British invaded and overthrew the king in 1886, it became their colonial seat of government and was renamed Fort Dufferin. The palace was further damaged by the Japanese in the Second World War, but was extensively restored during the 1990s.

Left: Thibaw Min the last king of Burma in 1880. When he came to the throne in 1878, he made no secret of the fact that he wanted to regain territory from the British.

THAILAND
Rama IX

Official title	King Bhumibol Adulyadej (or Rama IX)
Country ruled	Thailand
Born	December 1927
Accession to throne	9 June 1946
Royal house	Chakri Dynasty
Official residences	The Grand Palace — Wat Phra Kaew
Heir	Crown Prince Maha Vajiralongkorn (b. 1952, son)

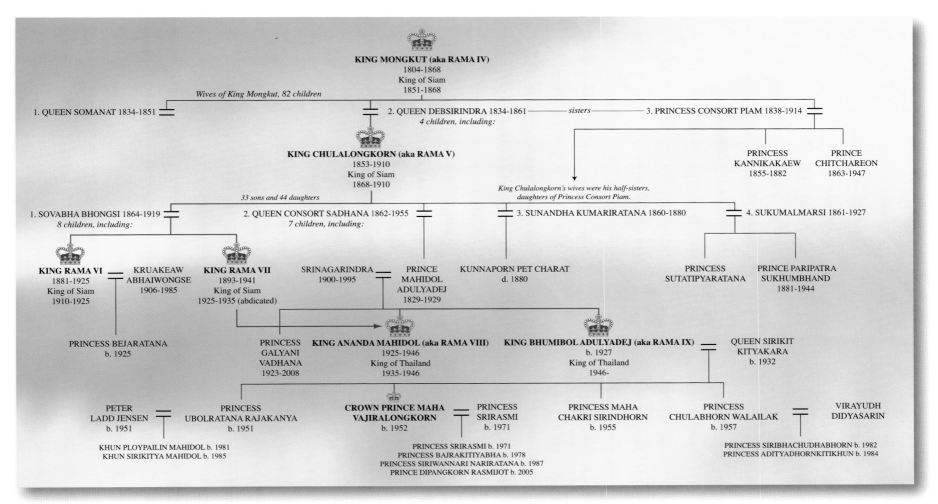

THE FOUNDER OF THE Chakri dynasty, the ruling family of Thailand, was Buddha Yodfa Chulaloke the Great (1737–1809). Also known as Phutthayotfa, he ruled 1782–1809, and was posthumously called Rama I the Great; at the time the country was known as the Kingdom of Siam. As a great warlord, he assumed power when his predecessor, King Thaksin of Thonburi was the victim of a coup d'etat, declared mad, and executed. He stabilised and united his country after a succession of wars and invasions into and from his surrounding neighbours, in particular Vietnam and Burma. One of his main achievements was the creation of a new law code – the Book of Three Seals – and the building of a new capital at Bangkok and his vast palace of Wat Phra Kaew.

The longest serving monarch in Thai history is the current king, Bhumibol Adulyadej, who came to the throne in 1946. He was born in Cambridge Massachusetts, USA in December 1927, the youngest son of Prince Mahidol Adulyadej (1892–1929) and a commoner, Mom Sangwal (1900–1995). He was taken to

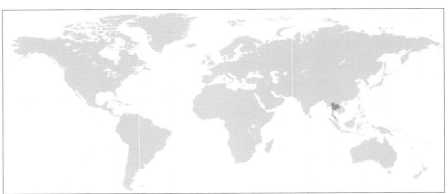

Thailand the following year, but was primarily educated in Switzerland and did not return home until 1945. He met Sirikit Kitiyakara his first cousin and wife-to-be in Paris when they were 21 and 15 respectively, and after a quiet engagement they married in April 1950 a week before the coronation. They have four children, Princess Ubol Ratana, Crown Prince Maha Vajiralongkorn, Princess Maha Chakri Sirindhorn, and Princess Chulabhorn Walailak.

Queen Sirikit became consort at the coronation and has

since been made Queen Regent (*Somdej Phra Boromarajininat*). When Bhumibol ascended the throne Thailand was under military dictatorship and his role was little more than ceremonial, but over the years his influence increased and a number of ancient royal ceremonies have been revived. Political unrest has marked his reign, but in 1992 Thailand finally achieved a democratic government, due in no small part to the king's intervention and influence. Since then his power has become considerable, reflecting in part his popularity.

King Bhumibol is hugely wealthy, with an estimated fortune in the tens of billion dollars. He has used some of this wealth to fund some 3,000 development projects, many of them in the poorest rural areas of Thailand.

A clear description of the Chakri dynasty is not at all straightforward as the kings and queens are known by different titles and several names at varying times, as well as by posthumously awarded titles. Members of the royal family rarely remain stable in rank, which in turn indicates the exact relationship of the individual to the reigning monarch. Currently there are 131 different branches to the Thai royal family and to differentiate between them all a complex system of ranking has evolved.

Below: King Bhumibol and Queen Sirikit with Crown Prince Maha Vajiralongkorn. The king ascended the throne in 1946 and is the longest reigning monarch in Thai history.

Above: Crown Princess Maha Chakri Sirindhorn prays
before playing on a ranadek, a traditional Thai instrument.

Below: King Bhumipol and Queen Sirikit.

Right: One of the many ornate royal barges on Chao
Phraya River in Bangkok.

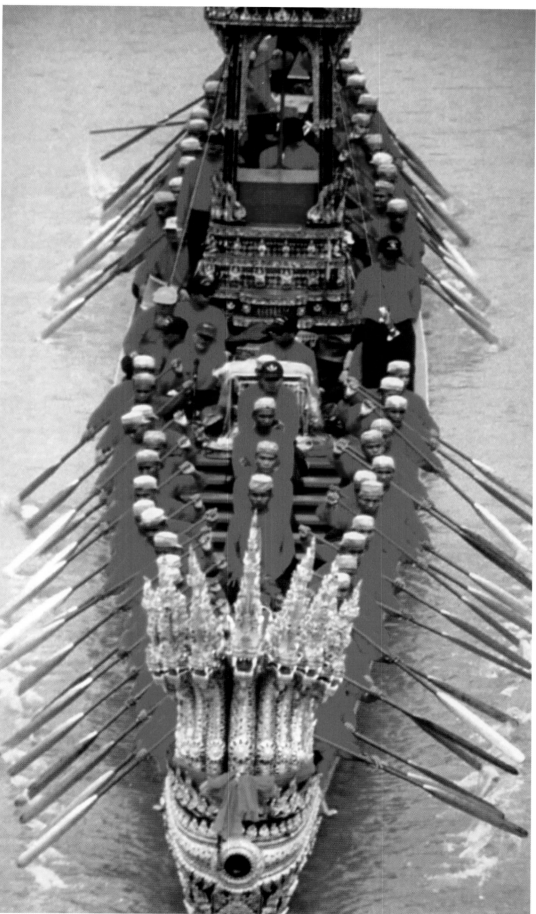

Left: Phra Ratchaniwet Marukhathaiyawan in Cha-am, southern Thailand. Built in 1923 for summer use by King Rama VI, it was designed by an Italian architect and built using golden teakwood.

Right: Dusit Mahallaprasat in Bangkok.

Below: The Grand Palace in Thailand is the seat of power and the spiritual heart of Thailand, although the royal family has not lived here permanently for around a century.

Below far left: The Phra Maha Monthien buildings were the main residence and audience hall for the Royal Palace.

Below left: Vimanmek was built by King Rama V and is the largest golden teakwood palace in the world.

CAMBODIA
King Norodom Sihamoni

Official title	His Majesty Preah Bat Samdech Preah
Country ruled	Cambodia
Born	14 May 1953
Accession to throne	2004
Royal house	House of Norodom
Official residence	Royal Palace of Phnom Penh
Heir	n/a

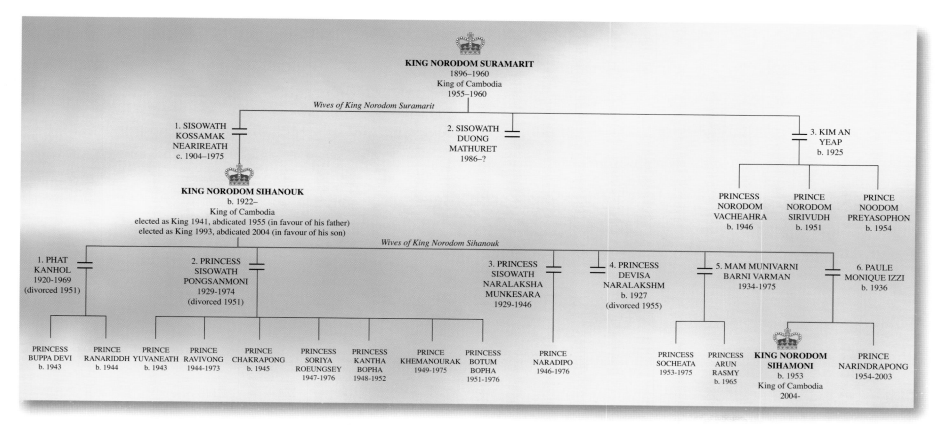

KING NORODOM SURAMARIT
1896–1960
King of Cambodia
1955–1960

Wives of King Norodom Suramarit

1. SISOWATH KOSSAMAK NEARIREATH
c. 1904–1975

2. SISOWATH DUONG MATHURET
1986–?

3. KIM AN YEAP
b. 1925

KING NORODOM SIHANOUK
b. 1922–
King of Cambodia
elected as King 1941, abdicated 1955 (in favour of his father)
elected as King 1993, abdicated 2004 (in favour of his son)

PRINCESS NORODOM VACHEAHRA
b. 1946

PRINCE NORODOM SIRIVUDH
b. 1951

PRINCE NOODOM PREYASOPHON
b. 1954

Wives of King Norodom Sihanouk

1. PHAT KANHOL
1920-1969
(divorced 1951)

2. PRINCESS SISOWATH PONGSANMONI
1929-1974
(divorced 1951)

3. PRINCESS SISOWATH NARALAKSHA MUNKESARA
1929-1946

4. PRINCESS DEVISA NARALAKSHM
b. 1927
(divorced 1955)

5. MAM MUNIVARNI BARNI VARMAN
1934-1975

6. PAULE MONIQUE IZZI
b. 1936

PRINCESS BUPPA DEVI
b. 1943

PRINCE RANARIDDH
b. 1944

PRINCE YUVANEATH
b. 1943

PRINCE RAVIVONG
1944-1973

PRINCE CHAKRAPONG
b. 1945

PRINCESS SORIYA ROEUNGSEY
1947-1976

PRINCESS KANTHA BOPHA
1948-1952

PRINCE KHEMANOURAK
1949-1975

PRINCESS BOTUM BOPHA
1951-1976

PRINCE NARADIPO
1946-1976

PRINCESS SOCHEATA
1953-1975

PRINCESS ARUN RASMY
b. 1965

KING NORODOM SIHAMONI
b. 1953
King of Cambodia
2004-

PRINCE NARINDRAPONG
1954-2003

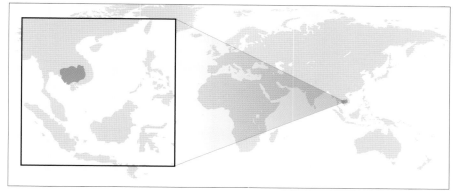

THE CURRENT REIGNING DYNASTY in Cambodia traces its lineage back to the Angkor (also known as Khmer) Empire that covered large areas of modern-day southeast Asia, including parts of Thailand, Laos, Vietnam and all of present-day Cambodia, between the 9th and 14th centuries. The world-renowned Angkor Wat temple complex that has featured on the Cambodian national flag since the mid-1800s, was built for King Suryavarman II in the early 12th century, and is still a source of great national pride for the people of Cambodia today.

More recently, the history of Cambodia has been a fraught and often bloody one, with numerous foreign nations and internal factions battling for control of the country. In the early 1990s the United Nations helped to broker a peace settlement between rival factions, and national elections were held, leading to the establishment of a new government and the formation of a new constitution. Under the terms of the 1993 constitution Cambodia became a non-hereditary constitutional monarchy with the succession decided within seven days of the death of the king by the Royal Council of the Throne, a body consisting of the president of the National Assembly, the prime minister, the first and second vice-presidents of the assembly and the Buddhist chiefs of the two major orders (Mohanikay and Thammayut). Although the monarchy is not hereditary, the new king must be aged over 30 years old and from the royal bloodline.

Following the introduction of the new constitution, Prince Norodom Sihanouk, the father of the current king, was re-installed as king, as position he had previously held between 1941 and 1955. Throughout the turbulence afflicting his country over his lifetime, Sihanouk has proved himself to be an adept politician, starting when the French crowned him as king in 1941. He was just 18 and it was assumed that he would be a compliant ruler. However, the French were soon proved wrong, and within a few years Sihanouk had become a nationalist leader, guiding Cambodia to independence from France in 1953.

As well as the hard-nosed politician and leader, there is a

more flamboyant side to Sihanouk. Known to enjoy an extravagant lifestyle, he has also maintained an interest in the arts, turning his hand to film direction and enjoying playing jazz music. To this day Sihanouk remains enormously popular in Cambodia, a fact reflected by the unanimous vote of the National Assembly that awarded him the title of Great King of Cambodia for life following his abdication in 2004.

King Norodom Sihamoni was seen by some as a surprise choice to succeed his father as he had spent much of his life outside Cambodia. Born on 14 May 1953 Sihamoni was sent by his father to live in Prague in 1962 where he stayed until 1975.

Sihamoni took dance, music and theatre courses at the National Conservatory of Prague and the Academy of Musical Art of Prague. Between 1981 and 2000 he worked as a professor of classical dance in Paris, and from 1993 to 2004 he served as the Cambodian ambassador to UNESCO.

Since his selection as king, Sihamoni has proved himself to be both a dignified and serious monarch. As well as undertaking numerous official trips abroad, he has devoted much of his time in Cambodia to meeting with his subjects and striving to help improve their lives, particularly in the fields of education and health.

Above and below: Prince Nordom Narindrapong, son of Nordom Sihanouk, studying in a Russian school in 1964 and (below) blowing a horn given to him by class mates for his birthday in 1963.

*Right: Prince Norodom
Sihanouk, with Prime
Minister Hun Sen, during a
parade in honour of his
return from exile 1991.*

*Left: The cupola atop the
Napoleon III Pavilion in the
grounds of the royal palace
in Phnom Penh.*

*Below: Norodom Sihanouk
and his wife Monique
receiving Fédérico Mayor,
the general manager of the
UNESCO at the royal
palace in Phnom Penh.*

Above: A reclining Buddha gold bas-relief decorates the walls of the royal palace.

Left: The Napoleon III Pavilion was the first permanent structure on the site of the royal palace, and it now serves as a small museum housing royal memorabilia and a photographic exhibition.

Above right: The current Chanchhaya Pavilion was built in the reign of King Sisowath to replace the earlier wooden pavilion built under King Norodom.

Right: The Stupa of Princess Kantha Bopha was built in 1960 in memory of the daughter of the former King Sihanouk who died of leukemia, aged four in 1952.

VIETNAM
Emperor Bao Thang

Official title	Bao Thang, Emperor of Vietnam
Pretender	Imperial throne of Vietnam
Born	1943
Pretender from	2007
Royal house	Nguyen Dynasty
Residence	France
Heir	Unknown

Crown Prince Bao Long, 1936–2007

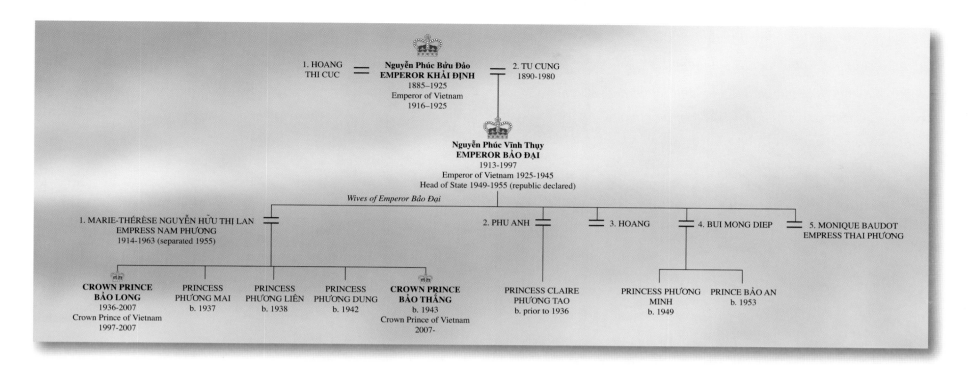

THE IMPERIAL THRONE OF Vietnam was finally abolished after many vicissitudes in 1955. Bao Dai, the last emperor of the Nguyen Dynasty, which had ruled the country since 1802, succumbed to post-colonial squabbling between the French, the USA and the Communist Viet Minh, and fled to exile in Hong King in 1946 when Vietnam declared independence from France.

Bao Dai, whose name means 'Keeper of Greatness' was educated in Paris, but his reign occurred in a period of enormous upheaval in southeast Asia, when the traditional imperial courtesies were roughly brushed aside by more powerful colonial forces. Bao Dai was not immune to modernism – his wife was Catholic and his children were brought up in that religion rather than the usual Shinto practices of imperial Vietnam. He also abolished several outdated customs, such as the need for courtiers to touch their foreheads on the ground when addressing the emperor.

He was restored to power in 1949, once the French had accepted the status of an independent Vietnam, but Bao Dai left the fine details of government largely to pro-French Vietnamese officials, preferring to stay in his highland hunting lodge and live up to his reputation as the 'Playboy Emperor'. In October 1955, after a national referendum, Vietnam became a republic and the last emperor retired to live in France where he was a

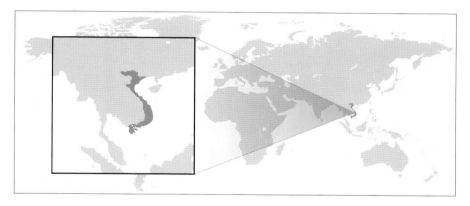

well-known figure in the Riviera casinos.

Bao Dai played no further part in the political maelstrom of Vietnam, only making one appeal in 1972 after his country had been ripped apart by war: 'The time has come to put an end to the fratricidal war and to recover at last peace and accord.'

In contrast to the flamboyance of his father's lifestyle, Crown Prince Bao Long lived a discreet life as a private citizen in France. He represented the Vietnamese family at the coronation of Elizabeth II in London in 1953 and during the 1950s tried to join the National Army of Vietnam to fight the Communist forces of the Viet Minh. Permission was refused, however, as no on wished to risk the life of the heir to the throne. Instead, Bao Long joined the French Foreign Legion and fought in Algeria, a colonial war on the other side of the world from his birthplace. His dedication and bravery earned him the

Croix de Guerre. After ten years with the Legion, he retired to work in a Parisian bank as an investment banker. When his father Bao Dai died in 1997, he became head of the Nguyen Dynasty, but made no public pronouncements on politics, let alone expressing any kind of opinion about the restoration of the monarchy in Vietnam.

Bao Long never married, so when he died in 2007, his younger brother Bao Thang became head of the family. He appears to be as discreet as his brother.

The family maintains a low-key public profile within Vietnam through the charitable work of the Order of the Dragon of Annam, a chivalric order once bestowed by the emperors. Crown Prince Bao Thang has delegated overall control to his cousin Prince Bao Vang, who serves as grandmaster of the order, using it to further educational and humanitarian causes within Vietnam.

Above: Born in 1936, Bao Long was proclaimed crown prince in 1939 in a traditional Confucian ceremony. lived in exile in France from 1947, where he was educated in Normandy and Paris. He served in the French Foreign Legion, and was decorated for valour. Although Vietnamese monarchists were keen to restore a constitutional monarchy, Bao Long lived a private life away from the limelight until his death in 2007.

Above: Marie-Thérèse Nguyen Hu Thj Lan became Empress Nam Phuong when she married the Emperor Bao Dai. From a Catholic family, she was the daughter of wealthy Vietnamese merchants and a naturalised French citizen. The marriage ceremony in 1934 was Buddhist, but she made sure that her children were brought up in the Catholic faith, which was slightly controversial, when previous Vietnamese rulers had practised Buddhism.

Above: Emperor Bao Dai and his family arrive in France, 1947.

Above right: Emperor Kai Dinh with his son Prince Nguyen Vinh Thuy (later Emperor Bao Dai) during th 1920s.

Below and right: The Emperor's throne room in the royal palace complex at Hue, and the magnificent gateway to the citadel at Hue.

BRUNEI
Sultan Hassanal

Official title	Hassanal Bolkiah Mu'izzaddin Waddaulah, Sultan of Brunei
Country ruled	Brunei
Born	15 July 1946
Accession to throne	October 1967
Royal house	House of Bolkiah
Official residences	Istana Nurul Iman Palace
Heir	Crown Prince Al-Muhtadee Billah, (b. 1974, eldest son)

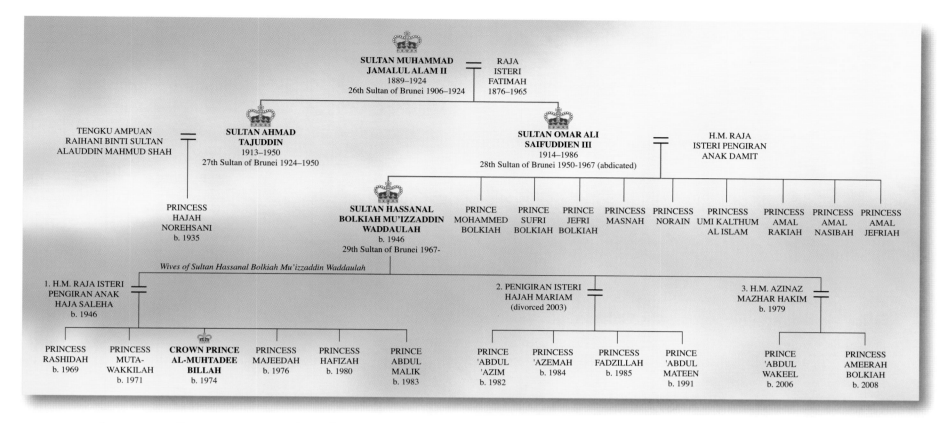

THE SULTAN OF BRUNEI, Hassanal Bolkiah Mu'izzaddin Waddaulah (born 1946) is the 29th sultan in a long line dating back to the first, Sultan Muhammad Shah who reigned 1405–1415. Hassanal Bolkiah became the head of state of Brunei, a country located on the north coast of the island of Borneo in south-east Asia, in October 1967 on the abdication of his father Sir Haji Omar Ali Saifuddien III (1914–1986).

Sultan Hassanal is head of state and prime minister with full executive powers, including, since 1962, full emergency powers; he also holds the positions of minister for defence and minister for finance. In March 2006 Sultan Hassanal changed the country's constitution to make himself infallible under Bruneian law. Then in 1991 the sultan introduced to his people a new conservative ideology known as *Melayu Islam Beraja* (Malay Islamic Monarchy), which gives the monarch the constitutional position as defender of the faith. He is a Sunni Muslim.

The sultan has had three wives: his first wife Raja Isteri Pengiran Anak Hajah Saleha (b.1946) has six children, his second wife Penigiran Isteri Hajah Mariam was divorced in 2003 after producing four children. The sultan's third wife is much younger former Malaysian TV presenter, Azrinaz Mazhar Hakim (b. 1979) who has given birth to a boy and a girl. Crown Prince

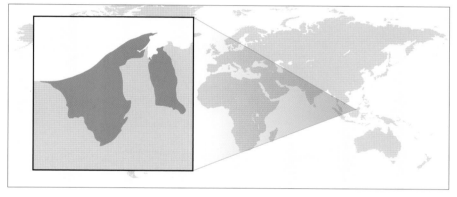

Al-Muhtadee Billah (b.1974) is the eldest son of his first wife.

Brunei is an oil-rich country and Hassanal Bolkiah, with his total control of Brunei, has become a very wealthy man. His personal fortune in 2007 was estimated to be around US$22 billion, down from an estimated high of £38 billion in 1997. He is probably still the richest man in the world, however. Aside from his political role, he is famous for his enormous collection of exclusive cars, which includes a reported 500 Rolls-Royces, as well as many other top marques, totalling somewhere between 3,000 and 5,000 vehicles, on which he has spent well over $4 billion. The sultan lives an extravagant lifestyle, which includes the use of a Boeing 747-400 which contains $3 million-worth of furnishings and gold-plated furniture. As a trained pilot, he also helms his six smaller planes and two helicopters.

The current Brunei ruling dynasty began with Awang Alak Betatar in the early 1360s, a prince from a powerful kingdom in western Borneo, who took over the throne from the previous ruling family. The current sultan is his direct descendant. Awang Alak Betatar changed his name to Sultan Muhammad Shah (ruled 1363–1402) in 1363 when he converted to Islam to marry a princess from Johore. Under his rule Brunei became the dominant trading power in the region and Islam the principal religion. Over the centuries the royal family of Brunei inter-married with other royal families across south-east Asia, especially with Malay and Japanese families, to strengthen trading and political relationships.

Perhaps the most adventurous was Nakhoda Ragam, the fifth sultan, responsible for the 'Golden Age of Brunei', and also known as the 'singing captain' or Sultan Bolkiah (1485–1524). He was a great sailor, journeying to Java, Malacca and the Philippines; he was also a great conqueror, extending his rule to the sultanates of Balongan, Banjarmasin, Pasi Kotei, Pontianak, Sambas, and the Sulu Archipelago, as well as to the Islands of Balabac, Banggi, Balambangan and Palawan.

Istana Nurul Iman Palace is the official residence of the Sultan of Brunei. Sitting on the banks of the Brunei River just south of the capital of Bandar Seri Begawan, it is the largest residential palace in the world and was designed by Leandro V. Locsin, the National Artist of the Philippines for Architecture in a mixture of Islamic and Malay architectural styles. It is rumored to contain around 1,788 rooms, 257 bathrooms, a mosque, five swimming pools, 44 sets of stairs and 18 elevators.

Above: The Sultan of Brunei (left) with his brother, Prince Jefri Bolkiah, after playing for the Cirencester Park polo team in June 1994. The brothers fell out over £8 billion of alleged fraud by Prince Jefri.

Above: The Crown Prince of Brunei, Al-Muhtadee Billah, (on the left) arrives at a state banquet with other members of the Bruneian royal family in September 1998.

Left: The Sultan of Brunei and his wife Raja Pengiran Anak Hajah Saleha. She is the first of his three wives and the mother of the crown prince.

Below: The yacht Tits (later renamed Samax) was owned by Prince Jefri and was allegedly extravagently decorated throughout.

Left: The Mosque Lagoon, Bandar Seri Begawan, Brunei.
The Omar Ali Saifuddien Mosque dominates the skyline of
Bandar Seri Bagawan. It was completed in 1958 in modern
Islamic style with marble minarets and golden domes
interlaced between courtyards and verdant gardens filled
with fountains. The mosque stands on an artificial lagoon
near the banks of the Brunei River and contains a replica of
a 16th century royal barge which was at one time used for
official state ceremonies. The mosque was named after the
28th sultan.

Right: Queen Elizabeth II meets members of the Thai
government and local dignataries at Istana Nurul Iman, the
largest residential palace in the world.

Below: The Prince of Wales and the Duchess of Cornwall
with the Sultan of Brunei and his two wives as they sit
down for dinner at the Royal Palace in Bandar Seri
Begawan in August 2008.

MALAYSIA
Sultan Mizan Zainal Abidin

Official title	Sultan Mizan Zainal Abidin, Yang di-Pertuan Agong of Malaysia
Country ruled	Malaysia
Born	22 January 1962
Accession to throne	2006
Royal house	n/a (elective rank)
Official residence	Istana Negara (National Palace), Kuala Lumpur
Heir	Unnamed (elective rank)

Name	State	Reign	Birth	Death
TUANKU ABDUL RAHMAN	Negeri Sembilan	1957-1960	1895	1960
SULTAN HISAMUDDIN ALAM SHAH	Selangor	1960	1898	1960
TUANKU SYED PUTRA	Perlis	1960-1965	1920	2000
SULTAN ISMAIL NAISIRUDDIN SHAH	Terengganu	1965-1970	1907	1979
TUANKU ABDUL HALIM MUADZAM	Kedah	1970-1975	1927	–
SULTAN YAHYA PETRA	Kelantan	1975-1979	1917	1979
SULTAN AHMAD SHAH AL-MUSTAIN BILLAH	Pahang	1979-1984	1930	–
SULTAN MAHMUD ISKANDAR	Johor	1984-1989	1932	–
SULTAN AZLAN MUHIBBUDDIN SHAH	Perak	1989-1994	1928	–
TUANKU JAAFAR	Negeri Sembilan	1994-1999	1922	2008
SULTAN SALAHUDDIN ABDUL AZIZ	Selangor	1999-2001	1926	2001
TUANKU SYED SIRAJUDDIN	Perlis	2001-2006	1943	–
TUANKU MIZAN ZAINAL ABIDIN	Terengganu	2006-	1962	–

The office of the king in Malaysia is not hereditary, but elective, and the country practices a form of government based on a constitutional monarchy combined with a parliamentary democracy. The office was first established in 1957 and in accordance with the constitution, the king is 'the Supreme Head of the Federation', and as such the head of state of Malaysia, retaining the position for a five-year term. As with most modern constitutional monarchies, the role of the king in Malaysia is mostly ceremonial in nature, although he is the nominal head of the armed forces and all laws and the appointment of every cabinet minister, including the prime minister, require his assent.

The king is elected by the *Majlis Raja-Raja* (Conference of Rulers) that is made up of the nine rulers of the Malay states (Negeri Sembilan, Selangor, Perlis, Terengganu, Kedah, Kelantan, Pahang, Johor and Perak), and the *Yang di-Pertua Negeri* (governors) of the other four states. However, only the nine rulers may vote in the royal election, and only one of their number can be chosen as king. In practice the kingship is generally rotated between the nine rulers in the order established by the first nine elections. Following the election of the king, the Conference of Rulers also appoints a *Timbalan Yang di-Pertuan*

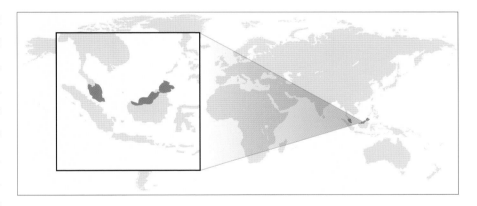

Agong (deputy king) whose role is to exercise the functions of the king should he become incapacitated. The deputy king does not automatically succeed the king.

The official residence of the king is the *Istana Negara* (National Palace) in Kuala Lumpur. The palace was originally built as a home for the Chinese millionaire Chan Wing, but after World War II the Selangor state government bought it, and following a program of renovation, it became the palace of the Sultan of Selangor. In 1957 the federal government bought the palace and continued to renovate and expand the building. In 1980 the palace was used for the first time as the venue for the investiture ceremony of the *Yang di-Pertuan Agong*. Prior to this, the ceremony had been held at the Tunku Abdul Rahman

Hall in Kuala Lumpur. At present there are plans for the construction of a new royal palace, but the expense of the project (estimated to be in excess of $113 million) has proved to be a contentious issue in Malaysia.

The current monarch, Sultan Mizan Zainal Abidin, was installed as Malaysia's 13th king on 13 December 2006. At the age of 44, he was the second-youngest person to hold the office after Tuanku Syed Putra (who was 41 when he became king in 1961). Sultan Mizan was born on 22 January 1962 at Istana Al-Muktafi in Kuala Terengganu. His received his early education in Terengganu, before going on to attend Geelong Grammar School in Australia, followed by the U.S. International University-Europe (now known as Alliant International University) in London, where he achieved a degree in International Relations. He was appointed as the Sultan of Terengganu in 1998 following the death of his father, and served two terms as deputy king before being elected as king.

Left: Queen Elizabeth II and the Duke of Edinburgh greet Sultan Azlan Shah, and his wife the Rajah Permaisuri Agong, outside Buckingham Palace at the start of a state visit to the UK in the 1990s.

Below left: Sultan Mizan, King of Malaysia (right) with Britain's Duke of York (centre) and the Sultan of Brunei (left) during the 50th anniversary of Malaysian independence in 2007.

Right: Malaysia's 13th king, Sultan Mizan Zainal Abidin and Queen Nur Zahirah during the coronation at the National Palace in Kuala Lumpur, April 2007.

Below: King Mizan inspects the guard of honour before the opening of parliament, 2008.

Above: The beautiful Forbidden Gardens at the Melaka Sultanate Palace. The palace was built in 1980s to replicate the original 15th century building

Right: The current Queen of Malaysia, Tuanku Nur Zahirah, during a visit to England in 2009.

Far right: The Istana Negara (National Palace) is the official residence of the Yang di-Pertuan Agong of Malaysia. It was originally built in the 1920s for a Chinese millionaire.

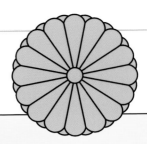

JAPAN
Emperor Akihito

Official title	Akihito, Emperor of Japan
Country ruled	Japan
Born	23 December 1933
Accession to throne	1989
Royal house	Yamato Dynasty
Official residence	The Imperial Palace, Tokyo
Heir	Crown Prince Naruhito (b. 1960, eldest son)

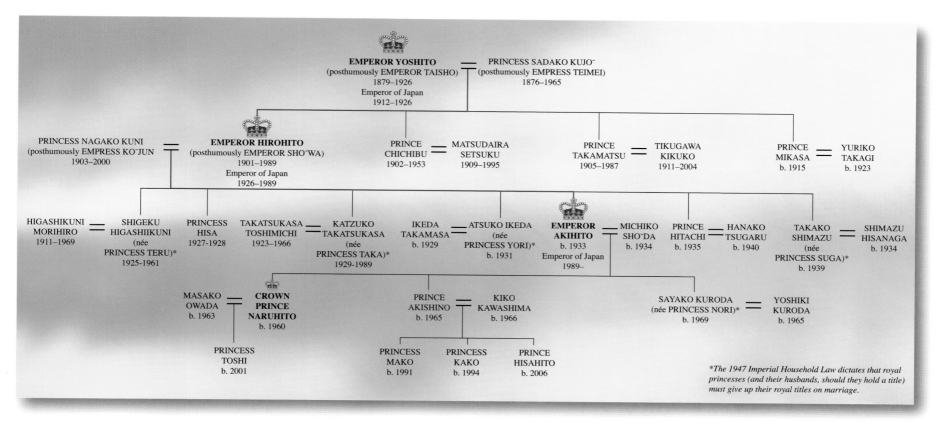

EMPEROR YOSHITO
(posthumously EMPEROR TAISHO)
1879–1926
Emperor of Japan
1912–1926
— PRINCESS SADAKO KUJO
(posthumously EMPRESS TEIMEI)
1876–1965

PRINCESS NAGAKO KUNI
(posthumously EMPRESS KO-JUN)
1903–2000
— EMPEROR HIROHITO
(posthumously EMPEROR SHO-WA)
1901–1989
Emperor of Japan
1926–1989

PRINCE CHICHIBU
1902–1953 — MATSUDAIRA SETSUKU
1909–1995

PRINCE TAKAMATSU
1905–1987 — TIKUGAWA KIKUKO
1911–2004

PRINCE MIKASA
b. 1915 — YURIKO TAKAGI
b. 1923

HIGASHIKUNI MORIHIRO
1911–1969 — SHIGEKU HIGASHIIKUNI
(née PRINCESS TERU)*
1925–1961

PRINCESS HISA
1927-1928

TAKATSUKASA TOSHIMICHI
1923–1966 — KATZUKO TAKATSUKASA
(née PRINCESS TAKA)*
1929–1989

IKEDA TAKAMASA
b. 1929 — ATSUKO IKEDA
(née PRINCESS YORI)*
b. 1931

EMPEROR AKIHITO
b. 1933
Emperor of Japan
1989– — MICHIKO SHO-DA
b. 1934

PRINCE HITACHI
b. 1935 — HANAKO TSUGARU
b. 1940

TAKAKO SHIMAZU
(née PRINCESS SUGA)*
b. 1939 — SHIMAZU HISANAGA
b. 1934

MASAKO OWADA
b. 1963 — CROWN PRINCE NARUHITO
b. 1960

PRINCE AKISHINO
b. 1965 — KIKO KAWASHIMA
b. 1966

SAYAKO KURODA
(née PRINCESS NORI)*
b. 1969 — YOSHIKI KURODA
b. 1965

PRINCESS TOSHI
b. 2001

PRINCESS MAKO
b. 1991

PRINCESS KAKO
b. 1994

PRINCE HISAHITO
b. 2006

*The 1947 Imperial Household Law dictates that royal princesses (and their husbands, should they hold a title) must give up their royal titles on marriage.

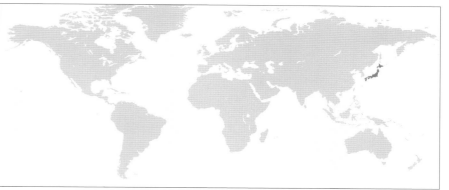

THE JAPANESE IMPERIAL FAMILY is the oldest hereditary monarchy in the world. Traditionally the imperial lineage can be traced back to 660 BC and the current emperor, Akihito, is considered the 125th Emperor.

The importance of the emperor and the power wielded by the holder of the title has varied enormously throughout the centuries. Early Japanese chronicles present the emperor as a mythical being with magical powers, and even up until the end of World War II the emperor was considered a divine being. Despite his divine status, for much of Japan's history real power did not rest with the emperor, but with the shoguns, the leaders of the warrior class of samurai. The power of the shoguns lasted from 1192 to 1867 when the Tokugawa shogunate was toppled and imperial power restored. During the Meiji Restoration (1867–c.1912), the imperial court was moved from Kyoto to Tokyo, which thus became the new capital city of Japan. Feudalism was abandoned in favour of centralised government, and Japan embarked on a course of rapid modernisation.

By the end of the Meiji period in the early 20th century, Japan had gone from being an isolated nation to being recognised as one of the world's great powers. The inheritor of this newly powerful nation was Emperor Hirohito. Born in 1901,

Horohito ascended to the Chrysanthemum Throne in 1926 and reigned until his death in 1989, making him the longest-reigning monarch in Japanese history. The defining event of Hirohito's reign was to be the Japanese involvement in World War II. The failure of the Allies to put Hirohito and other members of the Imperial family on trial in the aftermath of the war remains controversial, but even though Hirohito offered to abdicate, the American general Douglas MacArthur insisted that the emperor remain on the throne to provide a symbol of stability to the Japanese people during the American post-war occupation.

Hirohito announced Japan's surrender on the radio, uttering the immortal phrase, 'the war situation has developed not necessarily to Japan's advantage', and a year later in another broadcast, told his people that the emperor was not divine. These were astonishing actions for a formerly god-like figurehead, and in the years after the war, Hirohito made a point of travelling throughout Japan, making numerous public appearances to show himself to the Japanese people, something no emperor had ever done before. He opened up the imperial family to the scrutiny of the nation, and also became the first reigning Japanese monarch to make official trips abroad. In 1971 he undertook a tour of Europe, including a stay at Buckingham Palace, and in 1975 he made a state visit to the United States.

Following his death in 1989, his eldest son Akihito succeeded as emperor. Akihito himself had broken with over a thousand years of tradition by marrying a commoner, Michiko Shÿda, in 1959, an event that was hugely popular in Japan. From the start of his reign Akihito was keen to make amends for the past, and his public expressions of contrition have helped to mend relations with neighbours such as China, South Korea, and the Philippines. Akihito has also continued the path set out by his father in trying to bring the imperial family closer to the people of Japan. Like his father, Akihito also has a keen interest in marine biology and has had several scientific papers published on the subject.

A view of the rear of the Imperial Palace in Tokyo, with the palace moat in the foreground and the Otemachi Business Area Skyline to the right.

Left: An official photo celebrating the marriage of Crown Prince Naruhito and Masako Owada in 1993. They are flanked by the groom's parents, Emperor Akihito and Empress Michiko.

Below left: A dress rehearsal for the wedding of Crown Prince Naruhito, the heir to the Chrysanthemum throne, and Masako Owada.

Below: Crown Prince Naruhito visiting his old university town of Oxford during a visit to England in 2001.

Right: Emperor Akihito and Empress Michiko host a dinner for the Prince of Wales and his wife the Duchess of Cornwall at the Imperial Palace, Tokyo in 2008.

Below right: Princess Sayako of Japan at with the Taoiseach (the head of government of Ireland) Bertie Ahern during a four-day visit to Ireland in 2000.

KINGDOM OF TONGA
King George Tupou V

Official title	King George Tupou V (Siaosi Tupou V)
Country ruled	Kingdom of Tonga
Born	4 May 1948
Accession to throne	2006
Royal house	Royal House of Tupou
Official residences	The Royal Palace, Nuku'alofa
Heir	Crown Prince 'Aho'eitu 'Unuaki'otonga Tuku'aho (b. 1949, brother)

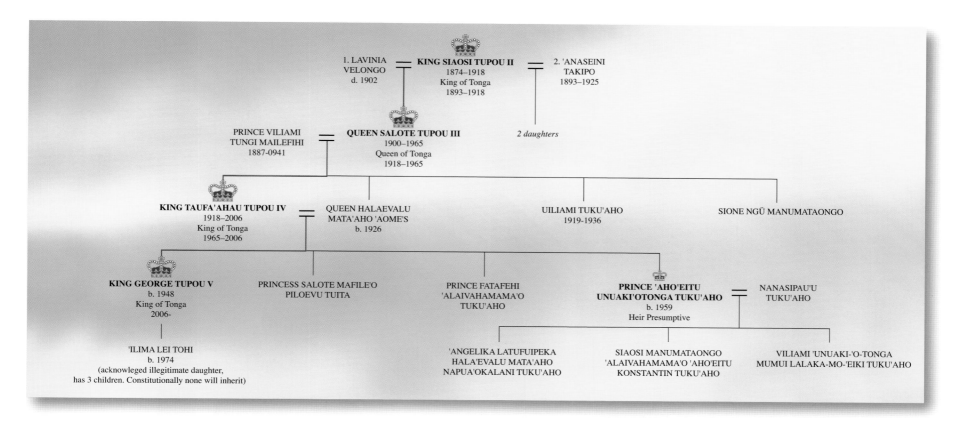

1. LAVINIA
VELONGO
d. 1902

KING SIAOSI TUPOU II
1874–1918
King of Tonga
1893–1918

2. 'ANASEINI
TAKIPO
1893–1925

PRINCE VILIAMI
TUNGI MAILEFIHI
1887-0941

QUEEN SALOTE TUPOU III
1900–1965
Queen of Tonga
1918–1965

2 daughters

KING TAUFA'AHAU TUPOU IV
1918–2006
King of Tonga
1965–2006

QUEEN HALAEVALU
MATA'AHO 'AOME'S
b. 1926

UILIAMI TUKU'AHO
1919-1936

SIONE NGÜ MANUMATAONGO

KING GEORGE TUPOU V
b. 1948
King of Tonga
2006-

PRINCESS SALOTE MAFILE'O
PILOEVU TUITA

PRINCE FATAFEHI
'ALAIVAHAMAMA'O
TUKU'AHO

**PRINCE 'AHO'EITU
UNUAKI'OTONGA TUKU'AHO**
b. 1959
Heir Presumptive

NANASIPAU'U
TUKU'AHO

'ILIMA LEI TOHI
b. 1974
(acknowleged illegitimate daughter,
has 3 children. Constitutionally none will inherit)

'ANGELIKA LATUFUIPEKA
HALA'EVALU MATA'AHO
NAPUA'OKALANI TUKU'AHO

SIAOSI MANUMATAONGO
'ALAIVAHAMAMA'O 'AHO'EITU
KONSTANTIN TUKU'AHO

VILIAMI 'UNUAKI-'O-TONGA
MUMUI LALAKA-MO-'EIKI TUKU'AHO

T HE KINGDOM OF TONGA sits in the south Pacific Ocean and comprises an archipelago of 48 inhabited islands and a further 123 uninhabited islands. The numerous islands of the archipelago were united into a single kingdom by the warrior Taufa'ahau (*c.* 1797–1893), eventually in 1875, after much opposition from rival leaders, Tonga became a kingdom and Taufa'ahau became George Tupou I, king of Tonga. By uniting his people and establishing diplomatic relations with other countries he prevented Tonga from being colonised. In 1838 he established the Vava'u Code, the first written laws in Tonga, and in 1862 he abolished serfdom across the archipelago. One constitutional change, which exists to this day, is that only people born in Tonga can own land. He was well into his nineties when he died, and all his children had predeceased him, so his successor was his great-grandson, George Tupou II (1874–1918).

In May 1900 Tonga became a British Protectorate under a Treaty of Friendship, and became part of the British Western Pacific Territories, but the government and rule of Tonga remained their own. This status changed in 1970 when Tonga joined the British Commonwealth. Perhaps Tonga's most famous ruler was Queen Salote Tupou III (1900–1965). She came to world attention when she attended the coronation of Queen Elizabeth II in London

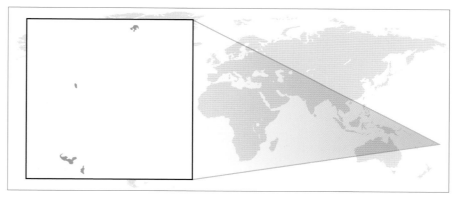

in 1953 and won the admiration and hearts of all who saw her as she smiled and waved through the rain.

Siaosi Tupou V (or George Tupou V) was born at Tongatapu in May 1948, the eldest son of King Taufa'ahau Tupou IV and his wife Hahaevalu Mata'aho 'Ahome'e. He can trace his ancestry back through the tribal rulers of Tonga to around 875 and the sacred founders of the Tu'i Tonga dynasty.

George Tupou was educated in Switzerland and New Zealand, before completing his education at Oxford University and the Royal Military Academy, Sandhurst. In May 1966 Siaosi formally became crown prince and heir apparent of Tonga. At this time he enjoyed being chauffeur-driven around the island in a black London cab, and acquired a reputation as something of a playboy. His business concerns made him a wealthy man, with financial interests in real estate, telecommunications, electricity and insurance. He became king in September 2006 following his father's death, and was sworn in as the 23rd *Tu'i Kanokupolu* (overlord), but was not ceremonially crowned until July 2008, the ceremony being postponed because of the Tongan riots of 2006. His constitutional position as monarch gives him executive powers, but the *Fale Alea* (legislative assembly) has the legislative power. In July 2008, just before his coronation, George Tupou V announced that he would relinquish most of his traditional legislative powers and be guided by his prime minister in most matters of state.

The king is yet to marry, but does, however, have an illegitimate daughter 'Llima Lei Tohi (born 1974), and through her, three grandchildren, but in the Tongan constitution none of them can or will inherit the throne. His younger brother, Prince 'Aho'eitu 'Unuaki'otonga Tuku'aho, is heir presumptive.

The Royal Palace is located in the capital Nuku'alofa, and was commissioned by George Tupou I as part of his modernisa-

tion programme. Built in 1864 in New Zealand using local kauri timber and then shipped to Tonga and assembled on site, it became the royal residence on completion. It remains the main home of the royal family and the surrounding area comprises the sacred royal compound. At the southern end of the palace is the sacred pangal (ceremonial area) where the king oversees official ceremonies and other regal duties.

Kauvai Royal Residence sits beside beautiful mangrove-fringed Holonga Lagoon on the outskirts of Longoteme on Ha'ano Island, and has historically been used to receive and entertain dignitaries and important guests. The original building was built on the orders of Queen Salote Tupou III in 1922 but the white wooden palace was destroyed in 1995. The replacement building was made from Norfolk Island pine and cocowood harvested from land 12 miles away around the older royal palace at Nuku'alofa, and is built as a conference facility for use by the royal family and their guests. The interior poles and rafters are decorated with traditional fabrics woven from coconut fibre.

Left: King Taufa'ahau Tupou IV and Queen Halaevalu Mata'aho 'Ahome'e and Crown Prince Siaosi Taufa'ahau Manumataongo Tuku'aho Tupou (later George Tupou V) attended by their pages, pose on the front porch of the Royal Palace after the coronation ceremony, 1965.

Right: Queen Elizabeth II shares a joke with King George Tupou V during a private meeting at Buckingham Palace.

Below: Crown Prince Tupouto'a arriving at Heathrow Airport from San Francisco before flying on to Brussels, in February 1984.

Below right: The Crown Prince of Tonga at a Royal Kava ceremony. As a show of their loyalty, the women prostrate themselves for him to step over. Kava is an intoxicating drink made from the root of the Kava plant. Only men are allowed to drink it, which they do in ceremonial rounds while they talk, sing or play music.

Right: Tonga's new king, George Tupou V during the coronation ceremony in the capital Nuku'alofa, Tonga. George Tupou V inherited the throne from his father, who died in September 2006 and who had for 40 years ruled the island with almost absolute power. The coronation had been delayed after several people died during demonstrations for more democracy.

Left: Sia ko Veiongo, or the royal palace of George Tupou II (1874–1918) as it was when photographed in 1932.

Right: The royal palace is located north-west of the capital, Nuku'alofa and close to the Pacific Ocean. It was built of white painted wood in a Victorian style in 1867, and was once home of Queen Salote Tupou III, grandmother of the present king. It is the official residence of the kings of Tonga and is surrounded by bars and fences to keep the public out, but the building is clearly visible from the waterfront. When the king is in residence the royal standard flies from the top of the palace.

AFRICA

MOROCCO
King Muhammad VI

Official title	Muhammad VI, King of Morocco
Country ruled	Morocco
Born	21 August 1963
Accession to throne	1999
Royal house	Alaouite Dynasty
Official residence	Royal Palace, Rabat
Heir	*Moulay* Hassan, Crown Prince (b. 2003, son)

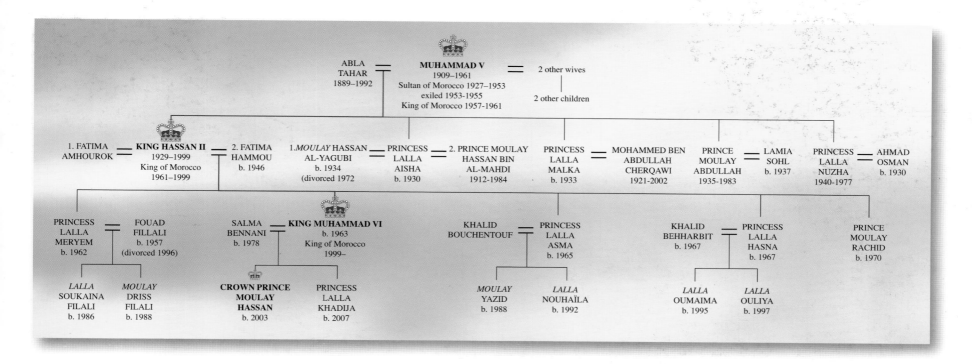

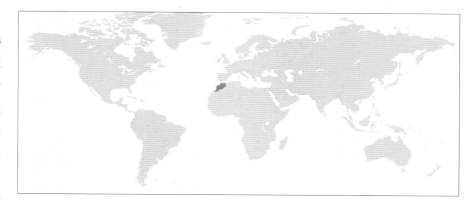

T{HROUGHOUT ITS HISTORY, VARIOUS} dynastic families, including the Almoravids, Almohads, and the Saadians (known as the first Sharifian dynasty) have ruled Morocco. The 17th century saw the rise of the Alaouite Dynasty (the second Sharifian dynasty) who remain on the Moroccan throne to this day. Like the Saadians, who they succeeded, the Alaouite dynasty claims descent from the prophet Muhammad through the line of the prophet's daughter Fatima.

The most notable of the early Alouite rulers was *Moulay* (Prince) Ismail Ibn Sharif (known as the 'Warrior King') who ruled from 1672 to 1727 following the death of his half-brother *Moulay* Al-Rashid (the founder of the dynasty). Ismail's claim was challenged by three rivals, all of whom were supported by the Ottoman Empire (which hoped to weaken Morocco by promoting divisions within the country), and it took him until 1686 to fully resolve the issue. During his reign Ismail successfully fought the Ottoman Turks in 1679, 1682 and 1695–96, as well as re-taking the important ports of Al-Mamurah, from the Spanish in 1681, and Tangier from the English in 1684. In order to bolster his position, Ismail forged an alliance with King Louis XIV of France (whose officers helped to train the Moroccan army). This led a strong French influence in Morocco that is still prevalent today. Ismail also moved his capital from Fez to Meknes and constructed an imperial palace that was modelled

on Louis XIV's great palace at Versailles.

Following Ismail's death there was another war of succession, and for the next 200 years crisis and disorder were punctuated by rare moments of peace and prosperity, until Sultan Abd Al-Hafiz was forced to sign the Treaty of Fez in 1912, which made Morocco a French protectorate. Almost immediately after signing the treaty, Abd Al-Hafiz abdicated in favour of his brother Yusef.

Despite the heavy investment in infrastructure that the protectorate brought, it was not universally popular with the Moroccan people, and in 1944 the independence party *Istqlal* was founded. The French exiled Muhammad V to Madagascar in 1953 but he was allowed to return in 1955. In March 1956, with the support of Istqlal, Muhammad was a finally able to secure Morocco's independence from France, and the following year he took the title of king. Muhammad was succeeded by his son, Hassan II (r. 1961–1999) who cultivated closer links with the West, and in particular the United States during the Cold War era.

The current king of Morocco is Muhammad VI who was born on 21 August 1963. From an early age his father (King Hassan II) was keen that he should have a balanced religious and political education to prepare him for kingship. To this end, Muhammad attended the Qur'anic school at the Royal Palace from the age of four, followed by primary and secondary education at the Royal College. In 1985 he gained a BA in Law at the Muhammad V University in Rabat. In 1988 he trained in Brussels with Jacques Delors who was at that time the President of the European Commission. Since coming to power, Muhammad has begun a process of political and economic reform aimed at liberalising Morocco. One of his key reforms has been the *Mudawana*, a law that grants more rights to women.

Above: Muhammad VI has introduced social reform within Morocco.

Left: King Muhammad welcomes the King of Jordan to Fez, 2009 (from L–R): Prince Talal of Jordan, Queen Rania and King Abdullah of Jordan, King Muhammad, Lalla (princess) Salma, Princess Ghaida of Jordan, and Moulay Hassan.

Top right: King Muhammad VI enjoying a family moment with his daughter Lalla Khadija.

Right: Lalla Asma, daughter of King Hassan II of Morocco, during her wedding to Khalid Bouchentouf in 1987.

Left: The sumptuous Royal Palace in the capital city of Rabat was built upon the ruins of an 18th century palace, which was strategically positioned to protect the trade route between Fez and Marrakech.

Above: The gateway to the Royal Palace is decorated with traditional intricate Islamic tiles.

Left: The Royal Palace lies in the heart of Rabat, Morocco's capital city and was constructed during the 1950s by King Hassan II.

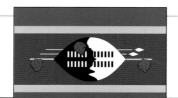

SWAZILAND
King Mswati III

Official title	King Mswati III
Country ruled	Kingdom of Swaziland
Born	1968
Accession to throne	1982
Royal house	Diamini dynasty
Official residences	Mbabane
Heir	Selected by council on king's death

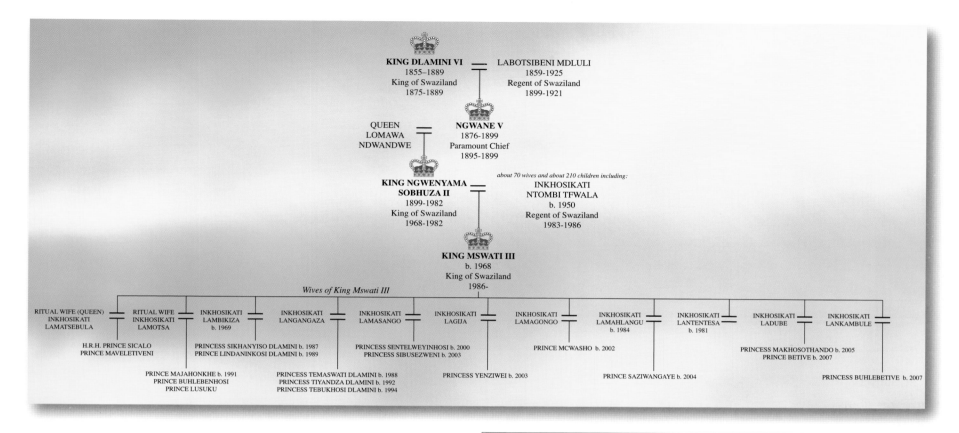

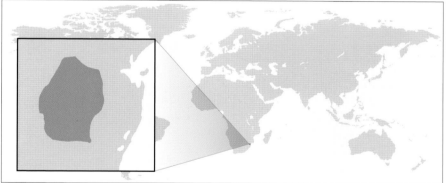

THIS LANDLOCKED COUNTRY IN southern Africa is named after Mswati II, a 19th century king, and is the last remaining absolute monarchy on the African continent. Swaziland was formally a British Protectorate from 1899 until 1968, and for all that time Sobhuza II was king. Born in 1899, he reigned from his earliest months until his death in 1982. When Sobhuza II died aged 82, he was the longest serving monarch on record. In his time he fathered some 210 children, 180 of which survived infancy and went on to produce around 1,000 grandchildren for the king.

The current king, Mswati III, was born in Swaziland in 1968, one of the many sons of Ngwenyama Sobhuza II but only son of Ntombi Tfwala, one of the youngest of the king's 70 wives. He was initially named Makhosetive (meaning 'King of Nations') and lived with his mother near Masundwini Palace.

After Sobhuza II's death in 1982 the Liqoqo (Great Council of State) selected 14-year-old Mswati as king. Two of the former king's wives then acted as regents while Mswati attended school in England. His mother Ntombi Tfwala was chosen to be the next queen regent, and a month later in September 1983 her son Mswati was declared crown prince. She partially relinquished power in April 1986 when Mswati turned 18 and was crowned king of Swaziland, Ntombi in turn was given the title *Indlovukazi* — meaning 'Great She-Elephant' and remains joint ruler with her son.

Mswati currently has 14 wives and 23 children. In accordance with Swazi tradition his first two wives come from the Matsebula and the Motsa clans: their positions are largely ritualistic and are chosen for him by his national councillors, but their sons can never be king. The king must take a wife from each Swazi clan, and once chosen, a girl is titled *liphovela* (bride) and will only become a wife once they are pregnant and have proved themselves capable of providing an heir.

Despite his enormous power, the king cannot choose his successor, as this is the job of the Liqoqo, which meets in special session. They choose the *Indlovukazi* — the Great She-Elephant and queen mother — whose son automatically becomes heir apparent. To qualify as *Indlovukazi*, the woman must be of good character and only have one son.

The king and his wives lead an extravagant lifestyle very different from the majority of his mostly very poor subjects, and he is frequently criticised for only slowly developing western-style democracy. His critics denounce him as a dictator, while his supporters claim he is just a traditional monarch who shares power with the queen mother and who enjoys the full support of the majority of his people.

As an absolute monarch Mswati appoints all the top government officials, but takes advice from the queen mother and his council. In the 1990s Mswati was pressurised into agreeing to greater democracy and political reform, but despite this, opposition parties are banned and civil rights are questionable. Swaziland has the world's highest prevalence rate of HIV/AIDS.

As head of state the king earns a high salary, as well as earning interest from his investments in Swaziland and abroad. In 2001 his attempt to use $45 million of government money to buy a personal private jet — the equivalent of Swaziland's health care budget for two years — was blocked, but in 2005 he paid $500,000 from his own pocket for a high spec luxury car. His use of power continues to attract criticism within Swaziland and his futile attempts to stem the AIDS epidemic ravaging his country bring massive foreign criticism. Mswati III is estimated to be the eleventh wealthiest royal in the world, with a personal fortune in the region of $200 million.

In 1830 a royal kraal (compound) was built at Lobamba, near Mbabane, the capital of Swaziland for King Sobhuza I, and was used as the royal residence for Sobhuza II. The current king, Mswati, uses nearby Ludzidzini Kraal (royal palace or the Ludzidzini Royal Village) as his private home for the royal family. It is forbidden to photograph the kraal except during the annual November festival of Ncwala, which celebrates the king and his prowess.

Above: Wearing red feathers, child prince sons of King Mswati III are followed by a guard of Emabutfo warriors at the annual Incwala ceremony which marks the end of the harvest.

Left: King Sobhuza II became king when he was less than a year old and spent his entire life on the throne.

Far left: King Sobhuza II, Lomakolwa Nkosi and their 16-year-old daughter, Gnapi.

Right: King Mswati III and King Letsie III of Lesotho at the latter's wedding breakfast in February 2000.

Left: King Mswati and his wife arrive at Westminster Abbey to attend a special ceremony marking the 50th anniversary of the Commonwealth in March 1999.

Right: Queen Elizabeth II receives King Mswati at Buckingham Palace, 2003.

Far right: The Prince of Wales and King Mswati III watch traditional dancers at the Ludzidzini Royal Kraal, after his arrival at Matsapha airport in Swaziland, 1997.

Below: Maidens carry reeds during the annual reed dance to honour the Queen Mother at the royal residence of Ludzidzini at Lobamba village near Mbabane, Swaziland. Some 20,000 maidens participate in one of the most important traditional ceremonies in the kingdom.

LESOTHO
King Letsie III

Official title	Letsie III, King of Lesotho
Country ruled	Lesotho
Born	17 July 1963
Accession to throne	1990–1995; 1997–
Royal house	House of Seeiso
Official residence	Royal Palace, Maseru
Heir	Lerotholi Seeiso, Prince of Lesotho (b. 2007, son)

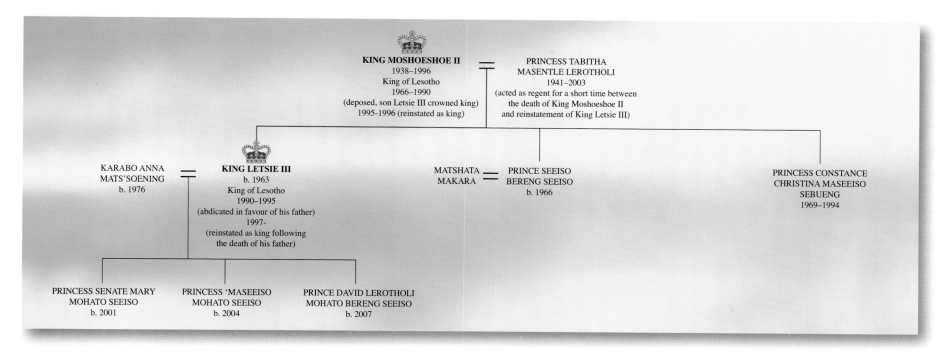

KING MOSHOESHOE II
1938–1996
King of Lesotho
1966–1990
(deposed, son Letsie III crowned king)
1995–1996 (reinstated as king)

PRINCESS TABITHA
MASENTLE LEROTHOLI
1941–2003
(acted as regent for a short time between
the death of King Moshoeshoe II
and reinstatement of King Letsie III)

KARABO ANNA
MATS'SOENING
b. 1976

KING LETSIE III
b. 1963
King of Lesotho
1990–1995
(abdicated in favour of his father)
1997-
(reinstated as king following
the death of his father)

MATSHATA
MAKARA

PRINCE SEEISO
BERENG SEEISO
b. 1966

PRINCESS CONSTANCE
CHRISTINA MASEEISO
SEBUENG
1969–1994

PRINCESS SENATE MARY
MOHATO SEEISO
b. 2001

PRINCESS 'MASEEISO
MOHATO SEEISO
b. 2004

PRINCE DAVID LEROTHOLI
MOHATO BERENG SEEISO
b. 2007

THE COUNTRY OF LESOTHO first came into being as Basutoland in the early 19th century when Moshoeshoe, the leader of a Basotho village, formed a number of alliances with other clans and chiefdoms. This was a particularly unstable time in southern Africa, when the aggressive policies of King Shaka of the Zulus were forcing many tribes to flee their lands, and white settlers had begun to arrive in numbers. Against this background, Moshoeshoe needed to find a safe haven for his people, and they sought refuge on the Qiloane plateau, later to be called Thaba Bosiu ('the Mountain of the Night').

Although Thaba Bosiu proved to be an impregnable fortress, Moshoeshoe still needed the assistance of powerful allies to ensure the survival of his kingdom. In the 1860s he appealed to the British for help and Basutoland became a British protectorate. For the next 100 years the country was frequently in danger of being incorporated into South Africa, but managed to resist this fate. In 1966 Basutoland gained full independence from Britain, became a constitutional monarchy and was renamed the Kingdom of Lesotho. Constantine Bereng Seeiso, the paramount chief and a descendant of Moshoeshoe, was crowned as King Moshoeshoe II.

As a child Seeiso was educated at the Roma College in Lesotho, but amid fears that there was a a plot to assassinate him, he was sent to England where he continued his studies at Ampleforth College and then Corpus Christi College, Oxford.

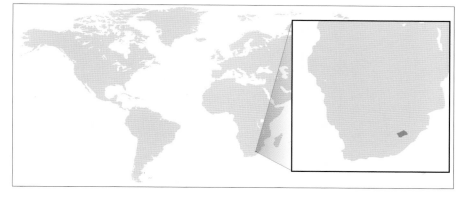

Whilst in England he stayed with a wealthy family and developed a taste for fishing, shooting and fox hunting.

From the outset Moshoeshoe II's reign was problematic, and despite being a popular figure with his people, he was dogged by political opposition. In 1970 he was deposed by the prime minister, Leabua Jonathan, placed under house arrest then forced into exile in the Netherlands; during his exile Moshoeshoe's wife, Queen 'Mamohato, acted as regent. In 1986 there was a *coup d'état* led by Major-General Lekhanya. As the military junta became increasingly unpopular in 1990 Moshoeshoe was deposed and once again forced into exile; his eldest son, Letsie III, replaced him on the throne. By 1993, with the assistance of Nelson Mandela and Letsie III, free elections were held in Lesotho and in January 1995, following Letsie's abdication, Moshoeshoe was returned to the throne. However, his reign ended abruptly less than a year later, when he died in a car crash.

Following his father's death, Letsie III again assumed the throne, following a short period when his mother once again acted as regent. In 1998 Maseru, the capital of Lesotho, erupted in riots, with demonstrators claiming that recent elections had been rigged, and calling on Letsie to overturn the result. However, international observers had declared the elections fair and Letsie, mindful of his non-political role, declined to act. The riots caused great unrest in Lesotho, but Letsie's marriage in 2000 to Karabo Anna Mots'oeneng went some way to uniting the nation. His wife has become a popular queen, working especially to alleviate the suffering caused by AIDS.

Letsie's younger brother, Prince Seeiso Bereng Seeiso, is the Lesotho High Commissioner to the United Kingdom. In 2006 Prince Seeiso and Prince Harry of Wales founded the charity Sentebale to provide aid to orphans and vulnerable children in Lesotho.

Right: Prince Harry of Wales in Lesotho promoting Sentebale, the charity that he founded with King Letsie's younger brother, Prince Seeiso Bereng Seeiso.

Far left: King Moshoeshoe II of Lesotho. Moshoeshoe was the first king of the renamed the Kingdom of Lesotho and was the father of the current monarch.

Left: Queen Tabitha of Lesotho, the wife of King Moshoeshoe II and mother to King Letsie III.

Left: The King of Lesotho, Letsie III is crowned with a hair band and feather, and wears his ceremonial cloak at his coronation in 1987.

Above: Princess Senate Mary Mohato Seeiso was born in 2001 and is King Letsie's eldest child. Her place as heir to the throne has been taken by her younger brother, Prince Lerotholi David Mohato Bereng Seeiso, born in 2007.

Right: King Letsie III married Karabo Matsoeneng in February 2000 at the National Stadium in Maseru, Lesotho. Now known as Queen 'Masenate Mohato Seeiso, she acts as regent in the king's absence.

MIDDLE EAST

IRAN
Reza Pahlavi II

Official title	Reza Pahlavi II, Shah of Iran
Pretender to	Throne of Iran
Born	31 October 1960
Pretendence	1980–
Royal house	Pahlavi
Residence	Maryland, USA
Heir	Prince Ali-Reza Pahlavi (b. 1966, brother)

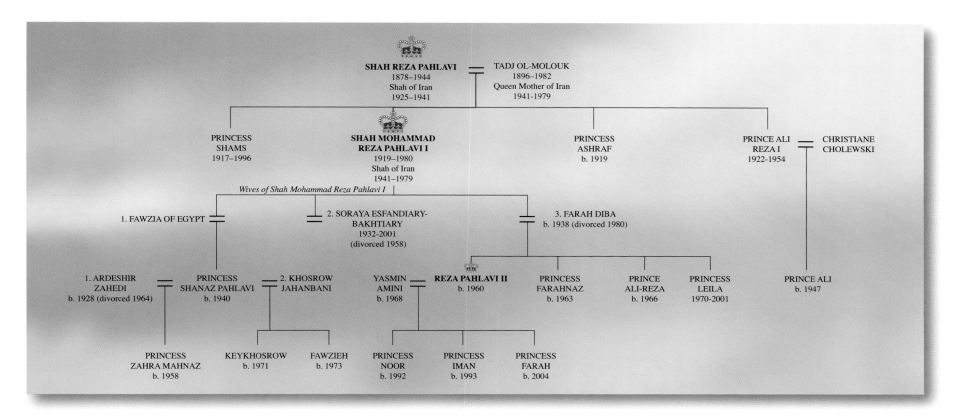

REZA PAHLAVI II, THE elder son of the last shah of Iran, lives in Maryland, USA, half a world away from the opulent palaces in which he was brought up. The eldest child of Mohamamad Reza Pahlavi, Shahanshah of Iran and his third wife, Empress Farah, 'RP', as he is known to his friends, has spent all his adult life in exile, in Morocco, France, Egypt and the USA.

Reza Pahlavi's grandfather founded the dynasty. A former army officer, Reza Shah gained power in Iran via a military coup, and was crowned shah in 1925, leading a modernising, anti-Communist regime that advocated religious tolerance. Germany's invasion of Russia in 1941, and the need for the Allies to preserve access to Iranian oil supplies marked the end of his reign. His son, Mohammad Reza Pahlavi, acceded to Iran's 'Peacock Throne' on the abdication of his father in 1941.

Courted by both the USA and Russia after World War II, Shah Mohammad Reza Pahlavi strove to introduce social reforms, and to move away from the traditional concept of despotic monarchy, building on the work of his father, who had done much to encourage the emergence of an educated middle class to modernise Iran. Oil made his country rich, but the wealth was not shared evenly throughout society. The wide dis-

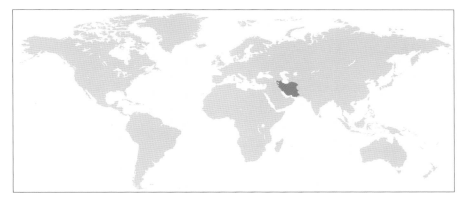

crepancy between the ruling classes and ordinary Iranians was brought into sharp focus in 1971, when the shah hosted magnificent celebrations at Persepolis, the ancient Persian capital, to mark the 2,500th anniversary of the monarchy. Abhorrence of the royal family's extravagant lifestyle, which was viewed by many Iranians as decadent, provided fertile ground for Muslim fundamentalists to preach a return to Islamic law. In 1979 having lost political control, the shah and his family left Iran. Shortly afterwards a revolutionary Islamic government was formed under Ayatollah Ruhollah Khomeini who returned from exile to a hero's welcome.

The shah died from cancer while in exile in Egypt in 1980 and his son inherited the title Shahanshah of Iran. Reza Pahlavi trained as a fighter pilot in the USA from 1978, and completed his education at the University of Southern California. After short periods of exile in Morocco, Egypt and France, he settled in the USA in 1984, where he married Yasmine Etemad Amini in 1986. The couple have three daughters. Reza Pahlavi does not use his royal title, but employs his high profile to campaign for human rights in Iran. An articulate, pragmatic man, he advocates a return to secular, democratic government in Iran – although whether or not he will head it is a moot point.

Above: Crown Prince Reza with his father the last Shah of Iran, 1978.

Left: Reza Shah, the ambitious army officer who founded the Iranian royal dynasty in 1925.

Above: Mohammad Reza Pahlavi, the Shah of Iran with Shahbanou (Empress) Farah of Iran at their opulent coronation in 1967.

Right: Empress Farah Diba with Crown Prince Reza , his wife Yasmine and their daughter Princess Noor, 1992. The former empress divides her time between her home in Paris and visiting her children in the USA.

Left: Crown Prince Reza Pahlavi receives an award from his mother the empress after training with the Imperial Iranian Airforce, 1979.

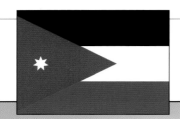

JORDAN
King Abdullah II

Official title	King Abdullah II of the Hashemite Kingdom of Jordan
Country ruled	Jordan
Born	30 January 1962
Accession to throne	1999
Royal house	*Bani Hashem* (Hashemites)
Official residence	Raghadan Palace, Amman
Heir	*Unnamed*

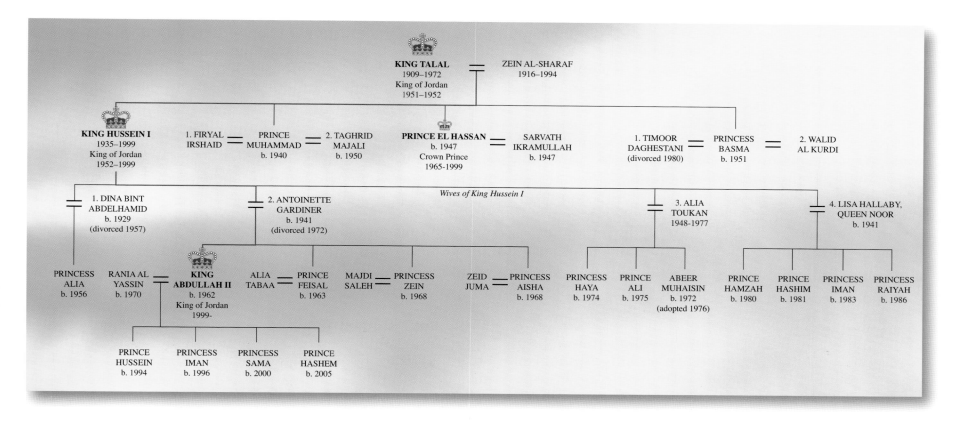

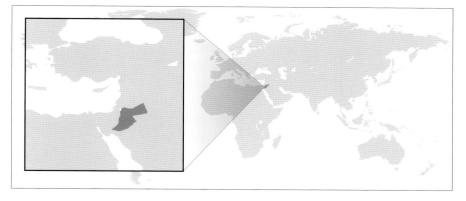

THE JORDANIAN ROYAL FAMILY traces its lineage directly back to the Prophet Muhammad through his daughter Fatima and her husband Ali bin Abi Talib. Ali and Fatima had two sons, Al-Hassan and Al-Hussein, the descendants of Hassan became known as Sharifs and the descendants of Hussein as Sayyids. The Hashemites are the descendants of the Sharifian side of the family.

The country that we recognize today as Jordan first came into being as the Emirate of Transjordan in 1921, following the break-up of the Ottoman Empire in the aftermath of World War I. Transjordan was ruled by Abdullah bin Al-Hussein, the great-grandfather of the current king. Initially, Transjordan was a British protectorate, but by 1923 Britain had granted a level of independence under the rule of Emir Abdullah. At this point, however, the British still retained effective control of financial, military and foreign affairs in the nascent state.

Full independence was finally gained after World War II, and by 1949 the Emirate of Transjordan had become the Hashemite Kingdom of Jordan, with Abdullah crowned as its first king. Abdullah's reign was brought to an abrupt end in 1951 when he was assassinated at the Al-Aqsa Mosque in Jerusalem. Abdullah's grandson, the future King Hussein, was also present and he only avoided death thanks to a strategically positioned medal on his chest.

Abdullah's eldest son Talal succeeded his father, but he abdicated for health reasons after only a year. Talal's eldest son, Prince Hussein, was declared king, but the Jordanian constitution specified he could not be crowned king until he reached the age of 18 the following year. In the interim a regency council led by Hussein's mother, Queen Zein Al-Sharaf, took charge of affairs of state.

For almost half a century King Hussein, known affectionately as 'the father of modern Jordan', led his country through a number of turbulent conflicts. His reign began during the height of the Cold War between Russia and the West, and encompassed several Arab-Israeli conflicts, as well as the first Gulf War. Throughout all this, Hussein managed the delicate balancing act of maintaining strong ties with fellow Arab leaders, as well as being seen as a moderating influence by the West. In addition to his work in foreign affairs, Hussein tried to modernise the economic and industrial infrastructure of the country and improve the lot of the Jordanian people.

In addition to being a keen sportsman, King Hussein had a great interest in technology. He was an enthusiastic 'ham' radio operator—using the call sign was 'JY1'—and in his later years he developed an interest the use of computers as an educational tool and issued a directive that all Jordanian schools should invest in information technology and have access to the internet.

For most of his reign King Hussein's designated successor was his brother, Crown Prince Hassan, but shortly before his death, Hussein altered his will in favour of Prince Abdullah, his eldest son by his second (British) wife, Toni Gardiner. King Abdullah was educated in Jordan, Britain and the United States, before serving in first the British and then the Jordanian armies. Like his father, he is an enthusiastic sportsman, indeed he is a former Jordanian National Rally Racing Champion. Since becoming king, Abdullah has continued the work begun by his father in modernising Jordan, promoting free market reforms and actively pursuing ongoing peace with Israel and Palestine.

Above: King Abdullah II of Jordan during a Sovereign's Parade at the Royal Military Academy Sandurst in 2006.

Right: Queen Rania arriving at the memorial service for the late King Hussein at St Paul's Cathedral in London, 5 July 1999.

Left: Queen Rania attending a reception and banquet at the Guildhall in London during a State Visit to Britain in 2001.

Below: King Abdullah II meeting with President Vladimir Putin at the Kremlin during a visit to Russia.

Bottom: King Abdullah II with British Prime Minister Gordon Brown inside Number 10 Downing Street, London during a visit to Britain in 2007. Diplomatic relations between Jordan and the UK are particularly strong.

Left: Born Lisa Halby in the USA to a family of Syrian descent, Queen Noor converted to Islam when she became King Hussein's fourth, and reputedly favourite, wife in 1978. She changed her name to Noor, which means 'light' in Arabic. King Hussein and Queen Noor had four children, Prince Hamzah, Prince Hashim, Princess Iman and Princess Raiyah

Above: King Hussein and wife Queen Noor attending the Thanksgiving Service as part of the VE Day celebrations at St Paul's Cathedral, London in 1995. Since King Hussein's death 1999, Queen Noor has worked for the King Hussein Foundation, which aims to continue the king's commitment to world peace and humanitarian causes. Stepmother to King Abdullah II,

Noor is now known as Her Majesty Queen Noor of Jordan, to distinguish her from Abdullah's wife, Her Majesty the Queen of Jordan.

*Above: King Hussein stand-
ing proudly with his wife
Queen Noor (left) and his
daughter (by his second
wife) Princess Aisha, the
sister of King Abdullah II.
Like her father and brothers, Princess Aisha attended
the Royal Military Academy,
Sandburst.*
.

*Above right: Prince Feisal,
the younger brother of King
Abdullah II, attending the
launch of the Thrust SSC
Land Speed Record
Attempt.*

*Right: King Hussein and
Queen Noor shortly after
the birth of their first child,
Prince Hamzah in 1980.*

KUWAIT
Sheikh Sabah Al-Ahmed Al-Jaber Al-Sabah

Official title	Emir of Kuwait
Country ruled	Kuwait
Born	6 June 1929
Accession to throne	2006
Royal house	Al-Sabah Dynasty
Official residence	Dar Salwa Palace, Hawalli
Heir	Sheikh Nawaf Al-Ahmad Al-Jaber Al-Sabah (b. 1937, brother)

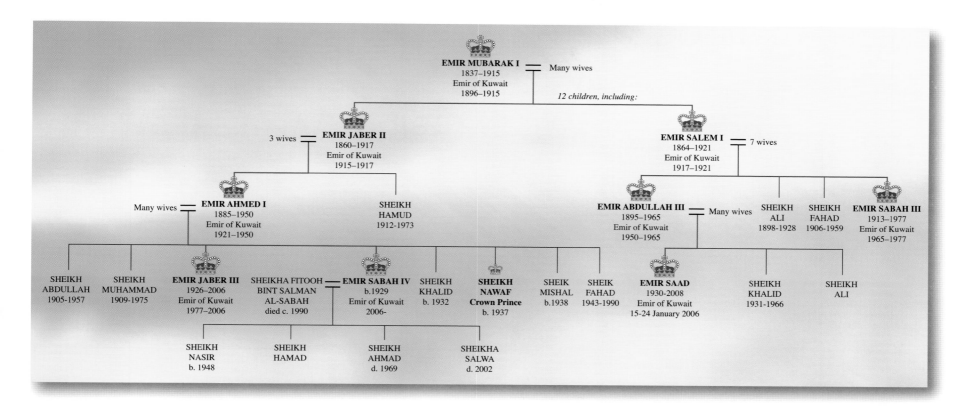

THE AL-SABAHS HAVE BEEN the ruling family of Kuwait since 1756 when the Banu Utub, a group of families of the Anizah tribe, living in the area that is now Kuwait (then called Qurain) appointed Sheikh Sabah bin Jaber as their leader. Although the sheikdom has remained with the Al-Sabah family, the line of succession is not strictly hereditary. Even though many of the emirs have, indeed, succeeded their father, the successor is chosen from within the family on the basis of suitability for the job; the current crown prince is the brother of the current emir.

Under the rule of the Al-Sabahs Kuwait began to prosper as a centre for trade, with pearls from the local oyster beds providing the mainstay of the economy along with trade in wood, spices dates and horses. Whilst internally Kuwait was prosperous, external pressures led the emirs to form an alliance with the British, who dominated the trade routes at that time. In 1899 Sheikh Mubarak Al-Sabah, known as Mubarak the Great, signed a treaty with Britain that established Kuwait as a British protectorate. Mubarak, who ruled from 1896 to 1915, is widely regarded as the founder of modern-day Kuwait. His two sons, Jaber Al-Mubarak Al-Sabah and Salem Al-Mubarak Al-Sabah, succeeded him, and it is from them that the Al-Jaber and Al-

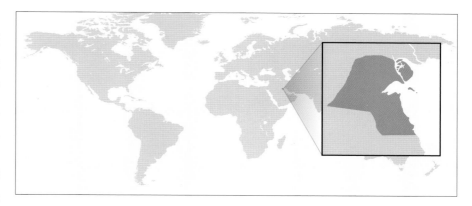

Salem branches of the Al-Sabah dynasty descend. Traditionally the position of emir has alternated between these two strands of the family.

On 19 June 1961, during the reign of Sheikh Abdullah Al-Salem Al-Sabah, Kuwait gained full independence from Britain. Following this, the title of the ruler was changed to emir and later in the same year, despite opposition from Iraq, Kuwait joined the Arab League.

The current emir, Sheikh Sabah Al-Ahmed Al-Jaber Al-Sabah, was born in 1929 and educated at the Al Mubarakya School, followed by private tuition. His reign began in controversial circumstances; on 15 Jan 2006 Sheikh Jaber Al-Ahmad Al-Jaber Al-Sabah died following a long illness, thus placing the crown prince Sheikh Saad Al-Abdullah Al-Salem Al-Sabah in the position of emir. However, Saad himself was also suffering health problems and just eight days into his reign he was voted out of office by the Kuwaiti parliament and replaced by Sheikh Sabah who was officially sworn in as emir on 29 January 2006.

Prior to becoming the Emir of Kuwait, Sheikh Sabah had held a number of posts within the Kuwaiti government. But it is for his work in the Ministry of Foreign Affairs that he is most well known, having played a key role in the formation of the Common Ministerial Council for the Cooperation Council for the Arab States of the Gulf (GCC) and the European Union, which endeavours to strengthen the economic ties between Arab and European nations. During his time as emir, Sheikh Sabah has overseen the introduction of some of the strongest press freedom laws in the Arab world. The emir is a widower, having married only once to Sheikha Fitooh who died in 1990. He has two sons, Sheikh Nasser and Sheikh Hamed; his third son Sheikh Ahmed died in a car crash in 1969 and his daughter Sheikha Salwa succumbed to cancer in 2002. In honour of his daughter, he named his palace Dar Salwa (the Palace of Salwa).

Left: Emir Jaber III meeting with British Prime Minister Margaret Thatcher during a 1990 state visit to Britain.

Above: Sheikh Sabah (then First Deputy Prime Minister of Kuwait) with British Prime Minister Tony Blair in 2003.

Left: A 1995 state banquet at the Guildhall, London hosted by the Lord Mayor and Corporation of London in honour of His Highness Emir Jaber III.

Below: Sheikh Sabah welcomes Austrian President Heinz Fischer to the sumptuous Bayan Palace in Kuwait City, 2009.

Left: A meeting between Sheikh Sabah and NATO General Secrtaty Jaap de Hoop Scheffer, 2009.

THE KINGDOM OF SAUDI ARABIA
King Abdullah

Official title	Abdullah bin Abdul Aziz Al Saud, King of Saudi Arabia
Country ruled	Saudi Arabia
Born	1924
Accession to throne	2005
Royal house	Al Saud
Official residences	King's Palace, Riyadh
Heir	Crown Prince Sultan bin Abdul Aziz Al Saud (b. 1926, half-brother)

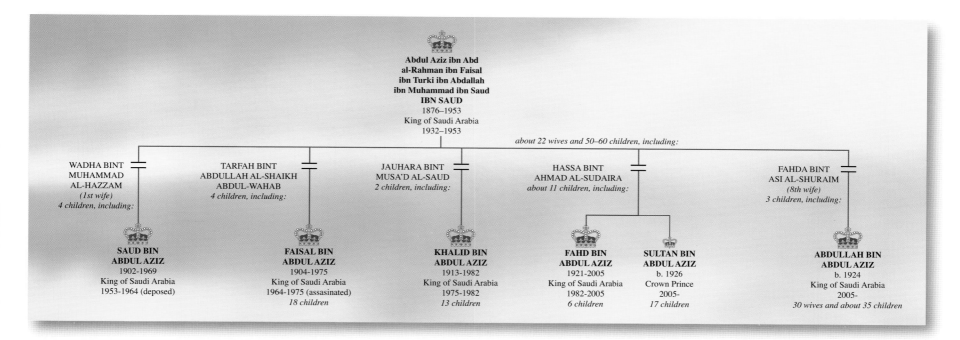

Abdul Aziz ibn Abd
al-Rahman ibn Faisal
ibn Turki ibn Abdallah
ibn Muhammad ibn Saud
IBN SAUD
1876–1953
King of Saudi Arabia
1932–1953

about 22 wives and 50–60 children, including:

WADHA BINT MUHAMMAD AL-HAZZAM *(1st wife)* *4 children, including:*	TARFAH BINT ABDULLAH AL-SHAIKH ABDUL-WAHAB *4 children, including:*	JAUHARA BINT MUSA'D AL-SAUD *2 children, including:*	HASSA BINT AHMAD AL-SUDAIRA *about 11 children, including:*	FAHDA BINT ASI AL-SHURAIM *(8th wife)* *3 children, including:*

SAUD BIN ABDUL AZIZ 1902-1969 King of Saudi Arabia 1953-1964 (deposed)	**FAISAL BIN ABDUL AZIZ** 1904-1975 King of Saudi Arabia 1964-1975 (assassinated) *18 children*	**KHALID BIN ABDUL AZIZ** 1913-1982 King of Saudi Arabia 1975-1982 *13 children*	**FAHD BIN ABDUL AZIZ** 1921-2005 King of Saudi Arabia 1982-2005 *6 children*	**SULTAN BIN ABDUL AZIZ** b. 1926 Crown Prince 2005- *17 children*	**ABDULLAH BIN ABDUL AZIZ** b. 1924 King of Saudi Arabia 2005- *30 wives and about 35 children*

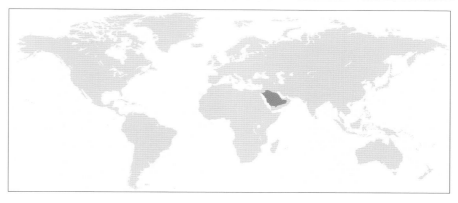

ABDULLAH BIN ABDUL AZIZ Al Saud became king of Saudi Arabia in August 2005 on the death of his half-brother King Fahd, although he had been effective ruler since Fahd suffered a major stroke in January 1996. King Abdullah is a cautious reformer with vast financial resources, thanks to Saudi Arabia's enormous natural gas and oil reserves. Saudi Arabia was a poor country until oil was discovered in the 1940s. The king himself has vast personal wealth worth in the region of over $20 billion.

The modern state of Saudi Arabia was founded in 1932 by King Abdul Aziz bin Abdul Rahman Al Saud (1876–1953, known as Ibn Saud). The 1992 Basic Law of Government states that the king must be a male descendant of Ibn Saud, the founder, who had some 22 wives, (although in accordance with Islamic practice, he never had more than four at any one time). Since Ibn Saud's death in 1953, his successors have all been from among his 37 sons: King Saud, 1953-1964; King Faisal, 1964–1975; King Khalid, 1975–1982; King Fahd, 1982–2005; and currently King Abdullah. The current Crown Prince is Sultan bin Abdul Aziz Al Saud, the king's half-brother (and a full brother of the late King Fahd). By a royal decree of October 2006, future Saudi kings (after the current crown prince inherits) will be selected with advice from a committee of Saudi princes. Saudi Arabia is the birthplace of Islam and is sometimes referred to as the 'Land of the Two Holy Mosques'. The king's

title, 'Custodian of the Two Holy Mosques', refers to the two holiest shrines in Islam, Mecca and Medina; Saudi Arabia is governed according to Islamic Sharia law, with the king as an absolute monarch.

King Abdullah was born in Riyadh in 1924 to Ibn Saud's eighth wife, Fahda bint Asi Al-Shuraim and was the first of their three children. Little is known about his early life other than he had a formal religious education at the royal court and spent some years living with Bedouin tribesmen in the desert to learn traditional Arab values. By 1962 Prince Abdullah was appointed commander of the Saudi Arabian National Guard (an appointment he still holds). In March 1975 he became second deputy prime minister when his half-brother King Faisal was assassinated, and another half-brother, Khalid succeeded to the throne. In June 1982 King Khalid died and another half-brother, Fahd, succeeded and appointed Abdullah deputy prime minister and crown prince. For nine years Abdullah acted as regent until King Fahd died in August 2005.

As is the custom, King Abdullah has been married perhaps as many as 30 times and is reported to have fathered around 35 children. Keenly interested in horse racing, he founded the Riyadh Equestrian Club and has his own thoroughbred farm outside Riyadh where he breeds pure Arabian horses. He is an avid reader and has founded the King Abdulaziz Library in Riyadh and another library in Casablanca, Morocco.

The King's Palace in Riyadh by all accounts is opulent, full of vast rooms filled with Italian marble and gigantic crystal chandeliers. The bathrooms are complete with gold taps and other gold fittings. White-robed royal guards are armed with gold swords. Elsewhere in Riyadh, the Grand Festival Palace was built in the 1980s as a traditional environment for meetings with important foreigners and significant guests, with a ceremonial hall for exhibitions and events. For government functions and state receptions Tuwaiq Palace was built in the mid-1980s.

Left: King Abdul Aziz Ibn Saud, seen in 1947 with some of his many children. Over his lifetime he is thought to have had around 22 wives and about 37 sons. But, in line with Islamic tradition, he never had more than four wives concurrently.

Right: King Khalid and his half-brother and successor, Prince Fahd. All the rulers of Saudi Arabia since its foundation in 1932 have been sons of Ibn Saud.

Far right: Lt. Gen. Prince Khalid Bin Sultan with his insignia of an Honorary Knight, Commander of the Order of the Bath in November 1991. He is the eldest son of Crown Prince Sultan.

Right: Russian President Vladimir Putin (left, background) and King Abdullah of Saudi Arabia (right, background) at a meeting in the Royal Palace in Riyadh. The royal palace is reportedly lavishly decorated with luxury details such as gigantic crystal chandeliers and Italian marble floors.

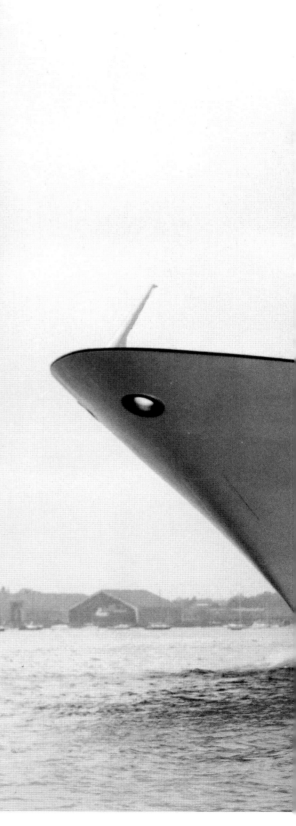

Above: Interior view of the Al Riyadh, *a 212-foot long luxury yacht belonging to King Khalid. She was built in 1978, but was badly damaged by fire in 2003 while undergoing a refit in Pireaus, Greece.*

Left: King Abdullah and the Duke of Edinburgh inspect the ceremonial guard at Horse Guards Parade in London. 30 October 2007.

Right: The 580-feet long Abdul Aziz *was the world's largest yacht for over 20 years until April 2005. She was built in 1983 in Denmark and fitted out in 1984 at Southampton Docks, then given as a gift to King Fahd. In 2002 her interior was completely rebuilt during a refit in Greece.*

BAHRAIN
King Hamad bin Isa Al Khalifa

Official title	Hamad bin Isa Al Khalifa, King of Bahrain
Country ruled	Bahrain
Born	28 January 1950
Accession to throne	1999 (as Emir) 2002 (as King)
Royal house	Al Khalifa Dynasty
Official residence	Riffa Palace, Manama
Heir	Crown Prince Salman (b. 1969, son)

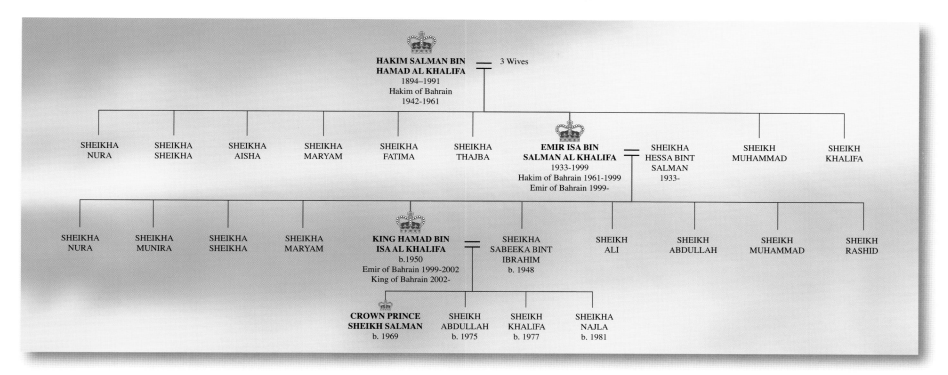

HAKIM SALMAN BIN
HAMAD AL KHALIFA
1894–1991
Hakim of Bahrain
1942-1961 — 3 Wives

SHEIKHA NURA • SHEIKHA SHEIKHA • SHEIKHA AISHA • SHEIKHA MARYAM • SHEIKHA FATIMA • SHEIKHA THAJBA • EMIR ISA BIN SALMAN AL KHALIFA 1933-1999 Hakim of Bahrain 1961-1999 Emir of Bahrain 1999- — SHEIKHA HESSA BINT SALMAN 1933- • SHEIKH MUHAMMAD • SHEIKH KHALIFA

SHEIKHA NURA • SHEIKHA MUNIRA • SHEIKHA SHEIKHA • SHEIKHA MARYAM • KING HAMAD BIN ISA AL KHALIFA b.1950 Emir of Bahrain 1999-2002 King of Bahrain 2002- — SHEIKHA SABEEKA BINT IBRAHIM b. 1948 • SHEIKH ALI • SHEIKH ABDULLAH • SHEIKH MUHAMMAD • SHEIKH RASHID

CROWN PRINCE SHEIKH SALMAN b. 1969 • SHEIKH ABDULLAH b. 1975 • SHEIKH KHALIFA b. 1977 • SHEIKHA NAJLA b. 1981

BAHRAIN HAS BEEN RULED by the Al Khalifa dynasty since 1783 when they seized control of the area. From 1783 to the rulers were called the *Hakim al-Bahrayn* (ruler of Bahrain); from 1971 to 2002 the title became *Amir ad-Dawlat al-Bahrayn* (Emir of the State of Bahrain); and following the adoption of a new national charter, establishing a constitutional monarch in 2001, Bahrain was proclaimed a kingdom in 2002 and the title became *Malik al-Bahrayn* (King of Bahrain).

For much of the time since 1783 Bahrain was a British protectorate, but in 1971, under the leadership of Emir Isa bin Salman Al Khalifa, the father of the current king, it gained full independence from Britain. Sheikh Isa ruled from 1960 until his sudden death in 1999, and during his reign he oversaw the emergence of Bahrain as a modern nation, with great improvements in housing, education and transportation, including the building of a causeway linking the country to Saudi Arabia in 1986. Although he initially attempted to bring in democratic reforms, women were not given a vote and a disagreement over the State Security Law of 1974 caused him to dissolve the National Assembly of Bahrain in 1975. Sheikh Isa was also reluctant to sanction the use of the death penalty, and he frequently refused to sign death warrants put before him.

His son Hamad bin Isa Al-Khalifa immediately succeeded Isa following his death in 1999. Hamad was educated initially in

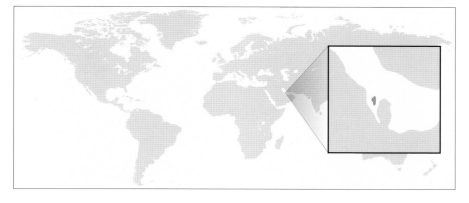

Bahrain, during which time he developed a love of traditional Nabati and Bedouin poetry. For his secondary education he attended the Leys School in Cambridge, England and subsequently went on to attend military colleges in the United Kingdom, where he studied at the Royal Military Academy Sandhurst, and the United States where he studied at the US Army Command and Staff College at Fort Leavenworth, Kansas.

On succeeding his father King Hamad set about introducing many social and political reforms. Unpopular security laws were repealed, a large number of political prisoners were released and the national charter of 2001 re-introduced the elected National Assembly. The 2001 legislation also gave women the right to vote and to run for political office for the first time in the Bahrain's history. As a result of this political reform Bahrain was able to negotiate a Free Trade Agreement with the United States in 2004, greatly enhancing the nation's economy. King Hamad's reforms have been widely applauded, but Bahrain still has some way to go before it fully embraces a truly democratic system. Although the country now has a constitutional monarchy, the royal family still occupy many government positions: the prime minister, for example, is the king's uncle Sheikh Khalifa bin Salman Al Khalifa.

Outside politics, King Hamad indulges in a number of sports activities and hobbies including falconry, golf, fishing, tennis and football, and maintains an enthusiastic interest in Arabian horses that led to the Royal Arabian Stud of Bahrain becoming a fully fledged member of the World Arabian Horse Organization in 1980.

Hamad's wife, Sheikha Sabeeka bint Ibrahim Al Khalifa, is actively involved in promoting the rights of women in the Arab world as the head of the Supreme Council for Women, and as chief patron of the Society for Women and Children in Bahrain.

Below: Britain is one of Bahrain's closest Western allies and relations between the two countries are warm. Queen Elizabeth II received the King of Bahrain, His Majesty Sheikh Hamad bin Isa Al Khalifa, at Buckingham Palace, London, 2004.

Right: In December 2008, King Hamad bin Isa Al Khalifa headed a Bahraini delegation that visited Russia to strengthen friendly relations between the two countries. Here is received by Russian President Dmitry Medvedev.

Above: Sheika Sabeeka is the cousin, first wife and Queen Consort of King Hamad, and Head of the Supreme Council for Women in Bahrain.

Right: King Hamad bin Isa Al Khalifa arriving at Sheremetyevo-1 International Airport, Moscow, during a visit to Russia.

Right: A view from Bahrain's Riffa Fort by night. Built in the year 1812, it was from here that the present emir's great-grandfather, Sheikh Isa bin Ali Al Khalifa ruled the kingdom of Bahrain from 1869 to 1932.

Below: The Prime Minister of Bahrain, His Highness Sheikh Khalifa bin Salman Al Khalifa (left) receives the Secretary of the International Federation of Journalists, 2009. The king's uncle, Sheikh Khalifa is the world's longest-serving prime minister, having been in the post since 1970.

STATE OF QATAR
HH Sheikh Hamad bin Khalifa Al Thani

Official title	Sheikh Hamad bin Khalifa Al Thani, Emir of Qatar
Country ruled	Qatar
Born	1952
Accession to throne	27 July 1995
Royal house	Al Thani Dynasty
Official residence	Royal Palace, Doha
Heir	Crown Prince Sheikh Tamim bin bin Hamad Al Thani (b. 1980, fourth son)

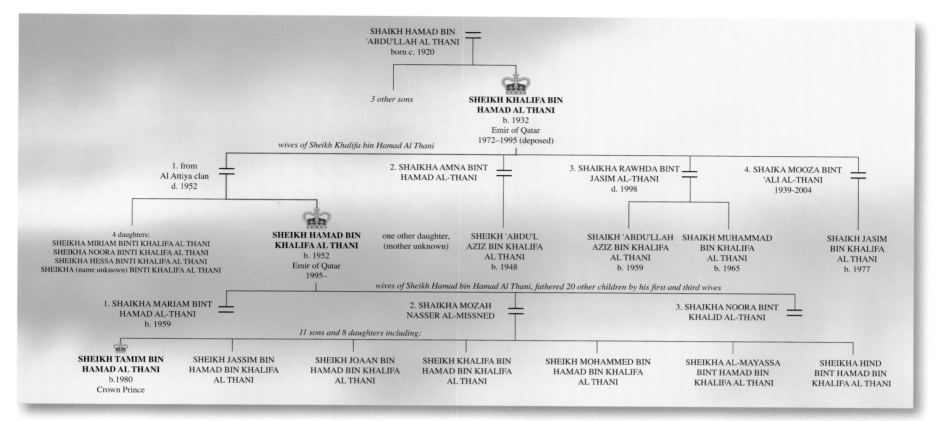

SHAIKH HAMAD BIN
'ABDU'LLAH AL THANI
born c. 1920

3 other sons

**SHEIKH KHALIFA BIN
HAMAD AL THANI**
b. 1932
Emir of Qatar
1972–1995 (deposed)

wives of Sheikh Khalifa bin Hamad Al Thani

1. from
Al Attiya clan
d. 1952

2. SHAIKHA AMNA BINT
HAMAD AL-THANI

3. SHAIKHA RAWHDA BINT
JASIM AL-THANI
d. 1998

4. SHAIKA MOOZA BINT
'ALI AL-THANI
1939-2004

4 daughters:
SHEIKHA MIRIAM BINTI KHALIFA AL THANI
SHEIKHA NOORA BINTI KHALIFA AL THANI
SHEIKHA HESSA BINTI KHALIFA AL THANI
SHEIKHA (name unknown) BINTI KHALIFA AL THANI

**SHEIKH HAMAD BIN
KHALIFA AL THANI**
b. 1952
Emir of Qatar
1995–

one other daughter,
(mother unknown)

SHEIKH 'ABDU'L
AZIZ BIN KHALIFA
AL THANI
b. 1948

SHAIKH 'ABDU'LLAH
AZIZ BIN KHALIFA
AL THANI
b. 1959

SHAIKH MUHAMMAD
BIN KHALIFA
AL THANI
b. 1965

SHAIKH JASIM
BIN KHALIFA
AL THANI
b. 1977

wives of Sheikh Hamad bin Hamad Al Thani, fathered 20 other children by his first and third wives

1. SHAIKHA MARIAM BINT
HAMAD AL-THANI
b. 1959

2. SHAIKHA MOZAH
NASSER AL-MISSNED

3. SHAIKHA NOORA BINT
KHALID AL-THANI

11 sons and 8 daughters including:

**SHEIKH TAMIM BIN
HAMAD AL THANI**
b.1980
Crown Prince

SHEIKH JASSIM BIN
HAMAD BIN KHALIFA
AL THANI

SHEIKH JOAAN BIN
HAMAD BIN KHALIFA
AL THANI

SHEIKH KHALIFA BIN
HAMAD BIN KHALIFA
AL THANI

SHEIKH MOHAMMED BIN
HAMAD BIN KHALIFA
AL THANI

SHEIKHA AL-MAYASSA
BINT HAMAD BIN
KHALIFA AL THANI

SHEIKHA HIND
BINT HAMAD BIN
KHALIFA AL THANI

THE TINY OIL-RICH Gulf state of Qatar has been ruled by the Al Thani dynasty since the early 18th century; they are descended from the Tamim tribe who come from the east of the Arabian Peninsula. The original tribal leader, Thani bin Muhammad extended his power across the whole Qatar Peninsula in the mid-19th century, and established the area that would become Qatar. It is not unusual in Qatar for a sheikh to be deposed by his own son. Qatar's wealth comes from vast oil and natural gas reserves, which give its population the highest per capita income in the world.

Sheikh Hamad, the current emir, was born in 1952, but after his mother died young he was brought up by his maternal uncle and eventually sent to England and the Royal Military Academy at Sandhurst. He graduated in 1971, the same year that Qatar won independence from Britain, and when massive natural gas deposits were discovered in Qatari waters. In 1972 his father, Sheikh Khalifa bin Hamad Al Thani seized power from his uncle Ahmad ibn 'Ali Al Thani and became the ruler of Qatar.

As the oldest of five brothers, Sheikh Hamad was ordered to return home to Qatar where he was commissioned in the Qatari army as a lieutenant colonel. He was quickly promoted up the ranks until he became commander-in-chief, with the par-

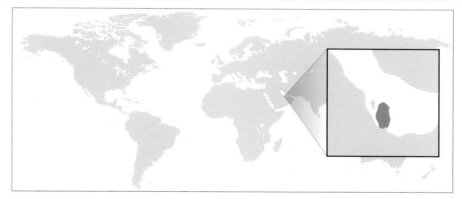

ticular brief of modernising the armed forces with increased personnel and state-of-the-art weaponry. In 1977 he was appointed Heir Apparent and Minister of Defence.

His father, Sheikh Khalifa, started huge reforms, including a benevolent welfare state with free healthcare and education for the Qatari people, as well as overseeing the creation of one of the highest per capita incomes in the world. As the years went by, he spent increasing amounts of time out of the country enjoying an extravagant lifestyle on the French Riviera, leaving Hamad to run Qatar from 1992. Allegedly worried that his country's wealth would be squandered, and the necessary reforms not undertaken, Hamad carefully consulted various of his Al Thani relatives, and with their support instigated a bloodless coup against Sheikh Khalifa on 27 July 1995. It is said he phoned Sheikh Khalifa at his hotel in Zurich to tell him of his changed circumstances and his father hung up on him! Sheikh Khalifa immediately disowned his oldest son and returned to Qatar to gather his supporters for a counter-coup. His funds were cut off, however, when Sheikh Hamad used the law to freeze billions of dollars in his father's bank accounts scattered around the world.

Sheikh Hamad has systematically modernised his country, including the funding of Al Jazeera, the Arab language satellite TV station which is based in Qatar (established in 1966, it is now English language too). In the late 1990s Sheikh Hamad eased press censorship and promoted ties with Iran and Israel, and allowed the US to use Qatari soil in 2003 prior to the invasion of Iraq. Since 2003 women have the right to vote and hold office.

Sheikh Hamad's first wife was his cousin in a politically expedient marriage. His consort, second and most influential wife was a love match: she is Mozah bint Nasser Al-Missned and together they have five sons and two daughters, including the heir apparent Sheikh Tamim Hamad Al Thani (b. 1980). She is the first royal woman to be seen with her face uncovered in public and is active in charity work and projects to promote Qatar. Sheikh Hamad additionally has about 20 other children from his first and third wives. There are around 3,000 members of the extended Al Thani family each of whom receives a monthly stipend.

Sheikh Hamad and his wife Sheikha Mozah have spent some of their vast wealth on assembling an impressive collection of modern and contemporary art displayed in the capital Doha, which includes a £9.7m Damien Hirst sculpture, and a Mark Rothko painting, reportedly purchased for $72.8m in 2007. In November 2008 the huge Museum of Islamic Art opened. Designed by I.M.Pei, it displays a multi-billion dollar collection of art that covers 13 centuries and three continents: the family has systematically bought virtually every important piece of Islamic art which has appeared on the market.

Right: Camel racing is a major sport across the Arabian Gulf. Here Injaz, *a camel owned by Sheikh Mohammed bin Rashid Al Maktoum, the ruler of Dubai finishes in first place at the annual Golden Sword race of pure-bred Arabian Camels held at the Shahaniya Race Course, Qatar.*

Left: Sheikh Hamad Bin Khalifa Al-Thani and Sheikha Mozah bint Nasser Al-Missned in London with the Blairs on 25 January 2006.

Right: Doha city combines the modern — such as the Doha Sheraton Hotel — with the old. Doha was founded as a fishing village in 1825 at which time it was called Al-Bida. The entire country was desperately poor until the late 1930s when oil was discovered and money started to roll in. Now oil and natural gas make up almost the entire economy.

Above: In a world of largely invisible women, Sheikha Mozah stands out as an educated and gracious consort who works with her husband Emir Hamad to promote Islamic and Qatari culture.

Left: Negotiations in the office of the Emir of Qatar held between Sheikh Khalifa bin Zayed Al Nahayan, President of the UAE and Russian President Vladimir Putin, (third on the right) and their advisors and secretaries.

UNITED ARAB EMIRATES
Sheikh Khalifa bin Zayed bin Sultan Al Nahyan

Official title	Sheikh Khalifa bin Zayed bin Sultan Al Nahyan, President
Country ruled	United Arab Emirates
Born	1948
Accession to throne	2004
Royal house	House of Al-Falasi
Official residences	Al Ain
Heir (as ruler of Abu Dhabi)	Sheikh Mohammed bin Zayed Al Nahyan (b. 1951, brother)

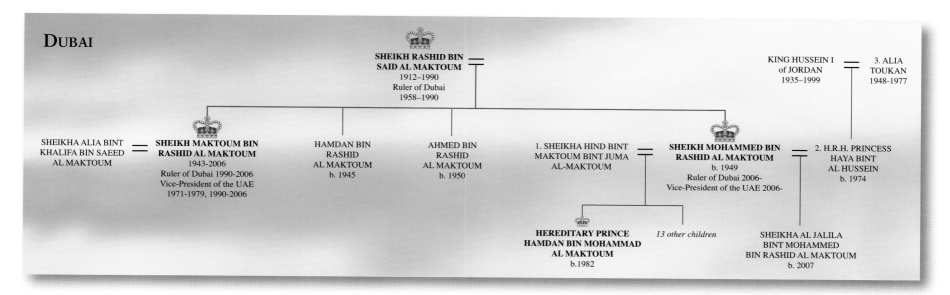

DUBAI

SHEIKH RASHID BIN
SAID AL MAKTOUM
1912–1990
Ruler of Dubai
1958–1990

KING HUSSEIN I
of JORDAN
1935–1999

3. ALIA
TOUKAN
1948-1977

SHEIKHA ALIA BINT
KHALIFA BIN SAEED
AL MAKTOUM

SHEIKH MAKTOUM BIN
RASHID AL MAKTOUM
1943-2006
Ruler of Dubai 1990-2006
Vice-President of the UAE
1971-1979, 1990-2006

HAMDAN BIN
RASHID
AL MAKTOUM
b. 1945

AHMED BIN
RASHID
AL MAKTOUM
b. 1950

1. SHEIKHA HIND BINT
MAKTOUM BINT JUMA
AL-MAKTOUM

SHEIKH MOHAMMED BIN
RASHID AL MAKTOUM
b. 1949
Ruler of Dubai 2006-
Vice-President of the UAE 2006-

2. H.R.H. PRINCESS
HAYA BINT
AL HUSSEIN
b. 1974

HEREDITARY PRINCE
HAMDAN BIN MOHAMMAD
AL MAKTOUM
b.1982

13 other children

SHEIKHA AL JALILA
BINT MOHAMMED
BIN RASHID AL MAKTOUM
b. 2007

SHEIKH KHALIFA BIN ZAYED bin Sultan Al Nahyan (properly known as Sheikh Khalifa) is the Emir of Abu Dhabi and President of the UAE. Born in 1948, Sheikh Khalifa succeeded his father Sheikh Zayed bin Sultan Al Nahyan as emir following his death aged 86 in November 2004, although he had been acting as president throughout his father's decline. Sheikh Zayed is credited with using the Emirates' vast oil wealth to create an efficient healthcare and education programme for his people, as well a working national infrastructure that united the various independent emirates of the area formerly known as the Trucial States.

The United Arab Emirates (UAE) comprises seven Persian Gulf states — Abu Dhabi, Ajman, Fujairah, Sharjah, Dubai, Umm al-Quwain and Ras al-Khaimah. Formerly known as the Trucial States or Trucial Oman, the area was more notoriously known as the Pirate Coast in the 18th and 19th centuries. Until oil was discovered in the 1950s, the entire area was predominantly poor, relying on fishing and a rapidly diminishing pearl industry. Since then, the Emirates have changed almost out of recognition into a wealthy economy drawing great fortunes from oil and natural gas revenues. The ruling families have almost all acquired vast wealth as a consequence. Each emirate is ruled by a hereditary ruler and retains a significant degree of independence; the seven emirs gather at the Supreme Council of Rulers to appoint the president, prime minister and cabinet.

The Al Nahyans are hereditary rulers of Abu Dhabi, but the presidency of the UAE is an elective position; as the richest emi-

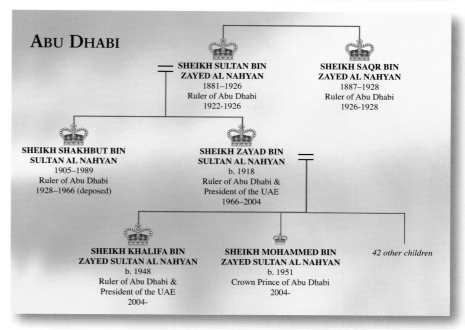

ABU DHABI

SHEIKH SULTAN BIN
ZAYED AL NAHYAN
1881–1926
Ruler of Abu Dhabi
1922-1926

SHEIKH SAQR BIN
ZAYED AL NAHYAN
1887–1928
Ruler of Abu Dhabi
1926-1928

SHEIKH SHAKHBUT BIN
SULTAN AL NAHYAN
1905–1989
Ruler of Abu Dhabi
1928–1966 (deposed)

SHEIKH ZAYAD BIN
SULTAN AL NAHYAN
b. 1918
Ruler of Abu Dhabi &
President of the UAE
1966–2004

SHEIKH KHALIFA BIN
ZAYED SULTAN AL NAHYAN
b. 1948
Ruler of Abu Dhabi &
President of the UAE
2004-

SHEIKH MOHAMMED BIN
ZAYED SULTAN AL NAHYAN
b. 1951
Crown Prince of Abu Dhabi
2004-

42 other children

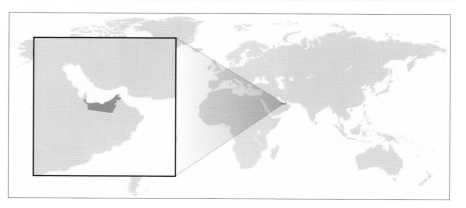

rate, Abu Dhabi provided the first ruler when the country was founded in 1971. When Sheikh Khalifa became ruler of the emirates in 2004, he appointed his brother Sheikh Mohammed bin Zayed Al Nahyan Crown Prince of Abu Dhabi, while the ruler of Dubai, Sheikh Mohammed bin Rashid Al Maktoum is vice-president of the UAE. The Emir stands for re-election as president of the UAE every five years.

The eldest of Sheikh Sultan's 45 children, Sheikh Khalifa was appointed to important position within the UAE's government from the time of its foundation in 1971. He is married to Sheikha Shamsa Bint Suhail who has an increasingly high profile role in the UAE and is president of the Arab Women's Organisation. His family, the Al Nahyan, were Bedouin Arabs belonging to the Bani Yas tribe who moved into the Abu Dhabi area in the late 1770s and built a port on the Persian Gulf coast. Abu Dhabi remained small until the discovery of oil in the region.

Sheikh Khalifa was born in Al Muwaiji Fort in the oasis town of Al Ain in 1948, to Sheikh Zayed, the local ruler and his first wife. Sheikh Khalifa spent his early childhood there and had his first education in the local public *majalis* (daily discussions), often accompanying his father as he went about his business. When Sheikh Zayed became leader of the emirates in 1966, he appointed his 18-year-old son to his former province of Al Ain to rule in his place, and made him crown prince of Abu Dhabi in April 1969.

Sheikh Khalifa is renowned for his love of horse and camel racing and has invested vast sums of money in the process. Financial sources put Sheikh Khalifa's personal wealth in the region of $20 billion, making him the second wealthiest royal after King Bhumibol Adulyadej of Thailand. He is a devout Sunni Muslim and not entirely hostile to modernising Western ideas.

Right: In 2007 Angela Merkel, Chancellor of the Federal Republic of Germany met with Sheikh Khalifa bin Zayed Al Nahyan in his role as President of the United Arab Emirates in his palace in Abu Dhabi. The UAE uses its near monopoly of Middle Eastern oil and natural gas supplies to promote Arab interests at the highest level of politics.

Left: Sheikh Mohammed bin Rashid Al Maktoum and his second wife Princess Haya, sister of the king of Jordan, at Royal Ascot, England in June 2004. They had married just two months earlier. Outside politics, the Sheikh is best known for his love of thoroughbred horses and racing. He owns stud farms in England, Ireland, the United States and Australia, as well as racing stables. His horses have won virtually every important title in the thoroughbred world.

Left: President George Bush, seated next to Sheikh Rashid of Dubai, enjoys traditional Arab hospitality during a visit to the UAE in 2008.

Below: The Maktoum family of Dubai have worked hard to make Dubai one of the world's most desirable tourist and business destinations, realising that the income from the country's oil reserves will not last forever. The Dubai skyline has altered completely in the space of ten years.

Right and below: Sheikh Zayed bin Sultan Al Nahyan, ruler of Abu Dhabi, and first president of the UAE. Emiratis frequently called him the 'father of the nation' because he did so much to capitalise on the UAE's oil revenues, using the vast wealth to improve education, healthcare and housing. His funeral (below) in 2004 was attended by heads of state from all over the world, but notable were his fellow rulers from the Middle East. Among the mourners in the second row can be seen (from left)

President Hamid Kharzai of Afghanistan, Sheikh Zayed's son Sheikh Khalifa, Crown Prince Abdullah of Saudi Arabia, the Sultan of Oman, and King Abdullah of Jordan.

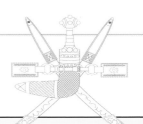

THE SULTANATE OF OMAN
Sultan Qaboos

Official title	Sultan Qaboos bin Said Al Said
Country ruled	Sultanate of Oman
Born	18 November 1940
Accession to throne	July 1970
Royal house	Abu Sa'id Dynasty
Official residences	Al Alam palace
Heir	No children, no designated heir

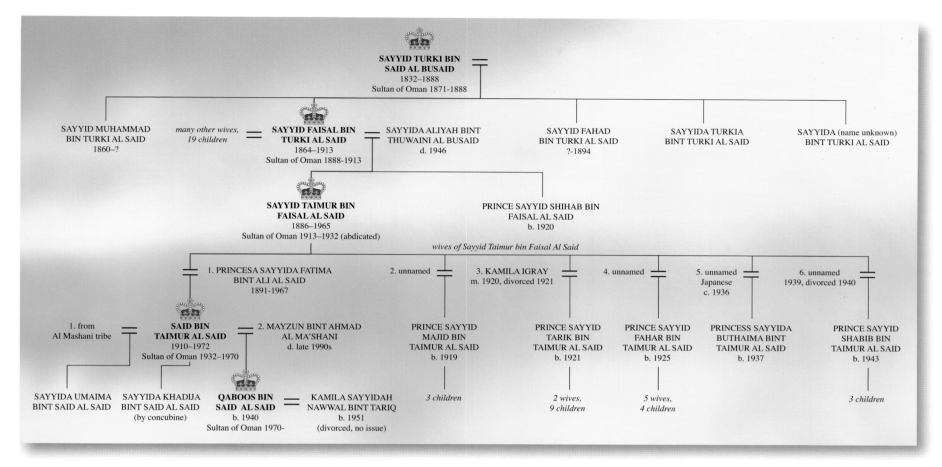

SAYYID TURKI BIN SAID AL BUSAID
1832–1888
Sultan of Oman 1871-1888

| SAYYID MUHAMMAD BIN TURKI AL SAID 1860–? | *many other wives, 19 children* | **SAYYID FAISAL BIN TURKI AL SAID** 1864–1913 Sultan of Oman 1888-1913 | SAYYIDA ALIYAH BINT THUWAINI AL BUSAID d. 1946 | SAYYID FAHAD BIN TURKI AL SAID ?-1894 | SAYYIDA TURKIA BINT TURKI AL SAID | SAYYIDA (name unknown) BINT TURKI AL SAID |

SAYYID TAIMUR BIN FAISAL AL SAID
1886–1965
Sultan of Oman 1913–1932 (abdicated)

PRINCE SAYYID SHIHAB BIN FAISAL AL SAID b. 1920

wives of Sayyid Taimur bin Faisal Al Said

| 1. PRINCESA SAYYIDA FATIMA BINT ALI AL SAID 1891-1967 | 2. unnamed | 3. KAMILA IGRAY m. 1920, divorced 1921 | 4. unnamed | 5. unnamed Japanese c. 1936 | 6. unnamed 1939, divorced 1940 |

| 1. from Al Mashani tribe | **SAID BIN TAIMUR AL SAID** 1910–1972 Sultan of Oman 1932–1970 | 2. MAYZUN BINT AHMAD AL MA'SHANI d. late 1990s | PRINCE SAYYID MAJID BIN TAIMUR AL SAID b. 1919 | PRINCE SAYYID TARIK BIN TAIMUR AL SAID b. 1921 | PRINCE SAYYID FAHAR BIN TAIMUR AL SAID b. 1925 | PRINCESS SAYYIDA BUTHAIMA BINT TAIMUR AL SAID b. 1937 | PRINCE SAYYID SHABIB BIN TAIMUR AL SAID b. 1943 |

| SAYYIDA UMAIMA BINT SAID AL SAID | SAYYIDA KHADIJA BINT SAID AL SAID (by concubine) | **QABOOS BIN SAID AL SAID** b. 1940 Sultan of Oman 1970- | KAMILA SAYYIDAH NAWWAL BINT TARIQ b. 1951 (divorced, no issue) | *3 children* | *2 wives, 9 children* | *5 wives, 4 children* | *3 children* |

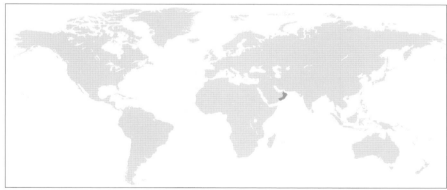

SULTAN QABOOS BIN SAID Al Said was born in Salalah in Dhofar in 1940, the only son of Sultan Said bin Taimur (1910–1972) and his second wife Mayzun bint Ahmad Al Ma'ashani (died late 1990s); she was the daughter of a sheikh of the Bayt Mu'ashani clan of the Qara tribe. At the age of 16 he was sent to private school in England and later attended the Sandhurst Royal Military Academy as an officer cadet. After a couple of years with the British Army he travelled the world for a year before returning to Oman in 1964 and studying his country's history and Islam.

On returning to his homeland, his father ordered Qaboos to be kept under virtual house arrest in the royal palace at Salalah. In July 1970 a British-backed, bloodless, military coup deposed the sultan and forced his abdication. Qaboos became the 14th sultan of the Abu Said dynasty and the Sultan of Muscat and Oman, inheriting a poor and dispirited country. It took another five years to quell the Dhofar Rebellion, the ongoing Communist insurgent attacks from Yemen via the Dhofar region in the south of the country, but by 1975 Sultan Qaboos was able to turn his attention to domestic matters.

In his accession speech Sultan Qaboos dedicated himself to Muscat and Oman and promised to unite his country and make it a modern nation. He appealed to the many Omani exiles around the world to return home and help him rebuild the country. In August 1970 Sultan Qaboos abolished the Sultanate of Muscat and Oman and instead announced the birth of the Sultanate of Oman and a new unity. A great deal of his energy went into general education at *madrasas* (schools) for both boys and girls, vocational training centres, and the establishment of the Sultan Qaboos University which opened in 1986. He has done a great deal to introduce the infrastructure of a modern state, improving education, healthcare and transport links for Omani citizens.

Sultan Qaboos is an absolute monarch whose powers are subject to no other authority, although an elected consultative council was introduced in 2003. His personal wealth is put at some $1.1 billion. He has not publicly named an heir, although he says that his successor is named in a sealed letter lodged with the defence minister. The country's constitution stipulates that the Ruling Family Council choose the successor after the incumbent sultan's death; if there is no consensus, then the previous sultan's letter is consulted. Under the sultan's leadership Oman has become a member of the Non-Aligned Group of Nations, as well as the League of Arab Nations and the United Nations.

Sultan Qaboos is a religiously liberal, but observant Muslim of the Ibadi School. In 1976 Qaboos married his cousin Kamila Sayyidah Nawwal bint Tariq (b. 1951) but the marriage quickly ended in divorce without producing any children. He has not remarried.

The sultan has the use of four palaces in Oman, the Al Alam palace in Muscat, Bait Al Barka Palace in Barka, Salalah palace, and Bahjat Al Andhar Palace in Sohar. The sultan is known to be a car enthusiast, particularly for luxury marques such as Ferraris, Rolls Royce, Bugatti and Aston Martin. His other great enthusiasm is for luxury yachts of which he is reported to own around six including the *Al-Said* which cost over $500 million in 2008.

Right: Sultan Qaboos, 1979.

Below: Sultan Qaboos bin Said Al-Said held talks with British Prime Minister Tony Blair in his palace in Muscat.

Below left: Sultan Qaboos and Prince Andrew, Duke of York, watch the final manoeuvres between British and Omani troops as they exercise in the desert in October 2001. The British were instrumental in supporting Sultan Qaboos in 1972 in his bloodless coup when he deposed his father Sultan Said bin Taimur. In return, he has made the deserts of Oman available to the British army for vital training.

Above: The royal emblem of Oman, two swords crossed by a curved khanjar *(dagger), decorates the gate leading to the ceremonial entrance of Al-Alam Palace, the sultan's royal palace in Muscat.*

Right: A view of the gardens and fountains of Sultan Qaboos' Al-Alam palace. The palace was built for ceremonial purposes in 1972, but the sultan does not live here. The façade has towering gold and blue pillars, edged in green with wrought iron detailing. The public are not allowed inside but can admire the impressive frontage.

Left: The Prince of Wales with his entourage tour the Sultan Qaboos Mosque in Muscat in 2003.

HOUSE OF GUELPH

Stuart dynasty ended 1714.-By act of settlement, the crown passed August 1, 1714 to the House of GUELPH, in the person of GEORGE 1, Elector of Hanover, great-grandson of James 1 of England.-To George 1 succeeded: 1727, GEORGE II;-1760, GEORGE III;-1820, GEORGE IV;-1830, WILLIAM IV;-and June 20, 1837, Her Majesty the QUEEN VICTORIA, Daughter of Edward, Duke of Kent, fourth son of George III

DIEU ET MON DROI

HONI SOIT QUI MAL Y PENSE

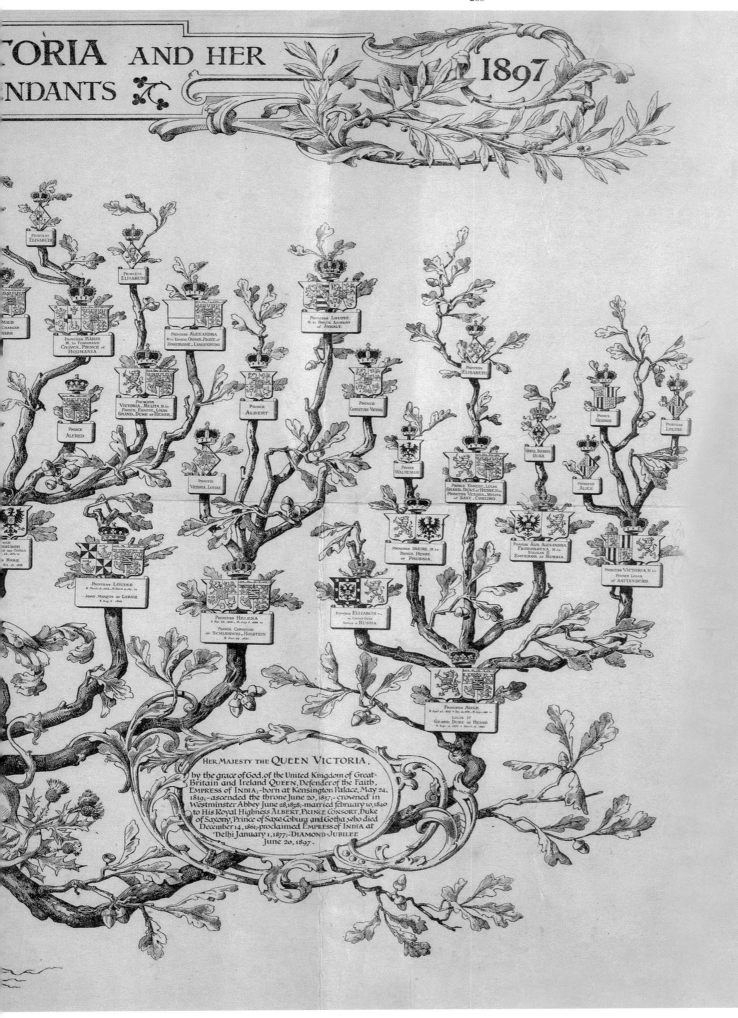

TORIA AND HER NDANTS ❧ 1897

HER MAJESTY THE QUEEN VICTORIA, by the grace of God, of the United Kingdom of Great-Britain and Ireland QUEEN, Defender of the Faith, EMPRESS of INDIA,-born at Kensington Palace, May 24, 1819;-ascended the throne June 20, 1837;-crowned in Westminster Abbey June 28,1838;-married february 10,1840 to His Royal Highness ALBERT, PRINCE CONSORT, Duke of Saxony, Prince of Saxe Coburg and Gotha, who died December 14, 1861;-proclaimed EMPRESS of INDIA at Delhi January 1, 1877;-DIAMOND-JUBILEE June 20, 1897.

This family tree, produced in 1987 to celebrate Queen Victoria's Diamond Jubilee, shows how closely related European royal families are to this day.

The queen's eldest daughter Vicky married the emperor of Germany, and her eldest son was Kaiser Wilhelm II; the current head of the house of Hohenzollern is his great-great-grandson. Ex-King Constantine of Greece and his sister Queen Sophia of Spain are also descended from Vicky. King Juan Carlos of Spain is descended from Princess Beatrice, the youngest child of Victoria and Albert, via her daughter Victoria Eugenie.

The Queen's British descendants flow from the children of Albert Edward, Prince of Wales, as does the Norwegian royal family.

Princess Alice's younger daughter Alexandra became tsarina of Russia and her oldest daughter Victoria is the grandmother of Prince Philip, Duke of Edinburgh. Prince Alfred's descendants acquired the throne of Romania.

The royal families of Sweden and Denmark are descended from Prince Arthur Duke of Connaught via his daughter Princess Margaret. who became Crown Princess of Sweden in 1905.

Main entries are indicated by page numbers in **bold**, illustrations and their captions are indicated by those in *italics*.

AP/PA pages 161 (below right), 162 below, 216, 219 (top right)

CORBIS/SYGMA/ Jean Pierre Amet page 72 (left); Jeremy Bembaron page 96; Alessandra Benedetti page 101;Brooks Kraft page 274; Stephane Cardinale page 123 (below);Stephane Cardinale/People Avenue page 99 (all 3); Antonio Cotrim/Pool/epa page 269; Dusko Despotovi page 131 (below right); Patrick Durand page 140; EPA pages 199 (top), 267 (top); Eric Fougere/VIP Images page 68 (right); Julien Hekimian page 68 (middle); Gavin Hellier/Robert Harding World Imagery page 274; John Hrusa/epa page 227 (below); Robert Jaeger/epa page 248; Alain Nogues page 70 (below); Reuters page 60; Eric Robert/VIP Production page 70 (middle); Patrick Robert 225 (below); RoyalPress/dpa page 213 (top); RoyalPress/Albert Nieboer/dpa pages 68 (left), 70 (top); Matthias Schrader/dpa page 123 (top); Shamshahrin Shamsudin/epa/Corbis page 199 (below); WAM/Reuters 275 (below)

GETTY IMAGES/AFP page 143 (below right); Karim Daher page 136; Dmitry Lovetsky page 150; Gent Shkullaku/AFP/ page 143 (below left); Koichi Kamoshida page 158; Pascal Le Segretain page 79 (top)

REUTERS 170

JO ST MART 135 (top), 164, 168 (both), 169 (both), 186, 200-201, 214-215, 218, 219 (top), 220 (top), 232 (top right), 234-235, 249 (below), 261 (left), 262, 262-263

TOPFOTO pages 21 (top), 25 (below left), 28 (inset right), 29 (inset), 42 (inset), 43 (top) 53 (top right), 64 (below), 72 (right), 76 (top), 86, 90, 91 (top left), 92, 94-95, 95 (both), 124, 126 (both), 127 (below), 131 (top), 132, 138 (left & below), 142, 144, 146 (below). 147 (top left), 150, 156-157, 176, 177 (right), 179 (top), 188 (left), 189 (top left), 195 (top), 208, 211 (below right), 238 (top and right) 239 (both), 255 (top left), 267 (below), 272, 276
AA World Travel Library pages 14-15, 43 (below), 102-103, 178 (top)
Africanpictures.net pages 228, 233
Alinari pages 71 (right), 98 (below right), 122 (below), 138 (top right), 172-173
AP pages 18 (below), 19 (top left), 25 (below right), 40 (below), 45 (right), 59 (both), 65 (top right), 77 (below) 116, 122 (top), 134 (left), 143 (top right) 146 (top left), 177 (top left and below), 206 (top & below left), 119 (below), 236, 244 (below), 245 (top left & below), 275 (top)
Art Media/HIP page 73 (right)
EE Images/HIP page 184 (top)
EMPICS page 207 (below)
Fiore page 167
The Granger Collection pages 73 (left), 153 (top), 154 (below)
Elmar R. Gruber page 213 (below)
John Hedgecoe page 91 (top right)

John Higgs page 204-205
Hubertus Kanus page (28 inset left)
The Image Works page 200 (top); 225 (top)/Lee Snider/ page 178 (below left & right); /Charles O. Cecil 280 (top)/David Frazier 179 (below)
Keystone pages 7, 50, 100, 108, 112
Mel Longhurst page 10, 54 (below)
Jon Mitchell pages 161 (below left)
National Archives pages 284-285; The National Archives/HIP 282
National Pictures pages 12, 19 (below left)
Novosti pages 11, 26 (top right), 66 (top), 80 (right), 84, 88 (below left), 91 (below), 128, 152 (both), 153 (below right), 154-155, 182 (left top & below), 202, 243 (top right), 255 (below), 258, 260 (right), 261 (right), 268-269
PA pages 1, 19 (below right), 25 (top), 42 (below), 44, 45 (left), 46 (top left), 47 (top right & below), 48 (below), 49 (all 3), 52 (right), 58 (top), 61 (all 3), 62 (top), 87 (top left & right) 98 (below left), 166, 174, 193, (top left & right), 195 (below), 196, 198 (both), 200 (below), 206 (below right), 207 (top), 282, 211 (top & below left), 226, 227 (top left & right), 231, 232 (left), 242 (both), 243 (below right), 249 (top right), 256 (below), 260 (left), 266, 278 (both), 280 (left)
Polfoto pages 16, 19 (top right), 22, 26 (top left), 26 (below), 27, 30, 32, 32-33, 34 (all 3), 35 (all 3), 36 (both), 37 (all 3), 153 (below left)
Print Collection/HIP pages 40 (top), 41 (below), 172 (both)
Prisma-V&W pages 20-21, 28-29
Ray Roberts page 90 (below)
Schofield pages 42-43
Spectrum Colour Library/HIP pages 67 (top), 185 (both), 194
Topham Picturepoint pages 82, 83 (top), 41 (top), 46 (right), 48 (top), 52 (left). 53 (top left), 76 (both below), 77, 78 (top), 130 (top), 143 (top left), 147 (top right & below), 160 (both), 161 (top), 210, 220-221, 224 (left), 254, 256 (top), 256-257, 279, 281
Ullsteinbild pages 2-3, 53 (below), 54 (top), 56, 62, 65 (top left and below), 66 (below), 67 (below), 87 (below), 88 (top), 89 (below), 104, 106 (all 3), 107, 110, 111, 114 (all 3), 115, 116-117, 118, 120 (both), 121 (right) 127 (top), 154 (top), 162 (top), 163, 172, 180, 189 (below left & right) 221 (top), 222, 246, 252, 270, 273
UPP pages 13, 18 (top), 24, 46 (below), 47 (top right), 55, 58 (below), 79 (below & right), 88 (below right), 89 (top), 135 (below) 139 (top), 148-149, 190, 192, 193 (below), 224 (right), 230 (both), 240, 243 (left), 244 (top), 245 (top left), 250-251, 264
Uppa/Bandphoto page 78 (below), 255 (top right)
Roger-Viollet pages 71 (left), 98 (top), 121 (left), 130 (below). 131 (below left), 134 (right), 146 (top right) 182 (right), 183 (both), 184 (below), 188 (right), 189 (top right), 212, 238 (left)
David Wimsett/UPPA/Photoshot page 74
Woodmansterne page 20 (top), 38

BISHOP OF URGELL 80 (left)

WIKIPEDIA 8-9, 83 (below), 139 (below)